RORY MOULTON

Europe by Milk Run

A Solo Travel Experiment from Copenhagen to Barcelona

First edition

ISBN: 978-1-954778-08-5

Editing by Barbara Noe Kennedy

This book was professionally typeset on Reedsy.
Find out more at reedsy.com

Milk Run:

"...an airplane or train trip with stops at many places.

...a regular trip during which nothing unusual happens."

Macmillan Dictionary

Contents

Europe by Milk Run   ii

The Mission   1

Copenhagen   8

Hamburg   24

Amsterdam   30

Brussels   88

Paris   97

Bayeux   126

Dinan   162

Saint-Jean-de-Luz   188

Pamplona   205

Zaragoza   226

Barcelona   244

Epilogue   272

Bits & Bobs   279

About the Author   281

Also by Rory Moulton   282

Europe by Milk Run

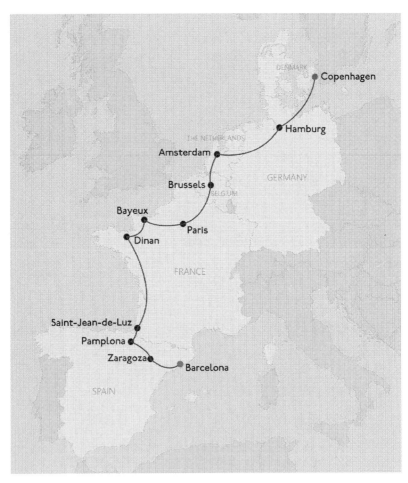

A solo travel experiment from Copenhagen to Barcelona

*With ample humor and humility, Europe by Milk Run uncovers
Europe's greatest treasures.*

When an acquaintance of author Rory Moulton declares that traveling
Europe "isn't real travel," Rory sets out to prove him wrong.
In this solo travel memoir, the author rides slow trains, explores
off-beat neighborhoods and attractions, eats at restaurants so lost in
time he's amazed they know when to open and befriends unforgettable
characters, some of whom actually like him. Rory embarks with little
more than a backpack, Eurail Pass and a vague notion of which direction
he should be traveling. Along the way, he:

· repels a cat invasion in Amsterdam,
· loses all his money and documents,
· witnesses a magical sunset in a ruined church,
· meets WWII-doubting Kiwis,
· investigates a haunted prison,
· explores Europe's most beautiful, albeit abandoned, train station
· and much more...

Europe by Milk Run shows that traveling Europe at ground level reveals
the Continent's greatest treasures.

The Mission

The train trundled into Bayeux's deserted two-platform country station, stopping fast with a jerk on *voie* one. The northwest-bound slow route had departed Paris' Gare Saint-Lazare (Monet's favorite), snaked through the Seine River Valley and reached the Normandy countryside in four hours. Lost in slow-train and farm-field revelry, I unstuck my forehead from the window, roused myself and realized: This was my stop!

Our sudden arrival caught me savoring Normandy's pasture-and-apple orchard daydream. I hastily threw my computer and notebook into my green backpack and stuffed my Eurail Pass and creased passport into my blue-canvas document holder. I jumped up, hoisted my pack and leapt off the train just before the doors closed and the TER regional train scampered toward the woodlands of the Cotentin Peninsula. Bayeux station's parking lot sat empty, and I was the lone disembarking passenger.

I was about halfway through my three-week solo train journey from Copenhagen to Barcelona and finding my travel groove. I had finally struck into the countryside after leaving Paris. This marked my visit to Bayeux. A gorgeous Airbnb room in a 17th-century home awaited me. The sun shone directly overhead with nary a cloud. I had no plans or pressing obligations. Best of all, it was lunchtime, and I was hungry.

Greeted with a smile, I settled into a table beside the River Aure at cozy La Garde Manger, near the Bayeux Cathedral, dripping with Gothic steeples and flying buttresses.

The cheerful waitress left with my order: spring salad, French fries, draft beer and *croque-à-cheval*—Normandy's equivalent of the *croque madame*, a grilled ham and cheese topped with a fried egg. In Normandy, where horses and heifers outnumbered pigs, locals used thinly sliced horse ("cheval") meat for ham. But as the French penchant for consuming horse waned, they substituted chopped steak. Thankful for the pliable nature of French palates, I patted my stomach expectantly, unzipped my backpack and reorganized my belongings, a jumbled mess after my frenetic dash off the slow train.

I reached in and dug around. Hmm, I touched my clothes, laptop, notebook, toiletries...Everything was in there. Everything except my precious document holder. I pulled the backpack onto my lap and dunked my head, searching for the blue document holder.

It wasn't there.

My passport, Eurail Pass, credit cards and the vast majority of my cash were now riding a northbound train to Cherbourg, while I sat at a café in Bayeux with a backpack full of dirty clothes.

I sprang from my seat, stumbled toward the door while zipping my backpack and frantically flagged the server in a manner resembling an aircraft marshaller parking a 747 while simultaneously fending off a severe bee attack.

"I'm so, so sorry. I must cancel my order. I left my, uh, my everything—passport, money—on the train."

"No problem, no problem." She appeared concerned, my desperate look said everything. "Yes, you go, go."

I sprinted back to the train station, alone in France without a cent or valid document to my name, my passport now inevitably circulating on the black market. I was a failure. My trip was ruined.

Was this the end? Would my wife have to wire me money, so I could slink home? My stomach turned over, my once-growling belly now gurgled with despair. I felt so dumb, so disappointed in myself that I dry-heaved in the parking lot. Which reminded me how hungry I still was.

As I knocked on the station manager's office door, consigned to a new life stuck in Bayeux, probably washing dishes or laboring as an orchard hand for my room and board, I wondered how I had even managed to get this far from Copenhagen without any other major mishaps. The simple act of stepping off a train had sent my whole trip into a tailspin.

* * *

A few weeks before leaving for Europe, my wife and I attended a dinner party hosted by two new arrivals to our little mountain town. We pulled our Ford pickup into the crescent-shaped driveway. A foot of snow covered the yard and unplowed driveway as steady snowfall filled the spindly branches of lodgepole pines. The headlights bounced off the ivory snow, illuminating two matching black Audi SUVs we'd parked behind.

"Ugh," moaned my wife as we stared at their house.

Like most recent transplants to our little mountain town, our dinner hosts were well-heeled professionals who cashed out their suburban equity and relocated to the mountains with remote jobs. And like those other recent arrivals, they'd bought a home with insufficient square footage, windows, granite and stainless steel, so a contractor's trailer sat next to a half-finished addition under a green tarp, awaiting the spring thaw.

Our hosts had recently completed a one-year, round-the-world trip. We sat around their massive dining-room table as dinner was served and prodded them for advice and stories. We began with Europe, their jumping-off point.

3

"We started in Ireland and then traveled down through the UK, France, Switzerland, Italy and Greece. But, ah, Europe doesn't feel like real traveling to me," the husband said.

"Oh?" I asked.

"Yeah, I don't know. It's just, I guess, so easy. Feels contrived. But after Europe we went to Africa." He grinned. "Have you been there? It's uh-mazing..."

The pork tenderloin was Death Valley dry. I gnawed my first bite and gulped it down with water and a big smile. "It's delicious," I lied.

In bed that night, I thought about what our host had said. (And the overcooked pork.) In fact, it wasn't the first time I'd heard the criticism. Europe had always been "soft" travel compared to the developing world. Sure. Had the modern conveniences, immense crowds and amusement-park infrastructure ruined it? Had the Continent gone so delicate that it no longer counted as "real" travel?

(Also: Why were such culinary injustices inflicted upon that innocent tenderloin?)

I fretted over whether Europe's commodification had really destroyed it. Surely, the Europe of old was out there. I'd find it and prove naysayers like the dinner host wrong. But finding it, I reasoned, might require a fresh approach. A little of something new and something old. It sounded like a worthy challenge.

I rolled out of bed with a determination bordering on obsession. I grabbed my bedside notebook and jotted down:

- Go solo.
- Ride slow trains. Or walk.
- Eat at markets, small cafés.
- Find Airbnbs and guesthouses owned by locals.
- Be spontaneous.
- Take setbacks in stride.

The next day, I reviewed my late-night diatribe and realized something was missing. I sorted through my dusty travel souvenirs—photos, back when photos were actual physical objects, retired guidebooks and old train and museum tickets. About halfway down my steam trunk of memories, I found it. The stapled white interior pages had yellowed long ago. The rumpled edges had been partially torn, but there was no mistaking it for anything other than my first and only Eurail Pass, circa 2000.

Over two glorious months, I woke up and decided where to go next, flashing my Eurail and swinging between storybook European towns. I'd ask locals and other travelers for recommendations, then check the timetables. Sometimes I'd go alone; other times I had companions.

My mission crystallized: With a Eurail Pass and the Airbnb app, I'd ride slowly but steadily across Western Europe. Using a low-key and low-planning approach, I'd *experience* the journey on local and regional trains included with my Eurail Pass. I'd secure scant reservations, scour off-beat places, up-and-coming neighborhoods, and travel at ground level where the locals are, eschewing tourist traps. At night, I'd ditch restaurant apps for walking around, reading menus and judging the atmosphere.

Easy, right? After all, it'd be a leisurely milk run, from A to B with minimal fuss. Yet, as the trip's outline fell into place and the departure date grew closer, concern gnawed at me: In tourist-soaked Europe, would hyper-organized 100-person tour groups covering 12 countries in five days and social-media rock stars with their fingers on the pulse run roughshod over me, outpace me, leave me scrambling for their leftovers?

I choked down the thought. Worrying what influencers or massive tour groups did was the wrong mindset, I reassured myself. Getting outpaced by selfie sticks and sun hats is exactly the thing I should *want* to happen.

Beyond the ground-level "Europe by milk run" experiment, I also harbored an ulterior motive. This would be my first solo trip in a decade. I love my world revolving around my wife and son, but I missed my carefree travel days and the restless tug of solo travel had recently returned. I wondered if a few weeks would sate the desire.

Or was I being selfish? A married, employed parent leaves a burden behind when they carve out three weeks for a solo jaunt through Europe. Don't they?

For my all-too-understanding yet skeptical wife and wonderful son, justification was necessarily necessary. When I first pitched the idea, they rightly and smartly demanded two weeks as a family in Germany and Denmark. I proposed the final plan one night at our favorite restaurant (naturally)—leading with the bit about Denmark and Germany (naturally). The log-cabin restaurant's fireplace roared as I said things like Eurail Pass, castles, trains, pastries, quality time and "Legoland" (the boy's ears perked). Then, I pitched my solo trip.

After years working as an editor behind the scenes at a travel website, I told them I'd use the trip to re-hone my ground-level writing chops. I'd make a little money selling articles while testing my Europe-is-still-cool-so-shut-your-dry-pork-filled-mouth thesis (working title). Oh, and might as well scratch that solo-travel itch, I suppose.

"Make...exactly...how little money?" asked my wife, flipping her blonde hair. Her job as a nurse practitioner is hard, much harder than mine. Yet, because of society's cruel misplaced priorities, we earn about the same. This disparity in effort-to-income ratio was never discussed, yet always present, lingering long in any discussion on household finances.

I stirred the sausage rigatoni, swimming in rosé sauce, and locked on two sets of pleading eyes eagerly awaiting my financial forecast.

My son chimed in, grinning with precocious pride, ever his mother's tiny echo. "Yeah, Dad. How much are you gonna make us? You gonna bring home the bacon or what?"

"Well, um, I'm not sure *exactly* how much I'll make." I forked the slippery rigatoni as I contemplated very complex algebraic equations. "I'll sell a couple articles on spec and snag a couple assignments." I chewed and swallowed a rigatoni, pausing for dramatic effect. "Maybe I'll write a book."

"Will you make enough to cover your expenses?" she asked between bites of pecan-encrusted halibut.

"Yes, yes, I think so. Maybe more."

Of course, I had no idea. The likelihood of breaking even, let alone profiting, seemed fanciful. But that satisfied them. At least enough to buy my Eurail Pass and the cheapest flight home I could find, Icelandair from Barcelona. Cope to Barca. That seemed a sufficient distance for 21 days.

Despite what countless memoirs and digital nomads preached, we'd never go whole-hog, sell the farm and travel the world. My wife's career demanded too much. Financial matters settled, however, we reached an agreement.

I couldn't shake the doubts, though. With tourist hordes mucking about, high-speed trains zipping across time zones and influencers swinging selfie-sticks, was Europe "real" enough for a ground-level adventure?

Let's find out.

Copenhagen

There I stood, heels together, tears welling, my right arm raised palm-up in suspended farewell as the train pulled away, leaving me totally and utterly alone in Europe. It was then I realized: The departing train exposed a crowded platform of commuters cowering in shock and horror as I gave a Nazi salute and tried not to cry about it. Thus began my solo European foray.

That morning, I fell hard for Copenhagen Central Station. Waiting with my family, I realized how easily the station lent itself to tender, memorable goodbyes. The red-brick gateway could be Europe's most romantic: Spanning the central concourse, arched wrought iron roof trusses, bisected by grand concave skylights, rested upon burnished-brick walls speckled with matching arched windows. Natural clay and black quarry tile floors completed the interior, which was stripped down to its exposed skeletal members.

The 1911 architecture captivated, thanks to Danish architect Heinrich Wenck who, it appears, specialized in train stations and sweet, juicy government contracts. Wenck designed over 150 depots in Denmark, all in the Art Nouveau-derivative National Romantic style.

Late 19th- and early 20th-century National Romantic architecture captured idealized Nordic nationalism. In a rapidly industrializing world, Scandinavian countries sought historical grounding, reviving national languages and propagating cultural folklore. The distinctly

Nordic style proliferated throughout northern Germany, the Baltics and even Russia. It expressed national solidarity and foreshadowed the progressive tidal wave that would cascade across Scandinavia culminating in the Nordic social welfare system.

So, yes, to some extent modern Scandinavians can thank artists and architects for their robust social safety net.

But architect Wenck wasn't concerned with health care and maternity leave. He fancied towering roof steeples and lots of them, massive brick arches, lofty slate roofs and corbel-stuffed facades, indulging his whimsy at Copenhagen Central. Wenck's exuberant exterior meshed in subdued elegance, like his minimalist interior that featured the building's structural supports instead of finishes and decoration.

As Europe's new train stations grow bigger, noisier and more plate-glass-covered every year (exhibit A: Berlin Hauptbahnhof), better resembling American malls than cultural crossroads, Copenhagen station emanated warmth, innocence and coziness. It felt like transiting through a fairy tale, a gingerbread building with the everlasting possibility of adventure shunting in and out along 13 peaceful tracks. Next stop: Narnia.

Neither Europe's oldest nor grandest, Wenck's creation isn't lauded in architectural circles, but Copenhagen Central Station is simply charming. It's perfect for a heartfelt moment, a compassionate farewell. Of all the ways to bid a lover *adieu* in grand old Copenhagen station, I don't recommend an awkward standoff resulting from an argument the previous evening that definitely, 100% had nothing to do with someone leaving alone on a three-week train journey and the other suddenly regretting her acquiescence to the plan.

Who knows how it started? (She knows.) There we stood, my son, wife and myself, about to spend three weeks apart and unable to muster a proper goodbye.

"Look, I'm sorry I was sassy last night. I'm excited, nervous and anxious. Very anxious." I apologized. Making amends would have to be quick—their train to the airport would depart any second.

"Excited, anxious to leave us?" She rolled her eyes and feigned dismay before locking into my sight. "Just don't do anything stupid," she said.

"Yeah, don't do anything stupid, Dad," my son affirmed.

"Don't ask the impossible," I replied, clowning a smile.

"That's all I'll ever ask of you," she fired back.

"Ask me what? To not be stupid?"

"No, for the impossible." Our stern faces softened.

We embraced and kissed, the boy squashed between us, before they leapt aboard.

After a courteous electronic warning, the train's doors slipped shut. My wife placed her open palm against the train window. I lifted mine toward her as the train lurched for Copenhagen Airport. Our plucky nine-year-old, threw up the rock 'n' roll "horns" sign with his left hand, while bursting into laughter.

Tears filled my eyes as I blinked to hold them, my right palm outstretched as I pivoted on my heels to face the departing train. Everyone waiting on the opposite platform recoiled in horror at what appeared like a Nazi salute. I sheepishly smiled, lowered my arm and withdrew to the main terminal, chastised just minutes into my journey.

My watch read 6:30 a.m., so I circled the 1:32 p.m. departure, enough time to explore a neighborhood and eat lunch. I'd still reach Hamburg, Germany, at sunset for a shower and email-check before exploring its notoriously hedonistic nightlife. I followed signs for the 2A bus into Copenhagen.

* * *

Why Hamburg?

Eventually, I had to move in a westerly and southerly orientation. So, for practicable purposes, I might as well lurch in that general direction. Plus, I'd never been to Hamburg, well, other than a brief stopover en route to Copenhagen the week prior.

The week before, the family and I devised a mission for our one-hour Hamburg layover: Find my son a German national team soccer jersey. My son was obsessed when Germany won the World Cup. After failing in small-town Fussen, Bavaria, I knew we would score a jersey in big-city Hamburg. An hour layover? Ha! I promised them: Give me 20 minutes, and we'd be positively awash in German soccer jerseys.

We stuffed our bags in train-station lockers and rushed to the nearest department store. We ran inside the first glass-and-granite box, which we discovered, after despondently shuffling around, was an office building, a realization that took far longer than it should have. Back on the sidewalk, we sprinted farther from the station as our 60-minute layover dropped to 45 minutes.

A few blocks away, we found a department store, a real one this time. I hunted for a jersey, throwing clothes off racks and dashing down aisles. And then I found it—a green-gray national jersey with a World Cup badge sewn on the front—but only in adult sizes.

That's when I summoned my travel superpowers. A traveler's ability to summon superpowers is never more potent than when an authentic sports jersey hangs in the balance. In this time of great need, appreciable urgency and supreme confusion, I mobilized my linguistic capacities.

The phrase "*Haben tot kinder*" popped into my head. How? Why? I don't know, but I felt like Neo unplugging from the Matrix: I speak German.

"Haben tot kinder."

It's worth noting: I'd never heard that precise phrase. Everyone knows *kinder* from kindergarten. I was pretty sure I'd heard *haben* used for have, tense be damned. I thought *tot* meant with, to or for. It seemed like it should be a preposition. Close enough! They'd comprehend, what with my wild flailing of the jersey and all. A traveler doesn't question his superpowers; he's just glad he has them.

My German flowed.

Some people, German speakers mostly, who overheard my rantings might disagree. But, reader, I promise flawless High German spewed from my mouth like the demon Pazuzu growling Latin. I bolted from baffled sales clerk to baffled sales clerk, thrusting the adult jersey in their faces and asked, "Haben tot kinder? Haben tot kinder?"

The first two clerks shrugged, looking even slightly mortified. What awful salespeople. I checked my watch: 20 minutes until departure. We had a brisk, 10-minute jog to the station. I told my wife and son to go; I'd brave it alone, locate a jersey and rendezvous on the train.

I really used that word: "rendezvous." I was becoming unstoppable.

Clutching the adult jersey, I raced upstairs as more flummoxed sales clerks shrugged or backed away from my frantic gesticulations and impeccable German. The sweaty, red-headed lunatic demanded: "Haben tot kinder?"

What's wrong with these people? Don't they understand their own language?

Finally, on the fourth floor, with nine minutes left, I found the kids' jerseys. The security guard eye-balled me as I paid, and I bolted from the store to the train station, mere seconds remaining. By the time I reached the platform, the train's doors had shut with everyone onboard. I pushed the green button and jumped through the sliding doors as they opened, exhaling as I landed. The doors closed abruptly behind me as the train lurched forward.

I patrolled the carriages for my family, holding the jersey above my head in glorious triumph, like Rafiki presenting baby Simba, but significantly sweatier. Elated at seeing the jersey, my son thrust it over his sweatshirt (it was two sizes too big). I slumped in the empty seat facing them and smiled, a modern-day Cnut the Great.

I think my spouse may have exulted, "You're the most amazing human being to bless this planet, and you're such a fearless traveler." Although we chugged toward Danish-speaking Denmark, I decided that capitalizing on my new superpower, while the linguistic capacity still coursed through my veins, would be a prudent use of the journey. I pulled a German phrase book from my tan backpack, feeling rather established.

I reviewed prepositions and couldn't find *tot* anywhere. I discovered that "for" is, gulp, exactly the same in German: It's *für*. I got the easiest word wrong. I should have said *für* not *tot*. "Haben für kinder."

"Huh," I said aloud. Okay, I was close. What the hell does *tot* mean? I flipped to the index and found *tot*. I thumbed back to the adjectives section (*uh-oh*) and my jaw fell in horror as I realized my error.

Tot means "dead."

I was asking the department store clerks if they had dead children.

So, why Hamburg? To spend one night in the famed city and experience its illustrious nightlife. Maybe apologize to a few department-store employees. See whether I was wanted for suspicion of child murder. You know, not for any unusual reasons.

* * *

But back to the destination at-hand, Copenhagen. Does your city have a squatter's commune? Mine (Denver) doesn't either. Boring, right? But Copenhagen does. It's called Christiania.

During the Ancient Times (1971), parents living in the Christian-shavn neighborhood sought playground space for their kids and broke through the fence at an abandoned military site, where acres of land sat unused since WWII. According to legend, hippies as far as Berlin heard the fences fall that day and upped-stakes for the Danish capital. One thing led to another and, poof, the anarchists, communists, hippies and mystics occupied what was once Denmark's largest military base.

Prized for its affordable housing (free) in a notoriously expensive city, Christiania's occupiers soon coalesced around a greater collective mission: building a self-governing micro nation. They considered Danish society too conservative and bureaucratic, and wanted the opposite. Christiania, as they envisioned it, would be a free, alternative and self-sustaining society within a society. The Freetown Christiania commune was born.

For utopia to flourish, however, they would need scads of cannabis.

Cannabis became the community's primary income source, upending its original spare-bicycle-parts- and hemp-bracelets-based economy. As the axiom goes, weed dealers beget weed buyers. Weed buyers bring cash and tell other weed buyers until it's an open secret that even cloddish tourists like me know about.

No matter a community's founding ethos, once no-tax, all-cash, free enterprise takes root, unrestricted avarice grows and evolves into an indomitable force. In a free society like Christiania, where rules just aren't cool, man, that evolution meant selling ganja on a brazen scale.

By the 1990s, Christiania's main drag, Pusher Street, was awash in pot sellers, many of whom authorities linked to violent biker gangs and criminal syndicates from outside Denmark. Authorities conducted periodic raids throughout the years, before reaching the current status quo where residents pay taxes and utility bills. In 2012, inhabitants agreed to buy Christiania's land, which the government still, technically, owned (talk about not cool, man). In return, authorities once again ignored Pusher Street's illicit cannabis market.

I think we all know the lesson here: Build bigger fences.

So, I wandered the dozen cannabis shacks on Pusher Street, looking to buy a joint. Hey, it's their fault for constructing substandard fencing.

I paced beneath prominent no-photography signs, cannabis vendors lined both sides of Pusher Street for a block. They worked from haphazard shacks assembled out of nailed-together 2x4s with tarps and camouflage netting stretched across the tops and sides. The stands were built to be abandoned: A complex community surveillance network alerts dealers of impending police raids. When dealers receive the warning, they grab cash and product and vacate in minutes.

Each 6x8-foot shack held two or three dealers clad in all-black, standing between a plywood sales counter and stacks of snap-lock rubber containers. They wore ski masks, gloves, hats and nondescript, monotone clothing.

My hunt led me down Pusher and its intersecting streets where tourists and residents sipped beers and smoothies, nibbled organic salads and puffed joints at rustic outdoor café tables. Natty-haired and dirty-kneed kids raced by me untethered, screaming and laughing, the entire community their playground.

Christiania was so incongruous, so ramshackle that I couldn't help but adore it. It shouldn't exist. At least not here.

In buttoned-up and tucked-in Copenhagen, where everything's in its place, the city's preferred color palette (outside touristy Nyhavn) seems to be various shades of gray (reflecting the sky, no doubt). In Freetown Christiania, unkempt vines grew across brick buildings, hand-painted rainbows surrounded doorways and wild rose bushes sprouted from forsaken bulldozer tires.

Copenhagen's playgrounds have rubber-coated swing sets and squishy artificial turf, ameliorating any chance of injury beyond a bruised ego. Christiania's playgrounds should require tetanus shots before entering and come with the understanding that your kid may re-emerge with fewer limbs.

Like I said, Christiania shouldn't exist. Yet, here it was—an anarchist sin city thriving in chaste Copenhagen.

After I walked the block once, surveying the stalls and periphery scene, I dove in. This was my first time evaluating cannabis shacks, and with no advertising, branding or marketing, my American brain had no idea where to start. My eyes roved across Pusher Street. What color tarps had the best weed? Should I go with the black tarp and camo-leaf netting combination? Or the stall with a camouflage tarp because it showed ingenuity and efficiency? How scary should the dealers look? Why were they dressed like Russian terrorists with British accents from a 1980s action movie?

Standing on Pusher Street, I weighed tarps against camo nets and ski masks versus neck gaiters. I felt searing anticipation as dealers eyeballed me, no doubt hoping I'd choose their shack as my cannabis port of call. Glad we went with the camo netting, they were probably thinking, because there stands a man who knows a quality marijuana stall when he sees one.

I approached one that looked as frightening as the rest.

"Uh, hello."

No reply. Well, then, let us dispense with the pleasantries.

I stared at jars of different flower varieties, pre-rolled joints, rolling papers, glass pipes, grinders and lighters sitting on the plywood countertop. One dealer stood at the ready and the other lingered beside the rubber storage bins.

"So, what kind are these?" I asked, assuming English as our lingua franca.

The lead dealer activated from Sleep Mode and replied in baritone and accented English, of the Eastern European, Russian or Balkan variety: "Dis one hybrid, cross of Sharknado #5 and OG Crème Brûlée. Dis also hybrid, call JackFruit Whisper. Dis sativa, Professor's Beard. Dis indica, Elf Lettuce. All skunk. Very strong. Vee also haff hash. Vich you vant?"

"I see. Sharknado #5 you say?" My eyes scanned the weed jars, pre-rolled joints in plastic cups and pipes and paraphernalia.

"Do all strains come in pre-rolls?"

"Yes, you ken pick any for pre-roll."

"How much for a pre-roll?" I asked.

"Ten euro."

"Do you take traveler's checks? Ha. Oh, I'm kidding, kidding."

Icebreaker?

"Cash only," he said.

Stoic and unimpressed as ever. Good for him. Too young for a traveler's check reference, anyway. I bet his dad would've loved it.

While the Elf Lettuce held a certain appeal, chiefly its name and me wanting to say it aloud, I pointed to a milder strain, JackFruit Whisper, and said, "One, please."

"And a lighter," I added, selecting one adorned with Christiania's flag, an homage to the military standard of the Roman Emperor Constantine: red background with three yellow discs, representing each dot above the three lowercase letters "i" in Christiania.

We exchanged cash and parted. The transaction raised more questions than it answered. I wondered what he looked like under that mask.

Where was he from? Was selling weed why he came to Copenhagen? Was he free to leave? Who was his boss? Where is the weed grown? If I devise a funny name for a cannabis strain, where do I submit it for consideration? What happened to Sharknados 1-4?

But Pusher Street is not a lobby for in-depth conversations and probing personal interviews. While Christiania may promote love and acceptance, Pusher Street is about money and generating as much of it as possible. These Pushers of Pusher Street wouldn't hesitate to express their displeasure at spending effort on anything other than making money. And may god have mercy on the foolish soul who puts themselves between the Pushers and their money.

Case in point: Two days later, a dealer shot and wounded two cops while leaving Christiania with a bag of cannabis cash. Shootings are rare in Denmark, where residents own less than 10 guns per 100,000 people (compared to over 120 guns per 100,000 U.S. residents). The perpetrator was a Bosnian refugee with a criminal history. Christiania's furious residents tore down the cannabis shacks. Nine months later, the weed stalls reappeared on Pusher Street.

I stashed the joint in my pocket and walked past an outdoor amphitheater on Christiania's eastern periphery to the Renaissance ramparts, where I dropped my daypack, sat down and lit the cone-shaped spliff. The last surviving section of Copenhagen's once-encompassing 17th-century city walls, the ramparts remain in remarkable condition. Like citing a hippie cooperative on a military base, the walls, once built to keep people out, now invited congregation. Kids ran and played, families picnicked and backpackers smoked weed and sipped bottles of Carlsberg and Tuborg beer.

The JackFruit Whisper worked as guaranteed. I stubbed out the half-smoked joint and opened the Airbnb app, hunting for a place in Hamburg. A private room with shared shower looked clean, had great reviews , was walking distance from the train station and only cost 15 euros a night. For a two- or three-night stand, it sounded ideal. I booked one night to test the waters. My roommate would be Hans, a blond 20-something photography student and part-time model. Of course, he was.

I strolled the ramparts north, periodically relighting and puffing the spliff. My stomach growled. I passed the critical darling, Noma restaurant, where elitists fork over a small country's annual GDP for a plate of grub worms and dandelions. Free-range grub worms, though. Not that farmed grub-worm bullshit.

I crossed a pedestrian bridge and entered Paper Island. The former wharf and warehouse served the bustling strait separating the two islands comprising the Danish capital, Amager and Zealand. In 2014, entrepreneurs redeveloped Paper Island into a bustling food-truck hall serving global street fare.

Hungry diners packed Paper Island. First stop: beers, which a hand-painted sign promised were "as cold as your ex's heart." (Ha! If they only knew.) A hoppy pilsner in each hand, I lapped the old warehouse, noting the extensive options. Brazilian steaks. Korean BBQ. French standards. Kobe sliders. Mexican street tacos. Ramen noodle bowls.

Paper Island's concept was straightforward: Repurpose a massive unused and central space into an inexpensive and casual foodie haunt. Reduce the aspiring restaurateur's barrier to entry by offering flexible lease terms and suppressing costs by sharing utilities and doing minimal renovations. Restaurateurs parked their food trucks or built slap-dash kitchens inside.

Taking food trucks off Europe's dense, narrow streets and putting them inside disused warehouses was an approach sweeping Western Europe, from Foodhallen in Amsterdam to Lisbon's Mercado da Ribeira, a natural progression of dining courts, food trucks and covered markets.

Hungry diners deep queued 10 deep at every one of the over two dozen food stalls, reaffirming my decision to buy two walking-around beers. I purchased fried cod strips from the only Danish-themed truck and duck-fat fries from a French one. Sunglass-wearing diners squeezed shoulder to shoulder at the outdoor tables eating and talking, savoring Scandinavian summertime.

With my fried bounty and remaining beer, I spotted a bench on the retired wharf and devoured my lunch under the fickle Nordic sun. Clouds gathered, and with the beer gone and all traces of duck fat licked clean, I hopped aboard a train to Germany.

* * *

My eyelids drooped as I leaned against the double-pane window. For a guaranteed nap, wash down copious quantities of duck fat and fried fish with strong beer, then sit on rolling stock. I jolted myself awake, though, and resisted the napping urge. You see, I wasn't riding some ordinary train. I sat aboard one of Europe's last train-ferries.

Train-ferries nose onto a docked ship where the entire goddamn train and its contents are loaded aboard ("shunted") for a short water crossing. The specialized ferries have bottom-level train tracks in line with the wharf and huge, swinging stern doors to accommodate idling carriages side by side. An adjustable ramp with counterbalancing weights and height fittings connects the boat and wharf.

Trust me, train people live for this stuff. They snap a thousand pictures, write blog posts, start Reddit threads and keep meticulous personal notes about the experience. They stand in silent awe, birders minus binoculars.

This time, I'd be right there with them. It's not every day you can observe a boat eating train cars. And I recognized this might be my last chance to witness the doddering spectacle, an Industrial Revolution-era relic.

The world's first train-ferry launched in 1850 in Granton Harbour, Scotland, outside Edinburgh. Engineer Sir Thomas Bouch designed a curious vessel he called the Leviathan, capable of mating with a railroad dock for roll-on, roll-off loading. The Granton Harbour train-ferry survived less than 30 years, shuttling an estimated 750,000 passengers in its lifetime. But the egg was hatched and their popularity soared for a hundred years before plummeting in postwar Europe.

The Copenhagen to Hamburg train-ferry opened in 1963, ferrying three passenger cars at a time across the 11-mile Fehmarn Strait between Rødby, Denmark, and Puttgarden, Germany. Predicting this might be my last chance to ride this train-ferry proved correct: The railways discontinued the 50-minute journey in December 2019, anticipating construction beginning on a controversial replacement, The Fehmarn Belt Tunnel.

Shunted train-ferry connections are a dying breed as bridges and tunnels flatten Europe's transportation landscape. The defunct Dover, England to Dunkirk, France line, rendered obsolete in 1995 by the Channel Tunnel, is the highest profile train-ferry casualty, but not the only one. Over 50 once operated in Western Europe, but by 2021, that number had fallen to one year-round route—Reggio Calabria (Italy) to Messina, Sicily (technically, also Italy).

As we approached the dock, I straightened in my seat. Here we go! Then we slowed down; not an unexpected move. Don't want to take that ferry at full ramming speed. We crept along until jerking to a dead stop.

Oh. We can't drive aboard, passengers included? How disappointing and unfussy.

We disembarked like lowly stevedores onto the four-decker ferry before actual stevedores shunted the train aboard. They forced us to watch from behind a thick yellow "safety" line, a demarcation of dubious efficacy promising if a train were to slide off the rails toward us, that yellow paint would stop it. Europeans are doing impressive things with paint.

Stowed behind the magic yellow safety line, I stood with 15 onlookers as workers disconnected the three carriages from one another and rolled them aboard one by one using a series of ceiling-mounted mechanical pulleys. A bespectacled middle-aged man, flipped-up sunglass attachments clipped to his wireframes, scribbled into a pocket notebook. He ceased scrawling, pointed his nose in the air—he could smell fellow English-speakers—and sidled beside me.

"Amazing, isn't it? Back home in the U.K., we retired our train-ferries. Sadly. Of course, our rail lines are a shambles. Compared to the Germans, that is."

"I didn't know train-ferries existed until a few hours ago," I replied.

"A Yank! Smashing." He outstretched his hand. "I'm Nigel. Now then, I'm sure I don't have to tell you we're witnessing a marvel of railway engineering." He was a short, squat and balding man who nudged my arm with his elbow as he spoke.

"Um, marvel might be a stre..."

But Nigel wasn't one to wait for clever ripostes. He started into a lecture on the wonders of shunting and train-ferries before illuminating the trains themselves.

"What we have here are DBAG Class 605s. They'll become redundant next year when Deutsche Bahn releases upgraded DMUs. Now then, I'm telling you something you already knew. Oh, forgive me. The carriages are stunning, beautiful and were beyond innovative at their inception.

"Notice something? Ah, of course you do. No locomotive. The carriages have integrated underfloor motors. They're tilters, too. I'm sure you knew that. First of their kind. Smashing upgrade to long-distance train travel. Leave it to the bloody Germans! What will they engineer next?"

"Trains that drive onto ferries without stopping?" I proffered. Bridges and tunnels would've been my next guesses.

While Nigel had been droning on about trains, train engines and train-ferries, I had devised a plan to save them: Drive the steel snakes straight onto the ship. Yes, slow the roll, but no stopping or disembarking.

Now that would be something. Don your life jackets, folks, our ferry is in sight! Sure, we'd need longer ferries, but demand and revenue would skyrocket tenfold. I'm confident it'd more than make up for all the trains we'd lose in the sea.

"Pardon me," Nigel asked, cocking his head and narrowing his eyes.

"They should look into it. Drive 'em right onboard. Now that would be a marvel. Right?"

Nigel stood in the dank hold staring at the idled DB Something or Others. He flipped down his clip-on sunglasses and shuffled off, muttering to himself, "He can't be serious." I think he spent the entire journey down there in the dank hold admiring the trains.

I took the staircase "topside," as boat-people say. (I know how boat-people speak because talking to boat-people is an industry hazard for travel writers.) Incredible 360-degree views greeted me. Okay, maybe debarking the train, which now sat tucked inside the ship's windowless industrial bowels, was the right move. Plus, I didn't see Nigel anywhere.

Panoramic views stretched for miles across the strait and down the German coast. I flopped onto a deck chair, soaking up sunshine and fresh air. Amid a deep-blue sky, the sun shone over the placid Baltic Sea as we cruised toward the dry land of mighty Deutschland.

Hamburg

Before reaching Hamburg Hauptbahnhof, I had already departed. Mentally, that is. As I laid on the sunny ferry deck staring back at the storm brewing over Denmark, noodling my route to Barcelona, I experienced a realization. Namely, that three weeks isn't nearly as long as it sounds.

I delegated a few nights to Amsterdam and Paris, perfect big-city laboratories for testing my ground-level approach. Fascinating countryside and second cities lay between Paris and Barcelona. Enormous, intense countries, I allocated a week each for France and Spain. That meant I had to get moving, if, ironically, I was to keep traveling slowly. I resolved to make real westward progress first thing tomorrow morning, eyeing the 5:46 a.m. departure for Amsterdam.

The plan assumed I survived Hamburg's rowdy nightlife. I'd heard the rumors. Strip clubs, sex shows, rowdy bars, bawdy clubs, Hamburg's St. Pauli nightlife district reveled in after-dark sin.

The Baltic evening sunlight strained for space between shifting clouds as I approached the brick duplex. A six-foot-two, lanky, towheaded Hanseatic god with high cheekbones and a breezy attitude that said "Yes, I know I have very high cheekbones" opened the black metal door.

"Ja! Rory, welcome. I am Hans. Come in. You find the flat okay?" I shook his outstretched hand as he tossed back his blond bangs.

"Yes, no problem. Nice to meet you, Hans. Wow, you speak awesome English. Most Germans do though, huh?"

"Ja, thank you. We do in Hamburg. And I studied in London last year. Ja, so, this is a tiny apartment. Your room is next to the kitchen. I'm here by the front door. Hey, listen, I have a little work, a photo retouching job. Then my girlfriend comes over and we go out tonight, ja. You will join us? We party in St. Pauli."

Oh, Hans, you beautiful stranger, you read my mind. St. Pauli's raucous reputation warranted me, a fragile interloper, following a local guide.

"That's nice, thank you, Hans. But I don't want to intrude. Be the third wheel. Uh, do you know that phrase?"

"Don't worry. It's no problem. We meet lots of people. Our friends will be there. Join us. We'll party-party." Hans shimmied his hips, smiled and solicited a response by raising his left eyebrow.

How could I resist? He was just so friendly and convincing. And, oh my god, I could just curl up and sleep in those mesmerizing blue eyes. Hans used Airbnb to meet people, not make money. He'd had great experiences as a guest and reciprocated as a host. No wonder his room came so cheap.

"Okay, sure. I mean...ja! Ja, I will go. First, I need a shower."

"Ja, gut!" Hans pointed down the galley hallway to my bathroom. "Please have a bath," he sniffed the air above me. "You smell of hashish and duck fat."

* * *

The last thing I remember with any reasonable clarity occurred while leaving the S-bahn station and walking toward the Reeperbahn with Hans and his girlfriend, Hannah (of course).

I said, "I'm catching the early train. I can't stay out late. But I'll have

25

a couple beers with y'all."

And I never say y'all. It just came out. Maybe I felt an urge to sound more American. I don't know. But the second it tumbled forth, Hans latched on.

"Haha! Y'all. How American," he said.

Hans did not acknowledge the "I'm-going-home-early" part.

He continued, "I think I hear this word—y'all—in American movies. I like this word, y'all. I will say it tonight."

We stood on the vaunted Reeperbahn, epicenter of St. Pauli. Not since a stroll down New Orleans' Bourbon Street had I seen such public debauchery. Heavy bass pulsed from nightclubs while neon lights advertised topless escapades and bottomless drinks. Groups of inebriated revelers heaved sideways as we dodged drunken college students, drunker tourists, and the drunkest of all—businessmen.

The Reeperbahn bisects St. Pauli and serves as the district's pulsating, sin-loving thruway. Despite its foreboding-sounding name in English, it means "Rope Walk" in German. (Don't worry, I didn't rely on superpowers and vetted this translation.) Before steam engines, the age of sail required prodigious amounts of rope for riggings, and this is where those rope-makers set up shop.

Hamburg is a historic Hanseatic port—a Baltic Sea-based trade league predating modern Germany. I credit those industrious Hanseatics. In a time when most Europeans lived in squalor under a nobleman's thumb, these clever, seafaring traders built their wealth independent of monarchs. They charted their own course by connecting trade routes throughout Western and Northern Europe with the Mediterranean. A leading shipbuilder, Hamburg relies on the sea to this day.

In the 18th century, the Reeperbahn started changing. Brothels and boarding houses sprang up to serve seamen on shore leave. Turns out selling booze and sex is more lucrative than rope. Hard-drinking sailors with more cash in their pockets than common sense in their brains blew their wages on prostitutes, gambling and multiday drinking binges. The Reeperbahn as we know it today was born.

Prostitution remains legal, though restricted to certain areas and times of day, and brothels, sex shops and strip clubs permeate the strip. The last live sex club, Safari, shut its doors in 2013. While still seedy, the Reeperbahn is now more likely to attract high school and college partiers than filthy seafarers. It's just as prone now to draw live-theater patrons for its Broadway productions than Johns looking for paid sex.

But whatever you desire, you can still find it on the Reeperbahn. (Except, ironically, rope. At least not rope you'd want to touch without first running an infrared light over it.)

I followed Hans, whom I started calling "Haaaansel" at some point, and Hannah. They knew everyone on the Reeperbahn, pulling in friends with each step. Our posse was tall, fashionable and double-take beautiful, and also I was there. After a block, our crew counted 10, 12, then 20 deep. We ducked into a club as the night devolved into pure chaos.

Drinks arrived, first beers and cocktails. Then trays of shots. More drinks and wine. I nursed beers until champagne arrived. I guzzled champagne until more champagne arrived, while declining multiple offers of white lines and little pills.

We danced. Well, they danced. I swayed, bounced and retreated to the bar attempting ill-advised conversations with bartenders that went something like:

"What's it like working on the Reeperbahn?" I shouted over house electronica.

"Vas ist vhat?" they inevitably replied.

"Vas ist de vork on de Reeperbahn?" I asked, having long-since lost my German superpowers.

"Vas ist gut ja?"

"Ja."

Propped up against various bars, I wondered just what the hell I was doing on the Reeperbahn—this Mecca of excess—with people 15 years my junior. Kids, actually. But German kids. Locals. I guess that made it okay.

From here, I can't confirm complete veracity, but at various points I seem to recall yodeling strippers, foul-mouthed midget waiters, elephants performing solid stand-up comedy, greasy late-night kebabs and emotional karaoke bouts.

I lost peripheral vision. We dashed between bars and clubs until I no longer grasped who, what or where I was. I'd still be stumbling somewhere on that ruinous street if it hadn't been for Hans' Germanic siren call, rising above the Reeperbahn's din and reeling me back to safety, "Y'all! Rory, y'all!"

The 15-minute S-bahn ride back to Hans' apartment sobered me enough to realize I wouldn't be Hans' only guest that night. Hannah and Hans, along with two tipsy and flirtatious women, one as blonde as them and the other a midnight brunette, sat on each other's laps in the seats across from me as the train pulled into Berliner Tor station.

"Y'all," Hans groaned as he struggled upright.

At the front door, Hans fumbled with keys while I checked my watch: 3:15 a.m. My train departed in two-and-a-half hours.

Instant regret.

Once inside, I heard whispered German and giggling behind me as I approached my door.

"Oh, Rory. They ask if you will join us?" asked Hans.

Hans stood in his doorway with three glassy-eye, half-naked women wrapped around him, all staring at me, waiting for an answer.

I wasn't sure what to say. I'd never been invited to an orgy before. My mouth moved, but nothing came out.

"Uh."

I edged through the doorway, my torso was now halfway inside my bedroom. I smiled, wagged my finger at them and said, "Y'all crazy. Goodnight, Haaaansel, Greta and, uh, you two lovelies."

"Y'all!" Hans screamed.

They piled into his chamber. Clothes sailed into the hallway as giggles turned to moans.

I closed my door and crashed into bed, melding with the down comforter. I couldn't move, but my mind raced. As I listened to Hans' bed squeak across the hardwood floor and the DJ's residual bass thump inside my head, I stared at the ceiling and smiled.

Oh, Hamburg. It's true what they say about the Reeperbahn.

I fell asleep knowing I'd never go back.

Amsterdam

The smell of bacchanalian, beautiful-people sex lingered as I tiptoed out of Hans' flat. "Smells of stale champagne and regret," I said before closing the front door.

I staggered through the damp and misty morning as dawn broke over northern Germany. Although it was dim, I couldn't free my eyes for more than a moment, not without squinting to block the street lights, car headlights and whatever other incandescent invasion pried open my eyes and ravaged my throbbing brain.

I downed copious water before leaving Hans' apartment, but I lacked real sustenance—coffee and food. In that order. Or I would collapse on the cold Hamburg pavement a few hundred yards from the salvation of roasted beans and leavened grains. And that would mean the Reeperbahn had won, which I couldn't possibly allow. My feet reeled side to side, resisting forward movement under the strain of my backpack.

The train station came into view. I was almost there.

European train stations vary. That's right, Denmark's old Heinrich Wenck didn't design them all. But big, small, old or new, one axiom holds true: You can always find a decent pastry and espresso drink. It won't qualify as gourmet, but it'll suffice. Plus, one can't be too fussy at daybreak after living a Reeperbahn nightmare.

Beads of sweat ran down my face as I limped into Hamburg Hauptbahnhof, my steel, glass and diesel-fumed Bethlehem. The mental image of pastries so flaky they peel apart in layers and dark coffee brewed in civilization's deepest truths had sustained me those last few steps. I discovered an open coffee shop, and the European train station axiom held true. My brain slowly awakened as the departures board came into focus.

High-speed trains crisscrossing Western Europe have dramatically transformed the transportation landscape. Italy's Direttissima was the Continent's first fast train, arriving in 1978. Impressive, but that's still 14 years after Japan unveiled their first "bullet" train. France and Germany quickly followed in 1981, and the network continues growing and getting faster, with some lines regularly exceeding 200 mph. For strictly speed's sake, high-speed trains dominate, halving or better travel times and even competing with some air routes when factoring in airport time.

But many of these same routes are also served by local and regional trains. Slow trains, that is. These trains use clunkier rolling stock and make stops galore, but they allow riders more time to appreciate the scenery and train journey itself. Plus, and this is crucial, many fast trains require reservation fees even for Eurail pass holders, but slow trains do not.

A slow train was scheduled to leave in 45 minutes, or I could hop a German Deutsche Bahn high-speed InterCity Express (ICE) right now. Eurail pass holders can board Deutsche Bahn's ICEs without reservations—in sharp contrast to French and Spanish railways—but they're subject to seat availability. Popular times on high-demand routes get booked out, so Eurailers foregoing reservations should ride early or late. Indeed, I had arrived early and would tempt fate with an ICE.

ICE trains reach speeds of 185 mph, and feature plush interiors with ample power sockets, steady Wi-Fi, a bistro car and comfortable four-across seating in second class and three-across seating in first. The saloon-style layout, which means the open carriage has no private compartments, comprises four facing chairs arranged around a table, double forward-facing seats and, in first class, doubles and two-seat tables.

This passage made 11 stops en route to a connection in Osnabrück, where I could roll the dice on another German high-speed train or finish on a slow train to Amsterdam. That totaled about six hours of travel time on two trains. I relished the opportunity to write, nap off my hangover and book a hospitable Airbnb.

The modern steel, plastic and blond-wood coaches on the ICE to Osnabrück possessed blue leather seats with adjustable headrests, open overhead storage and a wall of five-foot-wide curved windows that illuminated the coach in brilliant sunshine—even while parked in the station. At this ungodly hour, few passengers boarded the train and most seats hadn't been reserved, so I slumped into a four-chair table.

The frothy latte, two cloud-like chocolate croissants, and a liter of sparkling water settled my stomach and cleared my head. I felt alive again, en route to Amsterdam. I rubbed my face, feeling a tickle of beard, and made a note to buy a razor.

After displaying my writing implements, boarding passengers would realize I was a Great Writer engaged in Great Work. They'd leave me unmolested, so I could spread my backpack, laptop, guidebook, notebook, phone, pen and comestibles all over my rolling four-top of creativity.

You see, Europeans, my brethren from over the sea, appreciate, *nay*, revere the arts on a scale that, frankly, would disturb my fellow colonials. They are what's known as "refined," denizens of high culture who quote poetry and recite Greek tragedies, sometimes en masse upon gas-lit cobblestone squares.

In this second-class ICE carriage, the European reverence for the arts meant other passengers would leave me to enjoy this four-top undisturbed, preferring to squeeze together elsewhere so the next Great Writer could produce his next Great Work.

However, before embarking on the Great Work, this Great Writer needed an Airbnb. At a reasonable price, of course. An Airbnb not too far from the Great Writer's favorite haunts, naturally.

The previous few summers, Amsterdam was awash in cheap Airbnbs. I had stayed at several of them. One was filled wall-to-ceiling with erotic art. Great little apartment, perfect location, magnificent kitchen, super clean. Lots of erotic art. Four nights in that apartment taught me much about the hitherto mysterious grooming habits of gay men.

I plugged in my dates, price range, and swiped on the Instant Booking option. And...nothing. Where did all those Airbnbs go? I reviewed the search filters. Could I rebook last year's apartment? Is there a filter option for "Erotic Art?"

Maybe if I increased the price range a smidge, but I was already probing my budget's upper limits. Good lord, it might be cheaper to snag a hostel or small hotel room. This called for a reassessment.

I tried hostels, beginning with the city center's usual suspects—St. Christopher's Inn, the Flying Pig, Ecomama—but they only had dorm rooms left. I reviewed family run hotels in good neighborhoods recommended by my guidebook, like the Bicycle Hotel. No luck; all were fully booked or well outside my budget.

I returned to Airbnb, bumped the price range beyond comfort, and, wouldn't you know, options emerged. Another price-range increase displayed more apartments and rooms. Amsterdam's Airbnbs had doubled in price since last year.

If I was going to overpay, then I'd get fleeced in my favorite central neighborhood—De Pijp, an island neighborhood south of the city center bordered by the Amstel River to the east and three canals.

Zooming in, I spotted it: an attic micro-studio in a brick townhouse on De Pijp's southwest corner. The top-floor walk-up had large windows opening over a leafy courtyard, small desk with chair, double bed and full bath. Destiny had anointed it my writer's nest. I hit "Book" the minute we got into Bremen at 6:45 a.m., our second stop.

The stink of aftershave, bad cologne, cheap beer and cigarette butts washed over the carriage as the train's doors opened. Three broad-shouldered, beer-swilling men boarded, and the elation of finding my bohemian Amsterdam penthouse drained away.

To this day, I'm unsure what "they" were. Soccer hooligans? If so, I saw no evidence of soccer fandom. They could've played NFL Euro, competed on the Strongman circuit, or wrestled bears. Whoever these belching and grunting behemoths were, they were certainly not denizens of the arts. These were not admirers of high culture!

They crowded the gangway and inspected the Deutsche Bahn car for suitable spots. With XXXL t-shirts tucked into 45-inch-waisted blue jeans, they stood at least six foot three and must have weighed 325 pounds. Each lumbering giant held a plastic convenience store bag, sagging under the weight of individual cans of lemon "radler" beer and god only knows what else.

Freshly coiffed, they were prepared for something. That much was clear. But for what? A t-shirt-and-jeans wedding? A morning bachelor's party? A violent act of soccer hooliganism?

With the coach filling fast, I knew where they would sit. I sighed at the inevitability of it all. Without greeting, let alone warning me, the gargantuan Germans thundered down in the three open chairs beside me. Surrounded, I swiped my dispersed belongings into my lap and then stuffed them into the daypack at my feet.

It became abundantly clear that these Euro Strongmen didn't care one iota about writerly pursuits or how important I looked doing them. They didn't care about the Great Work! These were not cultured sophisticates!

They never acknowledged me, instead dispensing their convenience store goodies and passing around what appeared to be homemade purple hooch that smelled like cough syrup and turpentine. They ate raw hot dogs two at a time, pulled from a damp 50 pack. Raw. Hot dogs.

My new seatmates slurped beers, occasionally whole cans in two gulps, downing lemon radler after lemon radler. I suppose I should've been grateful for the lemon smell slightly diminishing the stench of cheap beer and raw hot dogs. When finished, they crushed the empty tall boys with one hand, leaned into the aisle and tossed them into the overhead luggage storage with no-look hook shots like wheelchair-bound Kareem Abdul-Jabbars.

They didn't speak German or English. Or any discernible human language. They communicated by waving uncooked hot dogs and shaking empty beer cans, grunting and burping, hot dog bits flying from their mouths. Between bouts of ingestion and expulsion, they stared outside or down the carriage, expressionless and emotionless as statues. The Strongmen Hooligans had no reading materials and, if they owned phones, they never once glanced at them.

They continued ignoring me, never making eye contact, speaking or even rubbing elbows with me by accident, an incredible feat considering they were about 75% larger than their seats. I no longer existed.

At first, I stifled the overpowering stench of raw hot dogs and bathtub booze to try speaking with them. Every time I opened my mouth, I shut it anew to choke down the vomit surging in my throat. Everything wanted out: The heavenly croissants and lifesaving coffee, beer, champagne and whatever the yodeling strippers had poured down my gullet last night on the Reeperbahn. (Perhaps it was the lilac booze these guys were swigging.)

Oh, curse you, vengeful Reeperbahn. This was all your fault, thou thoroughfare of doom.

I had to focus and remain calm. If I could survive this journey without vomiting on 325-pound Euro NFL Strongmen Hooligans, then I assured the travel gods I'd avoid that devious Reeperbahn forever. (Even though I had already promised myself that last night.)

I considered a tactical withdrawal to the restroom. Could I capture their attention to escape my window seat? Would I have to crawl? The mere theory of movement caused me dizziness. I peeked over the chair tops, scanning the train car for vacant seats. It was no use. Passengers had occupied every one in Bremen.

They had me cornered. I abandoned notions of retreat and melted into the window and watched as flat and spongy northern Germany farmland flew by, wishing I wasn't trapped among these Vikings-on-steroids and that I was out there on the soggy farms, or anywhere, anywhere else.

Except the Reeperbahn.

* * *

Most descriptions of Amsterdam, Europe's best-preserved 17th-century city, start with the canals, which, although obvious and, hello, cliche, is understandable. They're a storybook reminder of a bygone era. And we travelers love reminders of bygone eras.

Amsterdam's main canals date from the Dutch Golden Age. They fire the imagination with flower boxes lining wrought-iron bridge railings, brick arches supporting canal walls and charming canal-side townhomes.

The Golden Age canals are well and good. However, I start with a stern warning about the goddamn street crossings, Amsterdam's silent killers. Or vicious maimers at minimum. Crossing the road requires nerves of steel, acrobatic moves and a clockmaker's precision timing. With hours before my Airbnb check-in, I risked everything and ventured toward De Pijp...on foot. With nowhere to be, I set a leisurely pace.

First, I admired Centraal Station, a massive, bustling gateway to the Continent. From the outside, it looked like Copenhagen station got up-sized—corbels, a multitude of arched windows, countless steeples and copious red bricks (the Dutch do with brick what Germans do with steel, French with paint and the British with lack of self-awareness). The interior, however, has been updated and retrofitted to accommodate the depot's surging traffic. The station churns 250,000 people daily from 15 tracks and 11 modern platforms.

The street-crossing challenge launches immediately upon leaving Centraal Station. The main thoroughfare is a cobweb of trams, cars, bikes—oh, so many bikes—buses, pedestrians hustling in particular directions and something like 40 bridges with no clear walking path in sight. It's thrilling, I reminded myself. I counted no less than six trams, three buses and a steady stream of luggage-wielding passersby between me and my destination, the tourist information office.

Amsterdam's main TI lies across this transportation morass they call Stationsplein, a transit zone in front of Centraal Station featuring now less than six tram tracks, two lanes of car and bus traffic, and, as always, an ubiquitous fleet of angry bicyclists who pause for nothing. Combat soldiers, I believe, would call this a kill box.

Putting the TI inside Centraal station would've been boring and made altogether too much sense. With its stupendous red iamsterdam sign and promises of museum reservations baiting travelers into crossing, the precarious placement is no doubt a part of the city's tourist-thinning program.

The key to crossing 80 lanes of fevered traffic, as I learned in Southeast Asia, is confidence. Wait for a traffic opening, however fleeting, then stroll across the street. Drivers will acknowledge you seized the gap and slow down, regardless of what the traffic light says.

The mercurial northern sun shone, emboldening me forward. The pedestrian light had turned red, but my momentum carried me into the tram tracks. Confidence? Check. Proceed, sir.

I cruised past a parked tram. As it pulled away, I stepped forward, but another tram pulled in front and parked three inches from my nose. Before I could bypass it, another tram parked behind me, almost nudging my backpack.

I was sandwiched between two idling trams.

With inches to spare, I couldn't turn 90 degrees. I sidestepped, praying neither steel beast would pull away with me attached. As I crab-walked off, riders in both trams stared in disgust, confusion and, I think, awe.

The next obstacle was more familiar: automotive streets. Two horseshoe lanes buzzing with Mercedes-Benz, Renaults, Volkswagens and public VDL buses separated me from the safety of the next sidewalk. The pedestrian light held green, so I sprinted across. The street was lava.

Okay, maybe I had been making too big a deal over this. The bike lane represented the last impediment to Europe's Most Dangerous TI. How hard could that be?

I already knew the answer from previous experience: hard. For if intersections are the silent killers of Amsterdam, bikes are their ready assassins. Bikers are quiet, fast and legion. One learns fast that bicyclists rule Amsterdam. Don't stand or linger in the bike lane, and if you hear the cheerful dinging of a bell, dive for cover or get run over.

Today proved a different story. My traveler's luck prevailed and after a few bikers passed, the way cleared and I completed the perilous journey only slightly shaken. As I approached, I noticed a pedestrian walking zone circumvented the traffic snarl. I'd somehow missed it when setting out. It led to the TI.

I exited the waterside office where Stationsplein forks. The French-fry stands, weed shops and sex parlors made Damrak Avenue look bleak.

Hordes of American tourists devoured French fries. Booze-soaked stag parties bulldozed through crowds, while roving bands of black-leather-clad clubbers emerged from their hotels seeking booze-and-ecstasy hangover cures. Bewildered Chinese tour groups snapped sin-filled photographs, worrying how they'd self-censor this part of the vacation slideshow.

So, I veered right, diverting from the Damrak tourist quagmire down an old-world alley, the pedestrian Hasselaerssteeg.

Two blocks down, the Flying Pig Hostel put its debauched backpacker clientele on full display: The picture window revealed the lounge and bar area, packed today, like every day, with young, sociable travelers. They smoked weed, drank Gulpener drafts and plotted escapades, a menagerie of youthful indiscretion.

I peered through the window. Backpackers huddled over phones and beers at tall bar tables, but the activity, as I remembered, centered on the raised pillow lounge that's built into the facade window. Here, on natty oversized cushions around squat tables, lollygagging budget travelers, most in their twenties, met, flirted, bragged and got faded. Backpacks adorned with Canadian flags (a Canadian traveler's worst fear is getting mistaken for an American), dreadlocked blonds and nervous new arrivals sat around low tables. Europe's dirtbag backpacker scene endures, where poor decisions, on-the-fly STDs and experiments in beer- and muesli-based nutrition continue as they have since the 1960s.

I proceeded south on Nieuwendijk until it joined the tourist bog on Dam Square. Crowds and street performers milled before the Royal Palace of Amsterdam, festooned with colonialism's spoils.

My stomach growled for lunch, but I first sought a particular cannabis coffeeshop, Dampkring. I'd never been there, but it had attained quite the reputation for a couple reasons: First, its psychedelic Middle-Earth-meets-Alice-in-Wonderland decor. Visitors rave it's mesmerizing, even before getting high.

Secondly, film buffs will recognize its intersection with Hollywood royalty. Dampkring became famous when *Ocean's Twelve* shot a scene on location with Brad Pitt, George Clooney, Matt Damon and Robbie Coltrane. After shooting, paparazzi photographers later caught George Clooney shuffling his feet outside and trying to look nondescript while his *Ocean's Twelve* costars, Matt Damon and Brad Pitt, got blitzed inside.

At the center's southern tip, near the Singelgracht canal, I found it. Even the exterior exceeded expectations: The light-brown mahogany facade featured massive turned columns sitting atop carved corbels and multicolored leaded windows. Dampkring pioneered Amsterdam's cozy-psychedelic aesthetic that's been copied across the Netherlands.

However, the weathered wood and stained-glass exterior only teased a spellbinding interior; *dampkring* is Dutch for "atmosphere." I opened the door and slid down the rabbit hole, but with Frodo, Bilbo and copious amounts of the hobbits' pipe-weed. Everything was art—the walls, ceiling, furniture, bar.

Table, stool and chair legs were sculpted into faux-tree trunks. Table tops looked like warrior shields embedded with colorful shards and bits. The bar top was crafted from two-inch-thick brown tropical hardwood. Wood paneling flowed across the walls and bar like the grain in gnarled driftwood. Dark and earthy colors dominated. I couldn't spy any 90-degree angles. Master artisans had smothered every square inch of this place with Hobbit dreamscapes.

I had stumbled inside the Keebler elves' tree. Chinese lanterns swung from the ceiling and a three-foot-tall gold-leaf Buddha statue sat in the corner. The walls and lolly columns were sculpted into psychedelic trees with back-lit stained glass. The drinks bar, circled by a dozen velvet-topped stools, commanded the most attention, while the weed bar sat tucked in the back.

Some coffeeshops, the Old Guard, adhere to more discreet guidelines around selling weed, which isn't legal in the Netherlands. Authorities tolerate adults buying marijuana if shops restrict the quantity to five grams. Some parts of the country only permit Dutch residents to buy cannabis. Prudent establishments, and OGs such as Barney's and the Greenhouse, sell pot from a separate bar. (It likewise gives them more capacity to exhibit their weed, but I digress.) As part of this ruse, there's also an expectation, a de facto requirement, that patrons buy something besides pot, such as drinks.

Regardless, it's big business in touristy Amsterdam. Coffeeshops have cannabis menus showing the type, THC percent (cannabis' active chemical), strain derivative, intended effects and any awards won. I bought a gram of Thunder Chunder (who picks these names?) and stepped to the central bar, looking for a seat to call home.

Amsterdam's coffeeshops cemented their position decades ago as the world's only safe harbor for stoners. With legalization and decriminalization in the Americas, that's no longer the case. But while the rest of Europe remains under cannabis prohibition, they're a major tourist draw. Despite their enduring popularity, coffeeshops have declined by about 50% since 2000 as authorities rooted out criminal actors and restricted where they could operate. The surviving coffeeshops are crowded.

I surveyed the teeming room, thinking about hectic Damrak that morning. Amsterdam might be a city on the verge of total tourist meltdown. Had it grown too fun and notorious for its own good? Coffeeshop throngs were one symptom.

I scanned for seats; any small slice of action would do. Low-volume electronica played on house speakers as I lingered by the bar, ordered a coffee with milk and precariously rolled a joint in my left hand while leaning against Gollum's maypole.

A barstool cleared between two guys who had been chatting *en Français* around the stool's previous inhabitant. (Why hadn't they switched seats?) Without hesitation, the guy with wavy chocolate hair under a blue flat-brim ball cap and caramel skin scooted over to the vacant stool.

I grabbed his former seat and pocketed the red-and-yellow Christiania lighter. Except, for the first time in my life, I used the change pocket above the main pocket. I don't know why, but it seemed like the right move. It came across as *très* cool because the caramel-skinned Frenchman smiled and extended his right hand.

"Farid," he said, tapping his chest.

"Farid," I confirmed, nodding.

His friend extended his right arm across Farid's chest. "Antoine."

"Antoine," I repeated, shaking his hand. "I'm Rory. Parlez-vous anglais? O español si lo prefieres?"

I hate starting conversations by asking people if they speak English. So, I offer Spanish as well. Few take me up on it, but everyone instantly regrets when I begin stumbling through *mi español*.

"Ha, yes, a little English," Farid replied. "Not so good with this." He pointed to the tapered spliff protruding from his right middle and index fingers.

"Yeah, me too," I said, glaring at my joint. They laughed and nodded.

"But better English than Spanish. We try!" Antoine grinned and put his elbows on the bar.

"America?" asked Farid, exhaling a plume of smoke toward the ceiling.

"Yes. Where in France?"

"Rouen," they said in unison. They looked about 25-years old. I'd never been to Rouen, a city in Normandy, France's north. Rouen sounded so familiar. I'd heard it mentioned recently, but couldn't recall when or why.

"Where in U.S.?" Antoine asked. He had suntanned freckled skin, light brown hair trimmed tight, and he balanced a green flat-brim baseball hat on his knee. They were trim, like distance runners, and both wore skinny jeans and t-shirts.

"I'm from Colorado," I said. Their eyes spread wide, mouths dropped, and they leaned toward me.

"Colorado? Wow. Do you mountain bike?" asked Farid, grinning ear to ear.

"Yes! I love mountain biking. Do you?" We were now brothers.

"Yes," they both acknowledged, eager to plumb their favorite topic.

"Oui. It is...our life. We work in bike shop. We ride...uh," said Antoine, who lost his English, making a circular motion with his right hand.

"You ride a lot," I said.

"Yes, a lot! All the times. Colorado—epic mountain biking, yes?" Farid said, tapping his spliff into the ashtray between us.

I nodded and beamed at hearing his basic English included the word "epic." He gleaned the word, I assumed, from watching action-sports movies, where North and South American, Japanese and European athletes inevitably mixed it up together, making English the de facto lingua franca of skiing, climbing and, of course, mountain-biking media.

"Do you know this Colorado bike? Um, is it called..." Antoine turned to Farid for the answer.

Farid needed no further prompting. He faced me. "Yet...Yeti. You know Yeti?"

"Oh, yup. I know Yeti. Great bikes. Very expensive. You like Yeti?"

Colorado-based Yeti mountain bikes set the industry standard and can cost up to $12,000. People without six-figure incomes and trust funds take out loans to buy them.

"Yes, I like Yeti very much. This is the best bike. If I live in Colorado, I will have this bike," vowed Farid, who took a long, contemplative drag from his spliff and stared at the bartop.

"If I had a Yeti, my friend, I'd give it to you." We all chuckled at my blatant lie. "So, you are in Amsterdam on holiday?" I asked as my joint burned out.

They muttered a reply, bowing their heads at the glossy-varnished wood bar. I reached into my pants pocket for the red Christiania lighter, only to remember it was in the little change pocket that I never use. I brushed it with my fingertips, pushing it further down the coin pocket.

Change pockets, I was learning, are for putting things into, not taking them out. As Farid spoke, I leaned over his lap, stretching my torso so I could stuff my fingers into that little goddamned pocket. He continued speaking. I nodded and grinned as my fingertips searched the change pocket and my left ear hovered inches from his thigh. I made contact and the delicate retrieval operation went ahead.

"Uh, you good?" Farid asked.

Farid didn't possess strong enough English or sufficiently rude manners to ask why the hell my head was perilously close to his crotch. Lacking any French and all manners, I continued digging into my pocket with my face hovering his lap.

Found it!

"Yup, good, sorry." I returned upright and relighted my joint with the Christiania lighter. While I was fumbling through the lighter-extraction mission, they had been explaining what motivated their road trip. "Sorry, I missed that. Why Amsterdam?"

They both peered down. Farid said, "It is...hot. Too hot in Rouen." They exchanged dispirited glances.

Too hot? In Rouen? That didn't make sense. It had similar weather as Amsterdam, basically. But that face, that face Farid made when he said, "Too hot," was not the face of a man fleeing Europe's late-summer heat wave.

I realized, altogether too slowly: They weren't talking about the weather. Rouen had made the news about a month ago, even in the States. And it wasn't good news, because Rouen's good news would never reach the U.S., only its bad. Wherever I'd heard it—news article or CNN segment—the Rouen factoid slowly clawed its way back to my forethought. There had been a brazen church attack. I looked it up later: Two Islamic State-inspired militants had stormed St.-Étienne church during Mass on July 26 and slit the priest's throat.

No one said a word. They both avoided eye contact, touching their flat brims and ashing their spliffs, letting their realization sink in, probably thinking, "Even the idiot American who can't even pull things out of his pants pockets knows."

No doubt Farid's caramel skin came from North African or Middle Eastern lineage. He would fit right into the little Colorado town where I live or in hipster-happening downtown Denver. I'm sure most people would assume he was Hispanic.

But this was Europe, summer 2016, a particularly "hot" time for Europe's minorities. The Syrian Civil War had been raging for several years. The Arab Spring had jolted the region's totalitarian governments, themselves descended from post-colonial puppet regimes. Europe's Islamic communities, never assimilated by the colonial powers and often ignored, cleaved between radical and moderate factions.

The extremists fought in Syria, and some brought jihad home. France, with Europe's largest Muslim population, bore the brunt. Bataclan and cafés in Paris. Bastille Day in Nice. Charlie Hebdo. Sunday Mass in Rouen.

Brown-skin Europeans lived on edge; Farid kept flipping his hat and tapping his joint. The violence had no end in sight. We sat, silently drawing from our cannabis-and-tobacco spliffs.

"Oh, right, I see. Rouen. Right. I understand."

I had no clue. What did I know about Islam? Colonialism? Immigration? Third-culture kids? I'm a suburban sixth-generation American who six hours ago was shooting tequila on the Reeperbahn with a

German dude named Hans. *Hans!*

Ever the conversational matador, I should have steered the conversation back to bicycles, but instead blurted at Farid, "Are you Muslim?"

"I'm no religion." He looked at the ceiling and paused. "My father Algérien. My mother French. But it don't matter, I'm..." Farid pointed at his caramel-skinned forearm. "Police stop me, search me. They search the house of my father. People...curse me in street, at market. They stare at me. Too hot." Antoine handed Farid a lighter to re-blaze his joint. "Antoine say, we go to Amsterdam. Uh, and we go."

"Too hot," I concurred, nodding in solidarity, even though I would never understand Farid's situation. Or how so many second-generation European Muslims like him felt.

They were adrift, betrayed by religious fanatics from their neighborhoods and disowned by their fellow countrymen. Most sought acceptance in secular Western society, like their White friends and classmates. They dressed, spoke and acted the part, but they struggled for acceptance, never finding their orbit—destined to be neither immigrant nor French, somewhere in the in-between.

I gave Farid and Antoine my WhatsApp, promised them a bed in the States should they visit, wished them a more hospitable Rouen upon their return and, someday, Yeti mountain bikes of their very own. We smiled. I bid goodbye with a cordial "ciao."

* * *

In the late-Medieval/early Renaissance period, European farmers, traders and merchants, seizing upon unaccustomed surpluses, peddled goods from vital locations near city gates and churches. Local nobility, at first incensed their peasants might discover sustenance beyond gruel and clothing finer than rags, recognized a chance for increasing royal coffers and, I'm sure, foodie cachet...someday. Markets grew and codified, while royal authorities levied taxes on vendors for safe passage and secure, regular emplacements on public squares and city centers. The European market was born, a cultural institution that continues feeding and clothing the populace today.

European markets were things I'd only read about in Émile Zola novels or seen in movies, until a family trip to London and Paris. My parents made the questionable decision to let two teenagers roam London unattended while they strolled the National Gallery. My brother and I rode the Tube south to the imposing and thoroughly engrossing Imperial War Museum. After spending the day among artillery pieces, machine guns and tanks, two satisfied young men ventured farther in search of something we'd never find in a museum. What was it? We had no idea. But we hoped our parents wouldn't approve.

We hopped the Tube south to what my *Let's Go* guidebook promised was a worthy deviation from the tourist trail. That's when we face-planted into Brixton Market, a combination outdoor and covered-arcade market, teeming with food and goods vendors. After a thoroughly Anglo-British schooling at the Imperial War Museum, we found the exact opposite in Brixton.

For a starched boy from the Midwest suburbs whose idea of exotic food shopping up to this point was buying non-yellow cheese, Brixton Market appeared like another world, like a movie set. It was real, though, and, since the Tube didn't point skyward, I was still Earth-bound. My eyes couldn't have opened any wider.

North African halal butchers, with gray stubble chin beards, black fez hats and blood-stained aprons, swung skinned goat's legs in the air as they bartered and whooped with Pakistani patrons wearing dark tunics over khaki pants. Dreadlocked Caribbean grocers, standing behind wooden racks of jackfruits, mangos and tamarinds, advertised their goods in lilting, sing-song catcalls.

We dodged steam billowing from woks of hot rice as pungent spices tickled our noses. The mosaic of colored fabrics and vibrant produce swirled together like a painter's cherished and well-worn palette. The mishmash of languages bamboozled my virgin ears and indecipherable patois-English knocked me off mental balance. I couldn't process everything or anything.

I was hooked, hooked on the strange and new, the bewildering and enchanting and everything the market represented—travel's limitless opportunity for cultural and culinary awakenings.

I was also hungry.

We sampled falafel (meh), bit into juicy papaya and drank chai tea at a sheltered market counter, sitting between a wizened Rasta grandfather doting on his twirling granddaughter and a Muslim corner-shop owner very, very into his flip phone. My first hint of Africa, the Caribbean, Islam and the developing world at large happened in London, supposed capital of the Western world.

My universe had big-banged. Anything was possible. All thanks to a market!

Unlike the chaotic Brixton Market, De Pijp's Albert Cuyp was tidy and tame. Since the government recognized it in 1905, it had grown to over 250 sellers, which many now rank as Europe's largest. It's diverse and remarkable in its gentleness, an excellent toe-dipping opportunity for market newbies. Whenever I'm in Amsterdam and seeking nourishment from multiple continents and need textiles, bicycle locks and deodorant, I locate myself over to the Albert Cuyp Market.

A flood of people exited the tram behind me as I wandered beneath an extraordinary entrance gate. Hundreds of three-faced cyanotype lanterns bearing images of eats and merchandise dangled from a galvanized steel frame rising 50 feet above the pavement. The rigging held nine vertical lanterns, four deep and 10 across.

Standing on Van Woustraat, I peered down Albert Cuypstraat. White tents ran uninterrupted for a half-mile or so to its distant terminus on Ferdinand Bolstraat. Behind the stalls, I spied a narrow sidewalk connected bustling eateries and bars interspersed with clothing, housewares, bicycle and sundry shops conducting brisk trade.

North Africans, Middle Easterners, Poles and Asians ran shops next to pure-blooded Dutch folk. Bars with propped-open doors let muted tunes escape, but otherwise vendors stood quietly behind their counters, content to let the products persuade. Customers didn't haggle or yell. They fingered apricots, inspected greens and tried on hats, browsing in hushed towns as if guarding their finds.

Patrons looped through stalls, filling rolling baskets and oversize shoulder bags for their homes and hearth: Tomatoes, cabbage, potatoes and broccoli grown in Dutch greenhouses, the world's most productive. Carrots from Great Britain. Italian meats cured to mouthwatering perfection. Plump and tender Mediterranean olives swimming in oil and herbs. Istrian truffles sat beside gigantic wheels of Gouda cheese, the dairy glory of the Netherlands.

The food stalls emitted distinct, wonderful aromas. An old Asian woman, wearing a white visor and long yellow cleaning gloves, stirred gigantic noodle pots redolent of pork, onions, bok choy and mushrooms. Fresh cheeses, so smelly and rank, competed with spit-roasted, herb-encrusted chickens. Spice sellers hawked Moroccan saffron and Indonesian turmeric, cumin, cinnamon and the Dutch favorite nutmeg, a spice for which they committed vast genocide in Indonesia (a story for another book).

The most-alluring scent, however, came from the good, old-fashioned fry truck, serving a steady stream of clients near the lantern-bedecked entrance gate. Mr. Fry Purveyor spoke in calm, careful English, accent-free, like so many Amsterdammers.

"You were admiring our new gate," he said, scooping golden-brown steak fries into a paper cone. "Two Amsterdam artists, Reinder Bakker and Hester van Dijk, worked here all last summer hand-making the lanterns in the market. They used sunlight and special paper to capture the shapes and outlines, a very traditional process.

"Look there. See that?" He pointed to the top row. "That's my lantern on the end, see the frieten?"

His *frieten*, his calling card, his deep-fried pride and joy, sat atop the gate. The gate highlights the wondrous miscellany on Cuypstraat.

"Thank you, how cool. I see how they sifted through all this commotion, all this gear. They captured what matters, the reason shoppers come here."

"Yes, we say you come for the shopping and stay for the, um, friendship! It's not for the money," he said. "Here you are." He handed over the white-paper cone wrapped tight and filled with oily fries glistening and steaming hot. "Don't forget your toppings. We have many," he declared, hovering above nine plastic pump bottles. "Curry, peanut, chili, melted Gouda, gravy, garlic, Dijon mustard, honey mustard and, my favorite and the Amsterdam favorite, real mayonnaise. Not the fake stuff from Albert Heijn."

Crisped golden brown on the outside, fleshy and soft on the inside, the fries were so piping hot I stabbed at them with the plastic mini-fork. Every identical fry was flawless with none of the over-fried, inedible bits you so often find in French fry orders the world over. I devoured a few, savoring the raw salty and oily flavor, before pumping a dollop of mayonnaise on top.

Dutch pensioners debated the merits of assorted spices. Suited-and-booted professionals pushed their bicycles and discussed spreadsheets and Q4 initiatives (I assumed). Muslim mothers in black hijabs toted bored toddlers. They, like kids everywhere, gazed at me, awestruck. Perhaps it's my fiery passion for travel that only the purest of souls, like children, can sense. Or it's my snarled red hair that's drawn unhelpful comparisons to Ronald McDonald. Toddlers make terrible conversationalists, so I may never know.

Groceries and prepared foods comprised about half the market's offerings. Non-perishables included myriad clothing and fabrics, cell phone cases, knock-off soccer jerseys and spare bicycle parts. Others sold bins of cleaning supplies and light bulbs. A few carried Indonesian-built hardwood furniture, Turkish rugs and Baroque mirrors they claimed were antique. Stacked bolts of Egyptian-spun cotton cloth stood 10-feet tall, available in primary colors and an array of patterns.

Some people shopped hurriedly, sorting through second-hand clothing bins. Other market-goers lingered, leisurely ladling olive mixes into plastic cups and chatting with their wine merchant, cheesemonger, or cell-phone case purveyor. I was one of few travelers. I leafed through the clothing and fabric stalls for fun, finishing my fries and plotting my next snack.

One Dutch culinary curiosity elicits everything from bewilderment and disgust to adoration—the pickled herring. Okay, maybe not adoration. I counted three pickled herring stands while strolling Cuypstraat. One would seem sufficient. First salted, then pickled, this grub fueled Northern Europe's dietary needs from Sweden to Iceland and even provided the oil that lit Paris' first streetlights. But it's the Dutch who parlayed herring into an empire vastly disproportionate to its size.

The Dutch relied on herring, chasing stocks along the Danish, Swedish and Norwegian coasts, where herring schools were said to be so thick one could stand a halberd axe upright in them. The nation undertook a massive shipbuilding effort that churned out fishing and merchant vessels capable of sailing global waters.

This being the always-eventful 15th century, those global waters teemed with pirates. What's a good merchant fleet to do, but arm themselves? The Dutch fishing and trading fleets, now bristling with weaponry, birthed the powerful Dutch merchant navy and nefarious colonial corporation, the Dutch East India Company. They unlocked new trading opportunities in products far more lucrative than fish, like silk and spices. And what did all those sailors, soldiers, merchants and colonists eat on far-flung sea voyages? Protein and omega-3-rich pickled herring, of course.

I chose a white tent flying several Dutch flags, a promising sign of delectable—or at least edible—pickled herring. The three blonde women in French braids working the counter could have been triplets. I would've asked, but they were all business. And business was booming: I waited several minutes before approaching the stainless steel buffet pans piled with thin herring slices.

"Hallo, can I help you?" one triplet asked.

"Two, met brood, please," I said.

She placed a delicate slice of herring atop a dry cracker-like rye bread, then adorned it with pickles and onion. Okay, I admit, I was taking the cowardly way out. *Met brood* means "with bread," which is the wimpy way of taking herring. It's more palatable this way, what a rice roll is to sashimi. The Dutch way? They hold herring filets vertically above their mouths and slowly lower it in their gullets, chomping and swallowing until the tail.

Still, I braced myself. I last slurped a pickled herring years ago, and I'm pretty sure I was heavily intoxicated. Since then, I'd gagged on fermented shark in Iceland and spent days waylaid from mussel poisoning in Turkey. Seafood can scupper the finest travel plans. I stared at the paper plate, my doubts growing.

Well, I had already paid five euros. I ate them in three bites each. They were lovely. The spicy onion and pickle danced with the salty and meaty herring. The sour-rye cracker-bread rounded out the flavor and made each bite a mini-meal. Had I just become a pickled-herring convert?

The simple grilled cheese, or "*tosti*" in Amsterdam, is street grub to which I require no conversion. Europe's Great Cheese Countries (which is all of them except that slacker Liechtenstein), excel at melting farmhouse cheeses between hearty slices of rustic bread.

The grilled-cheese stand at the Albert Cuyp Market was no secret, drawing lines six deep, the market's busiest. Sorry, pickled herring! They offered 12 types, a few vegetarian and the rest with various cured meats, all grilled to order. I requested an "Amsterbammetje"—cheese and onion—from the grinning owner. He and a helper assembled the ingredients, slathered butter and flopped it onto an electric griddle. The sandwiches were triple-layered using both Beemster and Gouda cheeses—hard, yellow Dutch cheeses that, once warmed, melded together in perfect union.

If pickled herring represents the Dutch Golden Age era, then no food could be more symbolic of the developing modern Netherlands than cheese, specifically Beemster. And while the world loves Gouda, proper Beemster comes directly from polders. These reclaimed seabeds, lakes and marshes were drained by pumps and protected by dikes, levees and seawalls, an engineering marvel that doubled the Netherlands' landmass by 1961. It's not always particularly fertile land, especially dense and nutrient-poor sea clay, but the innovative Dutch found two profitable crops that thrive in polders—tulips and grass.

Accounting for some three-quarters of the world supply, Holland's dominance of the tulip market, thanks to vast polder fields, is well known. Its hearty polder grass, however, not so much. Cows graze the polder grass, then produce outstanding milk, which is processed by coops into cheese. Beemster, which refers to a region in North Holland province from which all Beemster derives, is exhibit A. While much of the creamy, high-fat Beemster buttermilk supply goes toward cheese production, not all of it does. The Beemster coop is the exclusive milk supplier for European Ben & Jerry's ice cream.

I ate the last crunchy, gooey bite, finished in spicy onion, and contemplated ordering another.

"Thank you," I said and waved goodbye, wishing I could hear his backstory. His magnetic smile invited conversation. He was dark-skinned with a serene, angelic face and a curious accent I couldn't place. Maybe a French North African? One who'd been in the Netherlands forever?

"Bon appétit!" he said with a wave and big grin.

My gluttonous rampage and all that salty, savory food called for a cold brew, which is about the only thing you can't get in Albert Cuyp Market. But, like vultures circling their prey, pubs and corner stores form a boozy perimeter around the marketplace. I surveyed the pedestrian-only Eerste van der Helststraat, a two-block affair of atmospheric bars, cafés and restaurants.

Modest Helststraat strategically intersected Cuypstraat and Sarphati-park, De Pijp's only green space. The dozen eating and drinking establishments and the lone coffeeshop, Katsu, hummed with young, hip customers, locals and expats.

Late afternoon stretched into blissful summer evening. The oak-table patios forming a quasi-beer garden on Helststraat made it feel like a Little Munich with each establishment a mini-Augustiner-Keller. I relaxed with my pilsner between young and hip groups of after-work, under-40 professionals sitting with cocktails and bar snacks. Everyone chatted, enthused to be off the clock and socializing. I realized Amsterdammers thrive on conversation. Happy hour drinks and coffee breaks are filled with friendly banter, the loquacious Dutch always laughing, debating and storytelling.

That's when my stomach started churning. Too many fried foods on a post-Reeperbahn belly. The herring must've triggered it, the straw that splattered the camel's pants. I gulped the pilsner and raced toward my Airbnb.

In a residential area three blocks from the apartment, the traveler's diarrhea hit me hard. I doubled over and concentrated my full effort on not soiling myself in public.

Oh, god, was it dripping down my leg?

I shuffled another step, then halted and stood upright, twisting my legs like a figure skater and groaned. Every muscle in my body contracted as I warded off the onslaught. Everything I had suppressed on this morning's train ride demanded escape via the other end. My valiant intestinal victory against Euro NFL Strongmen seemed destined for a terrible reversal.

I dropped my backpack and clamped my rear as sweat dribbled down my face. Then I noticed a two-bay automotive shop below a typical brick townhouse across the street.

The Airbnb was too far away. I couldn't keep it in any longer. The garage would let me use their bathroom, I hoped. Of all tradesmen, surely mechanics can sympathize with the shits.

"It closed. Not working," said the mechanic. He wiped his right hand on grease-stained blue coveralls without looking up from the reception counter.

Sonofabitch.

"Any other bathrooms nearby? It's an emergency," I pleaded.

He shrugged, eyes fixed to his desk.

After repelling the diarrhea once more, I staggered the last few blocks, unable to bend my knees. My body contorted like I had pins-and-needles everywhere. Somehow, I checked the gut tsunami brewing in my belly long enough to climb eight steps to the front door.

"Hello, welcome Rory. I am Elin." A six-foot-tall, blonde woman in her late 30s with tall, thick cheekbones and beaming blue eyes answered the Airbnb's door wearing stiff blue nurse scrubs.

"Hi, uh, Elin, I'm...," I paused.

I'm...I'm what? About to shit my pants? In need of a bathroom stat? A disgusting glutton who couldn't help but eat every damn thing at the

AC market?

"...I'm so excited to be here. What a lovely place you have."

She led me up four flights of stairs to my waiting pied-à-terre. She had places to go. Perfect, because I did, too. Dispense with the pleasantries and unveil the toilet!

I trailed her, climbing the staircase like an elderly coal miner, laboring to lift my feet over the tread without releasing my bowels. She must've assumed I suffered a serious back injury, spying my progress over her left shoulder. I smiled through the pain, beads of sweat now streaking down my face.

The corridor's steep pitch almost sent me flying backward under my backpack's weight and gravity's gentle, unyielding pull. Like the narrow, multi-level townhomes found throughout Amsterdam, Elin's main staircase was more like a firefighter's pole.

Narrow staircases mean nothing fits up them. People barely do, especially when they're gastrointestinally compromised. Amsterdam houses have top-floor hooks extending over the sidewalk to accommodate for this. The hook holds a block and tackle that hoists furniture, construction materials and (back in the day) merchant goods to the upper floors. If only a pulley had been hoisting me aloft Elin's house, then I could have concentrated maximum effort on not spoiling my underpants.

"Yes, well, here we are. Your new flat. You have bed, desk and the bath. It is tiny, like the listing says. I hope it is fine."

We stepped inside the renovated attic space. Well, Elin stepped. I shuffled with stiff legs clenched tighter than a razor clam. The agonizing pains pillaging my midsection and perspiration lines streaking down my face didn't hinder me from recognizing how incredible the room was.

I'd appreciate it later, though. Now—with utmost desperation—I needed Elin to beat it, so I could befoul this pied-à-terre's pristine bath. The tour was over; I held the key and Wi-Fi password. What more was there?

"Where are you from?" asked Elin.

Elin blockaded my porcelain savior. Her stern face wouldn't yield a smile, matching her placid demeanor, which swung between equal parts disinterested and unconcerned had crossed into Barbara Walters territory. Her eyes seared holes through my cranium.

You demand my entire life story, Elin? Now?

"Um, Colorado?" I responded.

Colorado? What's that? Who am I?

I spied the lavatory through the half-open door behind her.

"Oh, Colorado! I know this Colorado! I...," she said.

But I interjected.

"Sorry, Elin. I have to pee. May I?" I said and gestured toward the bathroom. I didn't wish to seem rude, but I also didn't prefer shitting my trousers. "We can chat more later. I'll come down to your apartment."

"Oh, yes, of course. I go to work now. Night shift at the hospital. Let's talk tomorrow."

"Yes! Tomorrow! I love tomorrow! Perfect!"

She walked toward the staircase. I followed a half-step behind when she performed an abrupt stop and turned at the bathroom door.

For cripe's sake Elin out of the way! I nearly cried.

"I almost forgot. The windows." She gestured at the two, four-foot-tall casement windows over the bed that opened to the shared inner courtyard.

"Remember to close them at night. No matter how hot the room is. Close them at night or if you leave at night."

"Sure, Elin, no worries. I'll close them, but...why? Are you worried about thieves?" I said, imagining black-masked cartoon burglars hopping from rooftops under the moonlight.

"Pfft! Thieves?" blurted Elin, stupefied.

She stared like I was the dumbest person in the world. Maybe she was right.

"No, not thieves. Cats," she said.

"Cats?"

"Cats."

Without further explanation, she stomped downstairs, while I leaped aboard the toilet.

"Cats? Feral roof-cats? Is she crazy?" I laughed.

With all evils now evacuated, I freed the laptop and took a deep breath. The tiny IKEA desk fit my 13-inch MacBook Air, a notebook, pen, beverage and nothing else. I worked, spinning words into currency.

* * *

During my manic dash to the Airbnb, I caught a fleeting glance of a quaint restaurant-bar, Cafe Lust, occupying a quiet triangle intersection. I grabbed my journal and paperback and drifted a block over to the snug bar.

The gray-brick patio sported a dozen weathered-oak tables. I stepped inside. Soft lighting illuminated the corners. Wooden booths lined the left side, tables ran down the middle, a countertop extended below the right window and a broad, dark wood bar filled the back. Servers rushed about as a bartender operated brass taps, poured cocktails and juggled orders.

Between the dim lighting, worn wood and brass and earthy paint, the café's atmosphere felt like sipping beers in a womb. The Dutch have a specific word for this feeling somewhere between cozy, secure and convivial: *gezelligheid*. A genuinely unpronounceable word (trust me), gezelligheid is the ultimate compliment for cafés, living rooms, art galleries and coffeeshops.

I ordered two draft beers from the blonde bartender and scrutinized the room; she filled two pint glasses and presented the bill before I could turn around. Cold, hoppy and satisfying, I quaffed them in rapid succession at the window counter and returned to the bar.

"One more, please," I said.

"Just one this time?" she asked, grinning and wide-eyed.

"Haha, yes. Only one, then home," I replied. "How do I say one more in Dutch?"

"One more? You say: Nog één. Knowg—ee-in. One more. Or say een bier, alstublieft." She rinsed and refilled my glass on the two-inch-thick wood bar. Beer foam crept over the rim and slid down the side.

Patrons packed Cafe Lust, engaged in animated conversation, in Dutch. One large group had commandeered the center tables. The booths were filled, too. Each party shared intimate dialogue over drinks, full of smiles, meaningful eye contact and an occasional wild gesture that prompted eruptions of laughter.

I turned to the bartender for another quick Dutch lesson, but she was tending new customers. Bars and waiters are not free language tutors, but sometimes I try. I checked my watch, gulped my remaining beer and shuffled home.

Outside the red-brick townhouse, I looked at the sky. The moon glowed, brightening the streetlight-free block. The humid summer afternoon and evening had become an almost-comfortable night. The neighborhood, full of almost-identical brick townhomes, laid quiet, but I swore I heard laughing, the clinking of glasses and joyous celebrations.

A twinge of restlessness rippled down my spine.

"Nope," I announced and bounded up the concrete stoop.

* * *

Was I alone? Hans, is that you?

I sat upright, eyes scanning the unfamiliar field from side to side. Ah, right, Amsterdam. I was in Amsterdam. I smiled.

My brain was distorted from sleeping an invigorating eight hours and dreaming nonsensical dreams, none of which I could recall. I could have slept through an earthquake, reeling from my brush with the Reeperbahn. I recalled a mythic figure named Hans—which must have been eons ago.

In fact, it had been 24 hours. Travel is life on fast forward.

Pale morning sunshine filtered through the leaves of the European beech that stood sentinel over the courtyard, branches reaching toward the bedroom windows. The tree had twisted itself over decades inhabiting the brown-brick patio. The attic's back windows, against which the bed sat, faced south and so followed the beech tree's branches. The first hairy sprout of a beechnut pushed out from the verdant shoot closest to the window like a newborn baby opening its eyes.

I wiped the morning slumber from my eyes, stretched my arms as I inhaled and surveyed the apartment, a dream find. Clean, sparse and comfortable, it had everything I needed—bed, desk, bathroom, closet—and nothing I didn't.

The white-vinyl IKEA desk doubled as the nightstand. A tiny closet with no doors, one clothing rod and four vertical shelves lined the attic's left knee wall, the five-foot wall created where the ceiling rafters contacted the building. Carpenters had somehow wedged a full bath on the right side between the knee wall, desk and landing.

The room had faux-oak tile flooring. The furniture, walls, and linens were bright white. A frying pan showerhead pierced the bathroom wall inside a one-person glass enclosure. An intimate space with beech branches tapping the window, the room was an adult tree house, long removed from the city bustle.

An omelet joint between the Airbnb and AC Market opened its doors for the morning just as I walked by. The aroma of fresh-brewed dark roast lured me inside. I slid into a booth and reviewed the laser-etched wood menu. My stomach had recovered sufficiently to gobble a bacon-and-farmer-cheese omelet. The fluffy eggs encapsulated salty and smokey bacon, and the gooey farmhouse *"boerenkaas"* cheese spiderwebbed between my fork and plate with each bite.

I requested another latte, and with Google Maps and a clear, caffeinated state of mind, my day took shape. I hopped aboard tram #24 going north. It was standing room only among the commuter crowd as the tram jerked and careened into old town. Trams may not be the smoothest ride, I thought, but they're simpler to hop-on, hop-off and afford a nicer view than existential subterranean nothingness on subways.

I veered six long blocks east. Amsterdam was still waking up, but already visitors crowded Damrak avenue, nursing hangovers, hunting for coffeeshops and posing for selfies along the waterfront.

I weaved between Chinese, Japanese, American and Australian tours and roving young men with heavy British accents shouting obscenity-laden singalongs and catcalling women as they downed canned beers, last night's revelers refusing to give up the night.

From St. Peter's in Vatican City to London's Westminster Abbey, Europe's churches come in all sizes and styles. But none are like the Lord in the Attic, or "Ons' Lieve Heer op Solder" in Dutch. Just as the name implies, wealthy merchant Jan Hartman built a secret Catholic church in his canal home, circa 1663. A Catholic from Germany, Hartman enlarged the home and hid a staircase leading from the second floor to a soaring three-story attic.

During the 16th-century Reformation, when Protestants broke from their Catholic masters, the Netherlands sided with Protestants and started the Dutch Reformed Church. Even then, the world viewed Amsterdam as an open-minded and tolerant city. At first, Amsterdam tacked toward neutrality while embracing Calvinist Protestantism. In fact, it welcomed Catholic (and Jewish and Muslim) refugees fleeing Protestant persecution from countries like Britain, France and Germany.

The Protestant-Catholic divide fractured along national lines, as the Protestant Netherlands folded the religious battle into its ongoing war of independence against Spain. They defeated Catholic Spain, achieving autonomy in 1648 after the devastating Eighty Years' War. In that war's heated late stages, Amsterdam's Catholics converted to Calvinism in droves. Some, however, refused and continued practicing Catholicism in seclusion, a practice that continued even after war's end. Since, you know, religion was still a touchy subject.

During the 17th-century third wave of Protestantism, Catholics built this clandestine house of prayer in Jan Hartman's attic. A museum since 1888, when Catholics consecrated the Basilica of St. Nicholas nearby, it's far too small to host big tour groups. It's neither grandiose in scale and construction nor does it have any relics or significant works of art. It's concealed from street level, unbeknownst to tourists who walk past it all day long. So, Lord in the Attic persists as Amsterdam's second most-famous hiding spot.

I was one of three people climbing the hidden staircase past period-furnished rooms to the surreptitious loft of God. For a tiny, cramped area, I had much to process. It was wide enough for a single pew across and five deep with enclosed viewing boxes installed on each side. A balcony hung along three sides, cantilevering one-third the way over the nave. Metal rods spanning the gap fought gravity to keep the sagging galleries from kissing.

The church's most striking aspect, besides its utter existence, was all the pink paint. Gaudy pink paint covered every stick of woodwork—roof beams, wainscoting, balusters, handrails—all pink. Beyond brightening the dim attic, the pink paint and other stylistic influences, like the gilded-top Corinthian columns, helped anchor the space to Baroque churches that weren't hidden in attics. Just because we're worshiping in an attic doesn't mean it has to feel like we're worshiping in an attic, they must've thought. To that end, they succeeded, capturing the exuberance of Baroque in the Barbie-pink attic.

Simple brass light fixtures adorned the balcony and directed my attention to the marble, candle-bedecked pulpit. Behind the lectern, the Baroque altar contained three ascending artworks. On the bottom, an oil painting depicting the Baptism of Christ by Jacob de Wit led my eye upward to a stucco statue of God the Father and continued skyward to the crescendo, a stucco dove portraying the Holy Spirit against a stark-white, divine ceiling.

It creaked underfoot and smelled like my grandparents' mothballed attic. The former place of worship was in immaculate condition. The pink paint contained no chips, and I detected no dust in the over 350-year-old church.

Docents didn't lead tours, and there wasn't an audio guide. Just a three-panel paper pamphlet and freedom to roam and investigate. I imagined the astonishing construction, workers discreetly sawing, hammering, planing and leveling, wielding their hand tools with extreme secrecy. I sat in the central pews, ran my hand along the wooden bench and imagined undercover Sunday Mass attendees wearing their Renaissance best tiptoeing up the veiled stairwell.

Neighbors, constables and fellow merchants—perhaps even Rembrandt, who lived nearby—no doubt noticed the stream of Sunday visitors and weekday carpenters at that upper-class merchant home in old Amsterdam's heart. After all, it had a not-insignificant 21-pipe organ. Whatever was happening in the canal home was their private business. If it didn't bother anybody, there was no need to fuss.

Decades of religious strife and political warfare certainly took its toll on Amsterdam's renowned tolerance. Lord in the Attic church is the only surviving of several Catholic churches that operated in secrecy out of private homes. So, what happened to the prominent Catholic churches when Amsterdam flipped to Protestantism? Two blocks south of Lord in the Attic, I found an answer.

Built to impress and intimidate at over 36,000 square feet, the Oude Kerk, or Old Church, was consecrated Roman Catholic in 1306. A church this vast couldn't hide à la Lord in the Attic, so it embraced Calvinism in 1578.

The conversion didn't prevent its sacking and looting, however, as mobs of angry residents stormed the church during the 16th-century Dutch Revolt. Looters destroyed precious artwork and left behind only the ceiling paintings, which they couldn't reach. By the late 17th century, the church had attained peak neglect. Inside the once-grand building, vagrants squatted and itinerant vendors set up ad-hoc markets during the tumultuous post-Reformation period.

Church authorities cleaned up, and today it serves Protestant worship and as a city-run art and history museum. It's the oldest building in Amsterdam, and a superb example of medieval architecture, on par with Paris' Notre-Dame Cathedral.

The immense wood ceiling drew my attention. Made of six- to 10-inch-wide planks cut from Estonian oak trees, the ceiling formed a broad, U-shaped arch. The graceful vault sat atop stone walls bound by immense beams sitting on massive oak corbels emerging from monolithic plaster columns.

It looked like an upside-down boat was lugged atop the walls and called a roof. Given Amsterdam's maritime legacy, that could be the case. Local artisans were experienced at building boats, but gargantuan churches? Not so much.

It also hosts Amsterdam's strangest holy event. Every year, Dutch Catholics meet here following the start of the Mirakelfeest, held the first Wednesday after March 12, to commemorate the Miracle of Amsterdam.

The Miracle of Amsterdam, according to an irrefutable Catholic legend that definitely happened, occurred in 1345. A dying man was read his last rites and given the Holy Sacrament, wine and biscuit representing the blood and body of Christ. He threw up the bread, which was tossed in the fire. But the cracker didn't burn. No, sir, it didn't. The next day, it sat intact atop the pile of ashes. (Ring the miracle bell!)

The man's wife sent for a priest who promptly conducted a miracle evaluation at the Old Church. (Back then, I assumed, they called it "the You're-Just-Big-For-Your-Age Church.") The next day, the priest opened the linen chest where he'd stored the potential miracle only to find the crisp floating inside. Clearly, it was time to involve a bishop.

Let's recap: A vomit-covered crisp didn't burn.

The Bishop of Utrecht, exercising his malleable interpretation of the metaphysical, declared it a miracle after a thorough one-year investigation. Ever since, Catholics assemble annually to silently walk from the Chapel of the Beguines, where the miracle occurred, to the Oude Kerk.

Here's where it gets murky on top of odd. Miracles should have significance in both the celestial and natural worlds, like Mother Teresa using supernatural powers to heal Earth's ill. This was a cracker, a symbolic host. It didn't feed thousands, cure a blind person, or save the elephants. It was just an unburnt, vomit-covered wafer...lying there.

The whole affair feels a bit like miracle-reaching, a rushed minimal-effort miracle. Before Liberace and David Copperfield, the wow factor required less gusto. We peasants were impressed by less, and mystical rumors survived generations.

I could've done well back then, I surmised.

* * *

Both Lord in the Attic and Oude Kerk stand in De Wallen, Amsterdam's Red Light District. I couldn't help noticing the incongruity of seeing the city's two most striking churches besieged by sin. They share a parish with prostitutes, cannabis cafés, bars, sex clubs, Thai takeout and psychedelic "smart" shops backed by lord knows how many criminal gangs. (Tip: The Thai takeout joints are the worst for you.) Not to mention, intoxicated 20-something Brits roamed the streets for weed and beer.

I wandered north under gauche neon lights, contemplating those churches' improbable locations, shining examples of Amsterdam's acceptance, tolerance, paradoxes and total lack of urban planning. It's a graceful and competent city, balancing prodigious demands from locals and tourists with admirable aplomb. It's survived a lot: invasions, world wars, famine.

Yet, I wondered, could Amsterdam survive modern tourism?

Tourists thronged the streets as I swerved toward Brouwerij de Prael. A college-age girl sat on the curb with her head between her knees. Her fellow travelers clustered around her, whispering and exchanging concerned glances, as one of them in butt-revealing shorts and a ripped oversize t-shirt comforted her.

A couple shared joints on the two-foot-wide brick skirting between the sidewalk and canal, oblivious to the pedestrians besieging them from all directions. Orange rental bikes swerved around groups and hopped curbs. I escaped the madness down a nondescript alley.

Brouwerij de Prael hosted no less than 8 million people that exquisite day. It was tucked in an alley and stood about two canal houses or 20-feet wide. I elbowed into a community table, ordering two glasses of 5.7% ABV Bitterblond beer and a platter of smoked salmon, pickled anchovies and steamed mackerel with rustic, flour-stained beer bread and a hefty cup of horseradish sauce.

Now early afternoon, the walk to Dam Square proved a minefield of tour groups and inebriated revelers, an old town overrun by rolling parties. On Dam Square, throngs gathered around buskers performing comedy routines, magic shows and live music. The line to the wax museum whose name we don't mention snaked around the intersection. Confounded tour groups, fresh off air-conditioned buses, walked in circles, wondering, is this all there is to Amsterdam? A palace, wax foundation, peddlers and nonstop crowds?

Desperate street salesmen, sweaty from hawking junk in the sun, offered trinkets, glass pipes and, when those were turned down, their top-shelf merchandise: "Cocaine? Ecstasy? Xanax?" they whispered, baiting eye contact.

I arrived in the Jordaan neighborhood via Raadhuisstraat. I ambled north on Herengracht, through the "9 Streets," an upscale shopping and dining area laced with Amsterdam's most breathtaking canals. While still touristy, the Jordaan gave me pause to catch my breath and plan my next stop as I traced the canals on foot—Keizersgracht, Prinsengracht, Bloemgracht.

Once a 17th-century working-class neighborhood noted for its leftist politics, the Jordaan devolved into a slum and narrowly avoided the wrecking ball after World War II. Gentrification in the 1970s changed it into one of Amsterdam's most charming areas. The narrow brick canal houses, once home to merchants who replenished their stocks via canal deliveries, leaned against each other, as if bearing themselves up after a night of too much drink.

Anne Frank and her family hid from Nazis where the present-day museum stands. Nowadays, boutiques, pricey restaurants and an excellent outdoor market, Noordermarkt, keep the Jordaan high-rent and often-Instagrammed.

On the Jordaan's edge, I pulled into the corner coffeeshop, La Tertulia.

A family-run establishment since 1983 meant it was an OG and a real outlier, since it wasn't controlled by shady holding companies and foreign subsidiaries. I peeked inside. Its artsy-shabby interior and low-key, "find-us-if-you-dare" vibe made it the antithesis of most neon-, electronica- and tourist-fueled coffeeshops inside the canal ring.

The bartender, a woman with blue-streaked hair and tattoo sleeves on both arms, considered my question. She filled a cappuccino order as she'd done countless times, cranking and pulling levers without looking. She stared at the potted bamboo and plants that formed a private garden near La Tertulia's entrance.

"Yes, it's always high season now. We used to have quiet time. Now, it's high season for tourism all year. No stopping."

Cannabis-infused, individually wrapped vegan "space" cakes filled a countertop basket. I followed her eyes to the indoor garden, on a half-level above the bar, being fed sunlight through large windows and fluorescent light from four long bulbs.

"Are you from Amsterdam?" I asked.

"Yes, I grew up here. I lived in London for two years, but I returned." She placed the cappuccinos on the counter.

"What's it like living here? Now that tourists are here all year."

"It's hard, expensive. Just look at what Airbnb does. It's impossible for normal Dutch people to live in the center. If I want to put up with the parties, drugs, clubs, drunken Brits, I can't afford it. Last year, I moved with a friend south, outside the canal ring. It's what we can manage and I appreciate it, but it's not Amsterdam," she said, sighing. "It's complicated. I feel like a stranger."

"Yeah, drats. Those Airbnb bastards," I muttered, searching sideways, praying she wouldn't inquire where I slept.

My wristwatch said 4:14 p.m. I resisted further cannabis-driven conversation and scooted to the nearby Museum of Canals before its 5 p.m. closure. Europe's famous and cavernous art, science and history museums stop admitting visitors an hour before closing. The Museum of Canals is neither famous nor cavernous. I would be admitted.

With La Tertulia's refreshments setting the mood, the exhibit featured alluring ambient lighting, interactive multimedia displays and meticulously designed city and canalhouse models. A dark hallway opened into a series of 3D models demonstrating Amsterdam's marshy founding and the canals' initial construction. The canals followed, re-routed and combined existing waterways while eking out some reclaimed land. Amsterdam soon ran out of land because it's not land, it's water. So, land-people moved to the canals and became barge-people. It's the real-life version of Kevin Costner's greatest cinematic masturbation, *Waterworld*, except the Dutch haven't evolved neck-gills. Yet.

I then studied wall-mounted, back-lit cross-sections showing Amsterdam townhomes sitting on millions of trees hammered into the marshland. Against all odds, piling by piling, brick by brick, a booming metropolis emerged, inundated with water; its stone, asphalt and steel sitting defiantly atop an underwater forest. It was engrossing, a feeling of true human accomplishment (that I had nothing to do with) washed over me. But perhaps I too could help conquer the sea. I might just become a canalman, I thought, flitting about Amsterdam's liquid cobweb, maintaining humanity's grip on the North Sea.

At 5:05 p.m., the security guard ushered me out.

"But there's more!" I protested.

* * *

Two happy hour pints later found me at a brown café, Festina Lente. An after-work crowd similar to De Pijp packed the downstairs, but I found a small, oval table in the loft. I sat facing the room and leaned against the wood-paneled wall. Above me, posters advertised a poetry contest. The busy server brought refills when my beer glass dropped below halfway. I wrote a page in my notebook, read my paperback and drank in the scene. And a few more beers.

I savored the day's fleeting sunshine while walking toward De Pijp. The Leidsegracht canal led me to the neighborhood north of Vondelpark, an area I soon discovered was rich with Indonesian restaurants specializing in elaborate *rijsttafel*. Dutch for "rice table," rijsttafel is a colonial adaptation drawn from the fertile abundance of Maritime Southeast Asia. At least, that's what Kartika's menu said, as I stood outside reading it. Big windows and lots of plants gave the restaurant an airy and charming atmosphere, like a winter garden or greenhouse. Long rows of tables ran on either side of a dividing wall covered with bamboo and palms, where I was seated at a two-person table.

The rijsttafel arrived 45 minutes, or two more beers, after I ordered. The round, pizza-pan-size platter contained several bowls of steamed, milked and fried rice along with 10 smaller clay pots of pork belly, chicken satay, curry, caramelized beef, roasted pork, banana fritters, spring rolls and various peanut and coconut sauces.

I ate everything and eyed the front door. Although servers began shutting down the restaurant, my feet refused to carry my bulging stomach. Had I actually been in Indonesia, I would've hailed a *tuk-tuk* to haul me away. Plus, the night remained as hot and muggy as the daytime, so I nixed the thought of walking home. I stepped aboard tram #3 to De Pijp. Soon, I climbed the four floors to my writer's nest, catching my breath at each landing, and plunged into bed, exhausted.

After lying in the sweat-soaked sheets for a moment, I couldn't fall asleep. My dreamy fourth-floor perch was way hotter than outside. I rose to my knees, louvered open the two windows above the bed, and let the nighttime breeze cool me off.

"Ah," I announced and slumped onto the mattress, closing my eyes. A gentle wind circulated, making the accommodation deliciously cool. I fell asleep dreaming about working a canal cleanup, fishing out rusty bicycles, saving damsels from canal-related distresses, and being a real, honest-to-god canalman. At last.

* * *

After midnight, it'd gotten cool enough for me to pull up the covers. I didn't open my eyes, but later on I felt the blankets move. I tucked them to my chin, eyes still shut, then after a half-asleep minute or two, they ended up down below my shoulders again.

This continued twice more before I scooched against the headboard and opened my eyes. My vision adjusted to the inky night. Over a dozen glowing eyes stared back at me. Two yellow eyes blazed two feet from my face, and a heavy weight pawed at my sheets. I pulled the sheets up. Yellow Eyes pulled them down.

"Meow?" it demanded.

"Crap. Roof-cats!"

I leaped from bed and saw another twelve-plus eyes on the beech tree, calmly waiting their turn to storm my Airbnb. I slammed shut the windows, turning to watch six, now seven cats, stalk around my room, eyeballing me and meowing demands. I had a full-blown roof-cat invasion on my hands. They sniffed the floor, pawed furniture and began settling in for the night.

"No, no way. Not tonight, goddamn roof-cats. Not my writers' nest," I declared.

I lurched at the nearest roof-cat, which sprang atop my desk and knocked over an empty glass, which I caught midair. All I seized was the glass, though. The cat sat on my bed, outside my grasp, staring at me like I was the dumbest man in the world.

I lunged at another. Then another. They taunted me as I chased them around the tiny apartment. They evaded my lunges, every "Meow?" a ridiculing blow. I thrusted at them with open, steady hands, only grabbing air or a puff of fur. (Hair? Fur? I don't know what covers these feather-footed beasts.)

The slippery felines spent little effort dodging me. Each time they vaulted onto or scampered under something, they tilted their heads at me like I was the crazy one invading their bedroom sanctuary.

"Meow?"

Corralling them like a madman wasn't working. I wondered what a bona-fide canalman would do in this situation. But who was I kidding? I was no heroic canalman, merely a simple traveler faced with a roof-cat invasion. I whistled, trying to lure them out the window, snapped my fingers and sweet-talked them.

"Here kitty-kitty. Let's go outside. Yay, outside. Yay."

"Meow?" They always responded.

Now's an appropriate point to mention: I'm a dog person. I have never owned cats, and I will never own them. Cats confound me. What's wrong with them?

If they entered through the window, then they'd leave through the window. Right? Seems logical. Yet, every time I corralled one close enough to open the window, they'd hiss and howl like I was coaxing them through a flaming ring.

I sat on the bed, dejected. Two cats meowed at each other. A nefarious plot was on the rise. They were banding together, scheming a coup d'cat. I had to act.

Desperation sunk in. My shoes sat beside the bed. Hmm. I pulled out the laces. Cats play with strings. That's an immutable law of nature. But these cats, the nefarious roof-cats of Amsterdam, were immune to the temptations of dangling strings.

If I can't trick them with laces, can I lasso the goddamn things?

Should I give up, pack my stuff and flee? Leave the world's most perfect Airbnb to the roof-cats?

No, no, I couldn't do that. The owner would shred me in the reviews, and I have a flawless Airbnb profile to maintain. I wouldn't dream of jeopardizing my Airbnb rep by doing something stupid like strangling a bunch of roof-cats, absconding at midnight, or, I don't know, smoking weed inside the townhouse.

Aha! Weed! That's it!

Cats like cannabis. Well, they could like it. They might like it. What the hell? I had nothing left to lose. My options had shrunk to luring them away with weed or abandoning my Airbnb to a roof-cat gang.

After retrieving my backpack and digging out the sparkly nugget I had leftover from La Tertulia, I approached the closest cat. I held the bud toward its snout. It tilted its head asking, "Meow?"

The cursed thing seemed interested, moving forward and puckering its nostrils.

"Meow?"

"Yes, yes, good roof-cat. Kitty-kitty want some weedy-weedy?" I urged the soulless beast and led it to the window.

The window opened after two turns and I held the bud outside, just above the beech branch. The cat strode over my pillow, never lifting its gaze from the glistening flower.

"Here ya go, kitty-kitty." I waved the nugget across its nose.

The cat climbed the branch toward the weed. I held it in my fingertips, extending my right arm. I play-tossed the nugget, which caught the cat's attention long enough for me to slide off the windowsill and close the window.

"One down. Six to go."

I became the Pied Piper of baiting roof-cats into a beech tree using nothing but Sour Thaddywhacker #2. I improved, once even leading two cats simultaneously. Twenty minutes later, the herding process relocated all roof-cats to roofs elsewhere. I sank into bed.

"Goddamn roof-cats," I muttered before drifting off.

* * *

A blue sky greeted me outside the restaurant and I faced the sunshine, patting my belly still bursting from an enormous breakfast of farmhouse sausage, spring greens, organic eggs and melted cheese—all sourced from the Netherlands.

I arrived outside the Rembrandt House Museum at opening. I'm a sucker for folk museums and historic workshops; where the art got made interests me more than the actual art. Once into the Rembrandt House, the artist's restored former residence came alive. The furnishings, wall hangings, woodwork and drapery were all faithful reproductions of how the famous artist lived, down to his re-created studio.

I ran my hands over the antique table tops, examined the furniture and door hardware—hinges, straps, handles and pulls. The assembly—"joinery"—fascinated me. Craftsmen wove together lumber using dovetails, grooves, some glue and plenty of skill, but no nails or screws, exhibiting an understanding of their mediums—wood, masonry, iron—on par with any artist, including Rembrandt himself. In Rembrandt's studio, I closed my eyes, feeling his presence and hearing the workshop clamor of mixing paints, shouting orders to assistants, requesting new sketches, reviewing original canvases.

Wertheimpark, a verdant canal-side patch of turf, trees and plants, caught my eye as I strode toward Flevopark via the Plantage neighborhood, the city's greenest and leafiest patch not called Vondelpark. The neighborhood is lovely, idyllic and unbeatable on a beautiful summer day. The pocket-sized Wertheimpark appeared vacant.

Dropping my daypack, I slumped aboard a wooden bench facing

the Nieuwe Herengracht canal and read my paperback. A vigorous hedgerow formed a half-circle niche around the oak seat. The brick canal homes across the canal appeared tidy and prosperous. A wee outboard puttered by, its ripple wake clapped the canal walls. Uncovering this spot was destiny. It was the middle of a weekday on Amsterdam's quiet east side. Nobody was around.

After reading and fidgeting with the red Christiania lighter, I thanked the pristine pocket park and lonesome waterway for the serene moment. While exiting, I noticed a sculpture, marker or something in the park's east corner. I followed the white gravel path and came upon Amsterdam's Auschwitz Monument. The haunting, shattered-glass memorial left me reeling. Near the gate, a young family with two eager kids charged through the entrance and bounded onto the plush grass.

I scampered down Plantage Middenlaan avenue past ARTIS zoo toward Flevopark and Amsterdam's eastern outskirts. After walking Lozingskanaal, lined with beautiful brick townhomes and modern flat-roofed houseboats, I entered Flevopark at Amsterdam's Graffiti Bridge. I ducked into the underpass, finding every inch covered in billowy, polychromatic tags, melting skulls, psychedelic teddy bears and fantastical mushrooms with human faces. On the opposite concrete pier, two painters wearing respirators sprayed a blue background before laying out a massive block "H" stencil.

Lush lawns were interspersed with ponds and shaded by umbrella oaks, towering beech trees and bulbous willows amid thickets of bushy undergrowth. Quite proud of myself for finding Flevopark, I sauntered an immaculate gravel path leading past an outdoor swimming pool full of rollicking children when I spotted something that couldn't possibly exist in Amsterdam. In fact, I observed a pair, squawking at one another, their silky-smooth lime-green bodies giving away their positions halfway up an oak. No, I thought, I must be mistaken. But the long tail feathers confirmed they were indeed parakeets, tropical parrots a long, long way from home.

I'd later learn that Amsterdam has a native parakeet population roosting in its parks. As the climate warms, they're positively thriving in Holland. No one's sure exactly how the parakeets got there, though some conspiracy theories posit American musician Jimi Hendrix released the birds while on tour in Europe. That's a stretch. I'm sure owners accidentally and intentionally released their pets, establishing the colony. (Sorry, Jimi.) Regardless, they've adapted, somehow, some way developing a biological niche in Amsterdam.

First Graffiti Bridge. Now, parakeets. That morning over breakfast, Flevopark was nothing more than a green blotch on the map, a convenient endpoint in eastern Amsterdam where I could hop a tram back to the city center.

Locals filled a grassy lawn, playing Frisbee, picnicking and feasting on UV. As the walking path turned past a playground and small restaurant, I encountered a pond lined with weeping willows whose branches patted the water's surface. A graceful chapel-like building boasting full-length arched windows and a multi-tiered pondside patio hosted happy groups chatting and clinking glasses. I traced the pond toward the sounds of revelry.

An overgrown brick path forked off the main walkway and led to a propped-open arched door from which locals streamed in and out. Its steep, red-tile roof terminated at alabaster dentil moldings above the arched windows, their black wooden shutters thrown open. Long beer-garden slab tables sat under trees next to the patio. Locals carrying cocktail glasses and beers buzzed back and forth between the white chapel of fun and its many outdoor areas. Shrouded in oaks and willows, I had stumbled upon a storybook tucked between trees and its own secret pond.

"What do you recommend?" I asked the brown-haired woman. She served drinks from behind a six-foot-long wooden bar. Shelves held myriad bottles of liquor painstakingly handmade from the in-house distillery. Besides the requisite gin in several variations and bitters decanted in narrow clear bottles, they advertised some 100 house-distilled drinks, including *genever*, eau de vie, liqueur, fruit-juice mixers and vodka.

"You'll like our gin sling, a three-year gin with angostura, lime, Cointreau, cherry juice." Her lean arms mixed several bottled contents and poured the iced-pink concoction into a delicate tulip glass and topped it with a lime slice. Patrons stood five deep patiently waiting to order, so I carefully navigated the gathering crush of humanity.

Distillery 't Nieuwe Diep sat in a gorgeous decommissioned pumping station of the Oetewaler Polder, reclaimed from the sea in 1630, then redeveloped in the 1870s as the city coveted more cobblestones and apartments. Flevopark occupied the southeast corner of the former polder.

Blooming hydrangea, their white flower bulbs the size of grapefruits, ensconced the stone patio. An open bench seat beckoned from the bottom terrace. Beelining to the bench only caused me to spill a third of my drink, but soon I was seated with my notebook and a refreshingly sweet-and-sour gin. I listened to the lilting Dutch conversations percolating around me, punctuated with guffaws. In the pond a few feet away, white geese and green ducks slurped algae while blue herons hunted along the shoreline and those wayward parakeets flitted between branches.

* * *

It was snack time and, in Amsterdam, snack time means *bitterballen* time. The breaded and deep-fried balls dominate the bar-snack scene, probably originating from Spain's 17th-century occupation of the Netherlands. Bitterballen look like croquettes, only rounder and shaped like a golf ball, not the Spanish-style egg. The real difference rests in the filling.

Beef, veal or a multi-meat mixture are the traditional Dutch fillings, though some creative types nowadays experiment with foraged edibles and game meat. Minced or chopped, the meat is combined with gravy and beef broth, with butter and flour added for extra thickness. A dash of salt, pepper, parsley and nutmeg (here it is again) round out the savory flavor profile. This is then deep-fried.

After alighting the tram near De Pijp, I skipped into a brown café. The female bartender nodded as I replied yes, I had, in fact, some understanding of the bitterballen craze.

"Yes, okay, so you know the bitterballen. Perfect. We have eight varieties here, all typical Dutch favorites. Veal, beef, spicy beef, spicy chicken, curry, rabbit and vegetarian."

The barkeep, wearing a white tank top, was polite and straightforward, standing behind eight brass taps mounted atop a half-circle mahogany bar. She moved with ease between taps, the glass case of bitterballen and three shelves of liquor bottles.

"Wow, huh, how about all of them? They look tasty. May I try spicy beef, rabbit and veal? Two each please."

"Yes, of course." She plucked two fried orbs from each pile using long stainless steel tongs she wielded as a natural extension of her arm.

She then plunged Dutch flag toothpicks into each golf-ball-size delicacy, and squirted yellow mustard into a shallow dipping bowl. She handed me the platter with a reluctant smile that assumed I'd hate them.

They were salty, spicy, flavorful and divine. The batter was crispy but not dry or crunchy. A warm, gooey spice explosion awaited on the inside. The curry ball had me wiping my runny nose and watery eyes as if I'd eaten a ghost pepper, crying tears of curry joy.

As I nibbled and sipped a pilsner, I pulled out my phone to locate an Airbnb in Paris. Just the thought of arriving in dreamy Paris sent shivers down my spine. Like many before me, Paris will forever hold an unassailable position in my heart.

The Airbnb map lit up with rentals, a wider and cheaper range than Amsterdam. I sorted, pinched and zoomed until zeroing-in on a couple intriguing options: A one-bed, one-bath on the border of the 3rd and 11th *arrondissements* on the Right Bank, an up-and-coming foodie area, and a studio in the Left Bank's Latin Quarter. Both were private flats. The Latin Quarter is busy and raucous. I didn't think I had it in me.

The 3rd and 11th arrondissements sat dead center between the historic center, the Canal St.-Martin area and several burgeoning neighborhoods like Belleville and the whole 11th. The listing showed several amenities, including a bona fide Parisian rarity: washing machine. I clicked Instant Book without thinking twice. How'd the Airbnb gods know my dirty laundry was overdue? I swigged my beer until only suds filled the bottom, paid the tab and strolled home.

I was feeling tired and achy en route to my attic Airbnb. Three weeks of travel had trashed my body. I needed water, the hotter the better. Whenever and wherever I'm traveling, swimming or soaking cures all. Wild, freshwater swimming in lakes, rivers, ponds, moats or whatever is my preference, but I'll make do in any submersible body of water.

Although Amsterdam *is* water, legal swims in clean water aren't exactly abundant. The canals are filled with bicycles and pollution (thanks, Canals Museum!), and the coast is a train ride away, too far for a late-afternoon excursion. By the time I pulled myself together, figured out trains and reached a destination, sunlight would be waning.

Elin was closing the front door in light-green nurse scrubs when I showed up at the stoop. How convenient. We said hello, and I turned the spotlight on her.

"You have lived in Amsterdam your entire life? On De Pijp?"

"Yes, all my life in Amsterdam, but I came to De Pijp last year. De Pijp is one of the last places in the center that normal people can afford."

Tugging at her nurse's badge, she stared at the sidewalk, then me, with her big, round vibrant blue eyes, plunging me into the Mediterranean Sea. Her cheekbones rose to just below those eyes with a prominent nose between. Her blonde hair was pulled tight into a ponytail. We stood roughly at eye level.

She released a protracted sigh and put her right fist on her hip. "But it's very expensive...getting more expensive every year. I love Amsterdam. It's my home, but it's becoming so crowded. I don't think tourists, all visitors, treat it well. I feel ready to leave, perhaps for two, three years. Travel or live somewhere else."

"Why?" If I owned an apartment in De Pijp, I'd never move.

"I guess I want a break. It's so full now. All the tourism makes it difficult to live a normal life. And, well," Elin smiled, "I'd like to live somewhere warmer with more sunlight. Maybe Dubai!"

The word Dubai hurt my ears. No region anywhere in the world interests me less than the gauche, authoritarian Gulf States. I mean, unless someone else is paying, then, fine, I'll see what all the fuss is about.

"Great, Dubai, what a place! I'm sure you'd love it there—plenty of sun," I replied. "Elin, I know you're going to work, but I have a question. Can you suggest a public pool or spa or somewhere I can go swimming? Or take a hot tub or sauna?"

"Sauna! Yes, of course. Dutch people love the sauna. Sauna Deco is my favorite in the center. It's in Jordaan, and it's beautiful, quite lavish. The decoration, furniture, windows, lights were salvaged from Paris. Everything removed and sent here."

"Sounds striking. What's it like? Are there pools? Dry, wet saunas?" I asked.

"Yes, small pools and both wet and dry saunas," she replied.

"Perfect. Tomorrow I depart early, so I think this is goodbye. I love the suite, and best luck with your decision about Dubai," I said.

"Thank you. Have fun travels," she said.

She stopped a few steps down the sidewalk as I ascended the staircase.

"Rory?" she asked.

"Yes?"

"Did you hear cats in the house last night?"

* * *

Tram #2 deposited me a few short blocks from Sauna Deco, where I contemplated my subsequent move. The thought occurred to me that I had no idea whatsoever what I was getting myself into.

Dutch sauna? Does that have water? Elin said plunge pool. Was it coed? Nude? If nude, I assured myself, it wouldn't be coed.

"Hmm." I studied the carved-wood door with a darkened rose window and intricate plaster surround. The brick building's arched windows were blacked out and barred. Two discreet, square brass nameplates listed the operating hours. Otherwise, it appeared to be a residence or an upscale private club.

Is it an *Eyes Wide Shut* scenario? Would Elin send me to an orgy sauna?

"Nude. I'm going with nude."

My nude-sauna primer occurred in Japan about 15 years ago. I was 24-years old then, had a flat stomach and substantial delineation between muscle groups, and the spa was gender-segregated. The protocol dictated an inordinate amount of showering before slipping into a series of natural spring pools. I'd scrub furiously for 10 minutes and peek up from my wash station only to find everyone else still washing. I almost drew blood. The emphasis placed on pre-bathing washing set the tone for an awkwardly soothing experience. From the moment I stepped into the showers to the final bath in an iron pool, I loved the hot water and the calming ambiance, but couldn't fully appreciate it all with my manhood exposed. Since then, I've tried an exhausting Turkish *hammam* in Istanbul, likewise separated by gender, and a couple nude beaches. But comfort with public exposure continues to elude me.

"Is this your first time at Sauna Deco?" asked Sem, the receptionist who quickly informed me he was no mere receptionist but a second-generation owner.

I arrived during a lull, so Sem stepped from behind the desk and showed me around the lobby.

Extravagant brass railings flowed along a scalloped staircase. Tropical wood wainscoting lined every wall. Leaded and stained-glass artwork covered fixtures, windows and room dividers. Plush leather armchairs and teak chaise lounges filled relaxation rooms. The reassuring cleanliness and pleasant smell, however, impressed me as much as the brilliant Art Deco decor.

"The building interior—all the wood, fixtures, glass—comes from a 1920s Parisian department store, Au Bon Marché. My father heard they were taking it down and doing a full renovation, so he rescued it. They dismantled everything, cataloged it and shipped it to Amsterdam." Sem said, guiding me around the lobby.

"Amazing." I ran my hand over the mahogany counter. "How long did that take?"

"Many months. Many trucks," he replied. Then he got to business.

"At the sauna we ask you to use our towels only and no swimwear allowed. All areas are coed. Showers are beside the changing area. Use them before going to the sauna area. Please sit on your towel in the saunas and furniture. We suggest starting in the dry sauna, then take a cold shower or plunge. Then wet sauna and cold plunge. Repeat as often as you'd like. We also have relaxation rooms, foot pools and massage. Please inquire with me or another attendant if you have questions. Here's your towel," he said.

No swimwear? No problem. I remained calm and forked over 25

euros, unfazed by the prospect of dropping trou...by myself...facing a bunch of strangers, many of whom would be tall, blond and attractive. My anxiety rose like a boiling tea kettle.

Sure, nude, coed, it's all good. Nobody cares these days, anyway. Like all good solo travelers, I go with the flow. Hell, I *am* the flow. I repeated my new mantra as I shuffled into the changing quarters: I am the flow.

The locker room was tiny and I grew preoccupied with keeping my butt from touching the two naked women I was changing between. A five-person coed group shuffled into the lockers just as the two women disappeared. We squeezed together, but it didn't deter them from stripping and stuffing their clothes in the wood-paneled lockers.

After showering, I slunk into the dry sauna, where a few men and women baked atop their towels. Had it been crowded, I think I would have fled. I unwrapped and sat down, hunching over my clenched knees, obscuring the line of sight leading to my penis. The intense heat relaxed every muscle, my shoulders slumped and thighs opened. The parched air stifled my breath, causing me to slow down, inhale with intention and control my exhale. My heart rate dropped. I decompressed and leaned back against the warm cedar slats. My knees unclenched. People showered or dipped, some returned while others withdrew to other delights.

I closed my eyes and let my mind wander. I daydreamed about Paris and my family, then thought about how hectic Amsterdam had become before the arid heat became too much, and I left for a plunge pool.

I sank up to my neck, the frigid water seizing and releasing my strained muscles, aching joints, painful childhood and buried regrets. Well, at the very least, it was relaxing. A blonde woman entered the icy pool as I bobbed.

"Oh, so cold," she said in accented English. She skipped the bottom step and submerged to her chin as I stepped back.

She grinned at me and shivered, jiggling her buoyant chest.

"I hate and love cold pool," she told me. "Is this your first time at sauna?"

"Yes," I replied in a combination shiver-chuckle. Sure is cold, this cold pool. I looked down. "How did you know?"

"Lucky guess," she laughed. "And I saw you in the sauna." She giggled. "You chose right time. Soon, it will become very busy. Do you enjoy sauna?"

She remained in the water next to me, the waterline a fingertip over her bosom. Her drenched blonde hair was slicked fast to the middle of her back.

"I like it. I love water and saunas. But it is intimidating being naked." I walked backward again, my lower back now pressed against the miniature pool's edge. "You Dutch are all tall, blond and gorgeous," I said.

She scoffed and floated onto her back, her nipples surfaced and pointed skyward. Her legs and waist then emerged, confessing a scorn for body hair. She rose upright.

"I suppose. But I'm not Dutch. I'm Russian."

"Oh, do you live here?" I asked. Why did I keep querying her?

"I live here two years. I'm flight attendant for Aeroflot. Are you traveling or staying in Amsterdam?" she asked.

"Traveling."

"Where?"

"I'm unsure. Paris next. For a few days. Then I don't know."

"Where is your wife?"

"How did you know I was married?" I asked.

"Your ring." She pointed at my left hand which, with my arms' crossed, settled below my chest.

"Right. She's at home...in the States...with my son. He's in school. I fly back in September. It's so cold, eh? Uh, I believe I'll visit the wet sauna."

"Yes. Let's go."

Let's?

Other sauna-goers wrapped themselves in towels when roaming between zones. I did the same. She did not; hers hung from her fist.

"What is your name?" she asked after placing her towel beside me in the steamy wet sauna. She threw her right leg over her left knee and faced me. Her gravity-defying breasts protruded, areolae the size of jelly-jar lids, and her hard nipples jabbed at me. She flipped her soggy hair over her shoulder.

"Rory. Yours?"

"Annika."

We shook hands.

"A pleasure. Do you always sauna alone?" I asked.

"I prefer with my girlfriends. But they are gone, working. What do you do?"

"I'm a writer and editor." I made a flourish with my right hand because writers still use quills. She laughed. Her breasts jiggled.

"Rory the writer. What do you write, Rory?"

"I'm afraid, uh, not much at the moment. I'm an editor for a travel website. I had a book under contract, but the publisher canceled it. I suppose one reason I'm here is to figure that out, decide what's next for my career, discover inspiration."

"What inspires you?" she asked.

"Ah, what inspires me?" I repeated. "Um..."

But all I could think about was her splendid boobs and not peeking at them. Don't look at her tits. Don't stare at her tits. Avoid her pointy, perky, bouncy and very-present boobs that swayed as she moved like errant torpedoes seeking targets. The closest breast jiggled centimeters from my right shoulder.

"I guess my inspirations are family, people I encounter, culture, adventure and, uh, beauty."

She smirked. "We plunge and start over," she said.

We sweated another round, chatting about flight-attendant work and the various places we've traveled. Annika stayed for more hot-dry-hot-dry, while I showered and retired for a golden-hour stroll through Vondelpark to Sarphatipark. I purchased canned Tuborg beers from a corner store in De Pijp, parked at the first open bench in Sarphatipark and said adieu to all the characters I'd never meet.

My body was detached, softened and detoxed. Even my toes spread out at ease. I soaked in the evening scene of picnickers, sunbathers, inflatable chairs, readers, Frisbee throwers, dog walkers, wine drinkers, singers and guitarists. The chirping birds mixed with ambient urban buzzing as the simple evening seared into my consciousness forever.

* * *

A final Cafe Lust nightcap found the neighborhood engaged in trivia hysteria. Laughter, debate, heckles, hugs and schemes permeated the diminutive bar as merrymakers passed around pitchers of brews and something resembling frozen margaritas. Tonight's crowd was too lively and demanding to attempt language lessons with the gracious bartender, who smiled at me as I strode to the bar.

So, I ordered double pilsners, shed a generous tip, and perched on a wooden stool at the side counter. My beard itched, reminding me I forgot to buy a razor. Tomorrow, in gay Paris, I'll grab one.

Light rain streaked down the window, just the excuse I needed for another round before going home in the cool, post-rain darkness. Sipping and writing, I was struck by how lovely Dutch sounded tonight in this candlelit café full of well-worn pine furniture and friendly hearts. Dutch sounds like German school children repeating English-dubbed dialogue of a Japanese cartoon. It's bouncy and familiar yet...off. At

Aachen Cathedral a few years ago, I'd followed the Dutch-language tour, wondering why the tour guide was so chipper, for a full 10 minutes before realizing it and sneaking off to find the English group.

Late that night, as I slumbered, hot but with a room free of roof-cats, I returned to the Sauna Deco plunge pool, the frigid temperature doing its cruel anatomical deed. A blonde appeared, her back to me. She said nothing. Her mid-torso blonde hair was slicked tight and her hour-glass backside crept toward me.

"Annika?" I whispered.

The blonde turned around, and it was my wife. I fumbled and stumbled, unable to speak.

"That's impossible," she snickered.

I woke up, sweating. It was only a dream. Then I swore I overheard the roof-cat gang returning. I locked the window, hunkered under my covers and girded for their onslaught. No roof-cat posse arrived, however, and I laid there, missing my wife.

Brussels

Slow trains do the Amsterdam-to-Paris journey in seven to nine hours. High-speed trains demolish it in about three hours, which, under other circumstances, would compel me to at least consider paying the Eurail Pass supplement. This trip was different—I refused to pay the high-speed tax.

But I had another reason to skip the high-speed route: Brussels, the capital of Belgium, a country called "the world's most successful failed state," by *The Economist*. Brussels lies halfway between Paris and Amsterdam, a perfect lunch stop to segment the flat, feature-less track. The posted timetables showed the slow lines, so I coordinated the two segments, arriving in Brussels for lunch and a quick nip before catching the Paris leg.

Once upon a time, you could book it as one high-speed segment, but the railways closed the loophole. Now, the best bet is taking the slow "Beneluxtrein" via Rotterdam and Den Haag to Brussels and connecting to Paris from there.

Brussels has its allure: chiefly, beer. Czechs may consume more per capita, and Germans may brew larger quantities, but the variety and quality found in Belgian beers remains unrivaled. From rustic farmhouse ales and crisp saisons to dry lambics and tangy sours, their bubbly, scintillating creations are the real champagne of beers (sorry, High Life). In 2015, UNESCO added "Belgian beer culture" to their intangible cultural heritage list. Belgium doesn't exist without beer. Camouflage-clad soldiers holding SCAR assault rifles patrolled Brussels Central. They were a grim reminder of the previous March's twin suicide bombings at Brussels International and a subway station that killed 32 people.

Usually its six antiquated tracks struggle meeting passenger demand, but I alighted at the Art Nouveau Brussels Central during a midday lull. Designed by famed architect Victor Horta in 1912, whose work garners UNESCO heritage designations like Facebook collects your personal information, the station didn't open until 1952 because those pesky world wars kept interfering.

It may rank as Europe's most unfortunate train station. Originally envisioned anchoring a master-planned urban neighborhood, Brussels Central sat unfinished, a maze of debris piles and water-filled pits, from 1914 until 1935. Authorities scrapped the neighborhood redevelopment plan and work resumed on the station, only for WWII to again halt construction in 1940. Amazingly, Victor Horta returned to the project and spearheaded its post-war recovery. He died in 1947, five years before the station finally opened.

It was clean and stark; my footsteps reverberated off the shiny marble and polished stone. The beige and white slabs sparkled with mineral flecks. Exiting the tunnel into the luminous main concourse felt like emerging from a granite quarry. I half-expected to find idling stone cutters. The wavy ceiling of coffered skylights bathed my face in sunshine.

Outside, a shallow "U" facade gave the building a sense of movement. The wedge-shaped station's brilliant execution led my eyes around the wavy front and down its ever-widening sides. Graceful windows separated by pilasters were perched above a shallow colonnade. I found the timetables posted near the exits.

The next slow train to Paris departed in two hours, arriving at 5:45

p.m. The calendar then had a peculiar four-hour gap in which the next departure wouldn't make Paris until 10 p.m. Still, I had enough time for a quick meander before cozying up at the Poechenellekelder, central Brussels' weirdest beer bar, where I'd indulged in a quick nip years ago.

Tour groups, students and business-folk on lunch breaks packed the avenue leading into the old town center. I weaved between them, noticing a lack of trees and grass, except for a leafy lawn thriving at Mary Magdalene Chapel. Curiously, a blue, two-person tent pitched in a worn-out section beside the chapel stopped me, an anomaly in Brussels' urban grid. Campers couldn't possibly be an everyday sight here, yet nobody else seemed to care or even notice.

I threaded a semicircle through Brussels' meandering but immaculate old town, ending at the UNESCO-protected Grote Markt, a public square bristling with stunning architecture. Rotating in place, I noted the different styles rested in relative tranquility—Flamboyant, Baroque, Gothic Revival—and chuckled at their exuberance. The Baroque guild halls' gold-leafed pilasters, flanked by the elaborately symmetrical Town Hall and imposingly needle-like City Museum gripped my interest. As an architecture enthusiast, I was perfectly overwhelmed.

Tour groups heaved about as I absorbed the moment, but Brussels felt like a breath of fresh air after jam-packed Amsterdam. The street scene was restrained despite tourist throngs. The visitors here acted tamer. On the surface, Brussels appeared buttoned up and subdued, following a more tidy and Teutonic rhythm than their Gallic brethren to the south and Dutch in the east.

Yet, straitlaced Brussels boasts an eccentric side, exemplified by the city's inexplicable mascot, the two-foot-tall bronze statuette known as Manneken Pis, which stands 15 feet from the Poechenellekelder's front patio. The toddler boy holds his winky, and there's little more to it. Oh, except that he's peeing full-throttle into a fountain basin below.

Hence the "*pis*."

Water streamed unhindered from his prepubescent bits as tourists crowded 20 deep, taking pictures and video. I waded through the cluster, bumping into a Japanese man with a gigantic telephoto lens and too big of a grin snapping pictures at a frantic pace, seemingly worried the sculpture might run off or run dry.

Tour guides attempted to explain the capital's strange predilection for statues of pissing children. (There's a "sister" sculpture elsewhere in Brussels' old town depicting a squatting young girl.) They offered various legends, all centered on kids urinating their way to historic miracles.

The leading fable claims a battle in 1142 inspired the statue. Godfrey III of Leuven suspended his two-year-old son...from a tree...in a basket...to inspire his armies. I bet you can guess where this ends. Yep, the kid peed onto charging enemy troops. This example of great parenting no doubt rallied Godfrey's forces, who vanquished their urine-soaked foes.

Here's what the tour guides weren't divulging: It's a replica. The original sits in the City Museum, which, I suppose, is a well-earned retirement for a hunk of bronze dating from 1619. The version tour groups marvel at now was installed in 1965.

This is a European "railside" attraction like the fake Romeo and Juliet house in Verona, the dreadful London Eye or all torture museums. It's the world's largest ball of twine, a UFO spotting platform or Carhenge. Sure, the Manneken Pis is a refined variant created by a "real" artist, but its prominence far outweighs its merit because the statue is semi-lewd and unexpected. It's simply meant for gawking at.

I don't pretend to fathom its worldwide notoriety and unassailable station on the Brussels tourist trail, but it's harmless and cheeky. I suppose. Sometimes he's costumed as a saxophone player or judo champ, though today he wore only his birthday suit.

Oh, the Poechenellekelder. If you love beer and creepy puppets, there's no better thirst-quenching tavern within five minutes of Brussels Central. That's a fact. It's a beer-lover's paradise, adored by tourists and longtime locals alike.

What's that? Back up to the puppets?

Besides art, posters and general bric-à-brac cluttering every inch of the dark and woody tavern, vintage puppets hung from the walls and ceiling. Poechenellekelder means "puppet cellar." These retired marionettes lent the tavern a conspiratorial vibe. The always-smiling handsocks glared across the room, judging beer orders and tourists' worthiness. Smug creatures.

The mob outside marveled at Manneken Pis as I settled into a patio table. The vast menu covered three pages with over 150 brews. And I couldn't understand any of it.

With Google's help, I deciphered a menu sent from brewing heaven. In French (take my interpretation with a grain of malted barley), four columns listed name, size, ABV and price over three pages. Ten sections organized the beers into drafts, browns, ambers, Trappists, a full page devoted to blondes, lambics, artisanal fruits, sweet fruits, Cantillon and flavored gin shots.

A casual beer drinker, I recognized several styles, but the Trappist, lambic, Cantillon and fruit beers demanded further investigation.

Trappist beers stand apart for two reasons: 1. Only Trappist monks, a cloistered Catholic congregation, brew them at 14 monastic breweries around the world, six of which are in Belgium. 2. Unlike other beers, they contain yeast and sugar post-fermentation, so they age in the bottle like excellent vintages.

Lambic comes from Brussels and the nearby Senne Valley. Lambic production, in many respects, mimics wine making more than beer making. Instead of adding brewer's yeast, lambics ferment with wild yeasts, a process similar to growing sourdough starter, and bacteria that impart a tart and dry taste. Lambics are brewed from fall to early spring when airborne organisms are ideal.

Once on the verge of closing after World War II, Cantillon has been a renowned Brussels beer maker since 1900, when it opened as a lambic blender. Cantillon started brewing their own beer in 1938. They blend the same way they have for 120 years, using wild-fermented sour ale aged 20 months with fresh fruit. They pump it into stainless vats and ignore it for two or three months. It's then blended with one-year-old lambic and aged in oak barrels. It's a transformational process revered by beer nerds.

The fruit beers come sweet and sour and undergo the same blending and fermentation process of lambics, but with particular fruits like apples or cherries. Some fruit beers only employ one brand. For example, *kriek* beers use only dark-red Morello sour cherries.

"Monsieur, welcome. Do you have questions or may I take your order?" asked the waiter, wearing the tavern's signature black apron over starch-white dress shirt. His cropped dark-brown hair was combed tight, and he conducted himself with the formality of a Parisian server at a Michelin-starred restaurant.

"Yes, thank you. My train leaves soon, and I would like to order drinks and food. May I have a croque monsieur...monsieur? Haha."

He did not laugh or smile as he recorded my request with pencil and notepad.

My right index finger traced the beer menu, unsure where to land. I didn't have time to ask questions or prowl my phone, so I stopped at the bottom of the blondes page—St.-Feuillien Triple.

Triples are so named because brewers add three times the hops used in Trappist beers. That breeds potency—St.-Feuillien Triple clocks in at 8.5% ABV. It occurred to me that I have made better decisions.

"Um, this one please," I asked, showing him the menu to avoid a verbal stab at "Feuillien."

"Oui, yes. What size?"

Size? Crap, I hadn't noticed sizes. This would be my only beer in Belgium, so I endeavored for grandeur.

"The one-point-five liter, please."

He raised his eyebrow and froze. Had he missed the part about me being in a hurry?

"One. Point. Five. The magnum?" he asked.

"The magnum," I confirmed.

Wait, what's a magnum?

But his dubiousness only hardened my stance. Yes, yes, of course, that's the one I want. He disappeared into the back.

I might've, just might've experienced slight panic in my haste. A magnum? How many ounces is that? What the hell had I just done?

I grabbed my phone and ran the calculation: One-and-a-half liters equals over four 12-ounce cans. Okay, that's not so bad. At home, four beers mean a full evening of drinking. Today, I'd have to condense that into—I checked my watch—20 minutes!

Somehow, I'd lost almost an hour. It wasn't spent admiring the Manneken Pis, that I was certain of. I must've ambled the old town longer than I realized.

I rechecked the timetable. The next train didn't arrive in Paris until 10 p.m., which meant I'd lose an evening in Paris if the 1 p.m. departed without me. No sir! I would catch the 1 p.m.

The waiter returned as a bead of condensation fell down the dark-blue bottle. He twisted off the metal seal, popped the cork and filled my tulip glass. I took a long, contemplative swig and refilled.

The numbers ran through my not-so-good-with-numbers head, as I gulped beer: Twenty minutes to knock back four beers boasting an alcohol content almost double what I drink at home. Oh right, the 8.5% ABV. I'd forgotten about that detail. It would feel more like consuming eight beers over 20 minutes.

Eight beers.

Nineteen minutes.

Or else I'd miss the train.

A 10 p.m. arrival would cause a headache for the Airbnb check-in, and I'd miss dinner in Paris. I couldn't let that happen.

Would I let a measly magnum jeopardize all that?

No, no, I would not. After inhaling the croque monsieur, a travel superpower washed over me: I could drink eight beers in 19, oops, now 14 minutes. I could do it!

Eight beers.

Fourteen minutes.

Not even 14 minutes. The station was at least a three-minute drunken scamper away.

Okay, recalculation:

Eight beers.

Eleven minutes.

I summoned my travel superpowers: Sure, I could drink eight beers in 11 minutes.

Another uneasy thought occurred to me: After Paris, I had no clue where to go—a realization that got me both excited and nervous as I guzzled St.-Feuillien, getting a bit googly eyed.

How would I reach Barcelona? Should I travel south through Provence? Cross over Switzerland, then to the coast? Or cut a diagonal through "l'Hexagone," mingle with Pyrenees' shepherds, and hop the border to Spanish Basque Country?

The Manneken Pis crowd thickened as another tour group arrived; its guide waved a yellow flag. Her face, ghostly from having to again recite the Pis tale, said she should have been waving a white one.

I needed to make itinerary decisions, and soon. But first, I had copious beer to consume and little time to quaff it. For I had a date with Paris, and no man, woman or child keeps sweet Paris waiting.

That's when my phone buzzed—my wife was calling. I had to answer it; I hadn't stopped thinking about her since last night's dream. But I also had to inhale a bunch of beer. My eyes danced from the phone to the tulip glass.

Phone.

Beer.

Phone.

Beer.

Soon, I'd polish off the glass, answer my phone, hoist my backpack and bound off with the magnum. I'd have minutes remaining, sprinting through bustling old town Brussels, dodging tour groups, couples holding hands and swerving past stroller-pushing families with my phone tucked between my ear and shoulder, feigning attention. All while gurgling a magnum of beer in my left hand, thanks to my latest travel superpower. I'd be a sweaty, burping mess, but I'd never give up.

I'd. Never. Give. Up.

But would I make the train?

Paris

I could be wrong, but I doubt there's a better way to enjoy a 28-euro magnum of beer than by chugging it straight from the bottle while sprinting through tourist crowds as thick as an Alaskan salmon run. You can take my word for it.

After tossing the empty St.-Feuillien, I hopped aboard the train with seconds to spare, found an empty seat and braced myself against the armrests, worried the bubbling keg of beer in my stomach might float me away. I wiped away sweat—the late-summer heat wave gripping Western Europe made my boozy gallop through Brussels all the more impressive and unpleasant.

The regional train chugged past Wallonian cities and towns before crossing into the French borderlands. My forehead was stuck to the window, eyes glued to tangled hawthorn bocage, enclosed livestock pastures, apple orchards and oak-forest fragments. The broad Paris Basin emerged with the Oise River on our right and soon we entered Paris' northern suburbs, docking at Paris-Nord.

After stepping off the four-hour, intercity train, I lingered on the platform, savoring Gare du Nord's striking light-filled terminal. The airy glass ceiling covering the train shed gave me giddy goosebumps, a much more mystical and inviting impression than Brussels Central's stark, granite cave. My eyes followed the riveted-iron frame, slathered in unmistakable Paris green paint, its main pillars met the iron roof trusses just below the ceiling's peak. Oh, that Paris green. Be it the iconic Métro surrounds designed by French architect Hector Guimard or Nord's ironwork, that green always signals my official arrival in the City of Light. But architecture aside, as the goosebumps persisted, I realized Nord has what all great stations have: the undeniable energy of possibility.

That possibility can seem endless here. Idyll equipment and various materials, part of a decade-long expansion to address skyrocketing demand, sat stacked behind metal fencing near the main hall. Since its completion in 1865, Gare du Nord grew from a humble suburban connector to the busiest train station in Europe, every day coordinating some 700,000 passengers and over 2,000 arrivals and departures. Jacques Ignace Hittorff, a German-born French architect, designed the station in unbridled Beaux-Arts, especially evident in the clean, chunky Neoclassical facade. It strikes an impressive balance between beauty and utility, quite a feat considering station officials add tracks and services every couple decades.

Gare du Nord's minimalist and practical interior—mostly brick, stone and iron—mirrored Amsterdam and Copenhagen central stations. Nord was built to dazzle, yes, but also to survive endless abuse. The stripped away interiors made prudent use of public funds. These 19th-century architects used only what was necessary and made sure everything necessary was beautiful.

Once upon a time, Europe's public infrastructure was meant to impress, endure and stay on budget. Nowadays, only prestige and press coverage matters and budgets serve as mere guesswork. Ongoing maintenance costs? Not a factor. New airports, train stations and public buildings all suffer from the same extruded-white-plastic and glass-panel disease: over-design with no concern for taxpayers.

Even simple pedestrian bridges aren't immune. London's Millennium Bridge opened $5 million over budget and spent two years closed as engineers addressed a "resonance" problem—it wobbled when people walked on it. But, hey, at least they could walk on it, unlike Venice's $8 million Constitution Bridge. Designed by disaster-artist Santiago Calatrava, who never met a public piggy bank he couldn't drain, the bridge's curved-glass walkway (yes, curved-glass...walkway) sent so many unsuspecting tourists and hapless locals careening on their asses since it opened in 2008 the city began replacing the glass with stone in 2022.

Pondering modernity's public architectural mistakes made me quietly appreciate Paris-Nord's simple, gritty and timeless embrace.

* * *

My Airbnb host, Cecilia, an Italian-named Peruvian living in Paris with her English boyfriend shook my hand outside her apartment building. After supplying the keys and Wi-Fi and giving a 10-second tour, we said "ciao" as I followed her through the front door onto rue Blondel, where several haggard, middle-aged women smoked cigarettes and pierced me with icy glares.

I turned right on rue Saint-Martin, crossed the Marais and entered Île-de-la-Cité. The Celtic Parisii tribe founded Paris' precursor on this Seine River island, so I figured lighting a candle at Notre-Dame Cathedral would be an apropos way to kick off my visit.

Stepping inside, the Gothic behemoth buckled my knees, sent my neck hair upright and compelled me into confessing my many sins, though I never got around to the last bit. I crossed the rib-vaulted side aisle, illuminated by candles and silent save for a dozen other footsteps, through the transept. I lit a candle in the ambulatory and shuffled through the nave, taking deep breaths while my body tingled with awe.

I hesitated at the three-inch-thick oak-and-iron doors, running my right hand down the interior face. Stories, voices, moments and memories from other lifetimes coursed through the ancient portal. I stepped forward and studied the facade, awash in floodlights, and I was overwhelmed by the incredible feeling, indeed blessing, of living and breathing in Paris.

On nearby Île Saint-Louis, a shadowy restaurant behind a weathered wood door with a fluted-column surround caught my eye. The menu, written in French on a chalkboard, featured all the standards from duck confit and onion soup to beef burgundy and escargot. I spied many vacant tables and entered.

"Bonjour, madame," I smiled.

She looked up from her reservation book, rectangle wireframe glasses perched on the end of her nose. Her drab hair was neatly pulled back, and she wore simple gold earrings and an elegant black, long-sleeve top.

"Bonsoir, monsieur."

Failed my first French test! It was after 5 p.m. and, therefore, we'd crossed from bonjour time ("hello") into bonsoir time ("good evening"). Travelers can set their clocks to trains in Switzerland or time-sensitive greetings in France. Both are equally accurate.

"Parlez-vous anglais?" I asked, knowing the answer.

She nodded, "Yes."

"I don't have a reservation."

We looked at the empty dining room, one of 20 tables in use.

"Oui, oui, no problem, monsieur. Come." She grabbed a leather-bound menu and ushered me over to a cozy corner table, farthest from her maître d' stand.

Diamond-shaped muntins divided the two vertical sashes into 2x6 grids, each topped with two stained-glass panels. The furniture was genuine wood, chunky French oak finished in simple oil and wax. Even the pass-through—where servers grabbed ready dishes—stood clad with French oak base cabinets and drawers below the stainless steel counter. Exposed blackened ceiling beams bowed under ever-persistent gravity and the second floor's ceaseless desire to meet the first. The artwork and wall mosaics featured knights and bishops. A six-person party finished their meal while I ordered, leaving me alone in the 17th-century space.

Well, not entirely alone. The chef worked unseen in a cramped 6x8-foot kitchen. The proprietor stood at her maître d' stand, worrying over the reservation book after fetching me the house red wine.

After the second spoonful of onion soup, I picked up my bowl, wine carafe and cutlery, and marched over to the table opposite her maître d' stand. Without moving, she lifted her eyes. "Do you mind?" I looked left and right. "We're the only ones here."

I set the table, sunk into the cushioned bench seat facing her and dunked my spoon into the soup. She said nothing and returned to her reservation book.

"Excusez-moi, are you the owner?" I asked, blowing on a steamy spoonful of caramelized onion, red-wine broth and Emmental. A stringy cheese zipline linked my spoon and soup. "It's delicious."

"Oui, merci," she replied, only lifting her eyes enough to meet mine.

I locked on, lifted my eyebrows, leaned toward her and gulped another spoonful. Briny steam washed over my face. Sweet onions and fatty cheese sent my taste buds spinning, while the wine broth gave the soup a satisfying depth and hearty body. The gooey Emmental and vaporous broth's heavenly aroma filled the room.

"When did you open?" I asked, eyes still locked.

She dropped her pencil and folded her eyeglasses onto the reservation book. The bench creaked as I reclined against the red upholstery.

"My husband and I, we open in 1992," she smiled and paused, her eyes glazed over in memories. "He was a chef. We were starting a family. We say if we want a family but have to work all day, we should do it together."

A new pork, duck and bean fragrance signaled the chef had pulled my cassoulet from the oven. We both lifted our noses.

"Was it difficult?" I asked.

Her smile vanished. "Difficult, yes. We put everything into it. Money, time, love, heart, everything. Michel, my husband, passed away four years ago. He," she tilted her head toward the kitchen, "is not as good. Un moment, monsieur."

She returned with the house cassoulet, traditionally a whatever's-in-the-pantry dish whose ideal consumer, according to Julia Child, is "a 300-pound blocking back who has been splitting firewood nonstop for the last twelve hours on a subzero day in Manitoba."

Duck meat slipped from the bone as I asked, "What changes have you seen in Paris in all those years?"

"Humph, plus ça change," she snorted and tapped the reservation book, organizing her thoughts.

"We have many more visitors, yes. But where in Europe doesn't? Now, I see different tourists—Chinese, Arab, Indian. With the EU, we have even more Europeans living here. Of course, technology has changed. Everyone walks around looking at their phones. Why come to Paris to look at your phone?" We laughed.

"And I must have a website! Put my restaurant on other websites and these apps. N'importe quoi! Many changes. Even so, always Paris." She stared out the window.

"Yep, always Paris," I concurred, chasing my last bite of cassoulet with a swig of red wine, thinking back to my earlier candle-lighting at Notre-Dame.

Now a half-dozen women with painted faces and tight skirts inhaled cigarettes and adjusted their nylons when I returned to narrow rue Blondel. Wearing three-inch black heels with matching mini-skirt and a leopard-skin blouse, one leaned against the wall a few feet from my doorway, staring me up and down as I fumbled with unfamiliar keys. Why does a one-door apartment require seven keys?

"Mon Airbnb," I informed her, finally inserting the correct key.

"Oui," she replied, exhaling cigarette smoke as I pushed inside the apartment.

Elsewhere in Paris, street prostitution was declining, but not on rue Blondel, a hunch I later confirmed with prodigious Google results. This little street, barely more than an alleyway, celebrates a notorious history of prostitution and brothels that would shock even modern Moulin Rouge performers. Tolerated since the Middle Ages, *maisons closes* ("closed houses"—so named because they kept the shutters closed 24/7) flourished during the naughty and decadent Belle Époque era that lasted from the late 1800s until World War I.

The neighborhood's most famous brothel, a lavish Belle Époque affair called Aux Belles Poules ("The Beautiful Chicks"), once entertained clientele just a couple blocks from my Airbnb. Known for its elaborate erotic wall mosaics and equally elaborate sex shows (euphemistically known as "living paintings"), Aux Belles Poules closed along with all Paris bordellos in 1946 during a postwar morality crusade. Almost overnight, Paris' 30,000 *horizontales* became streetwalkers.

While shrewd developers renovated most of Paris' 224 formerly legal brothels to attract more, uh, discreet tenants, Aux Belles Poules remained in original condition, erotic wall mosaics and all. Different commercial and residential tenants moved through its halls over the years, but the sex walls remained. It's now a registered historic monument and event venue (available for private parties should the inclination strike you).

I flipped open my laptop and plied my trade, while on the opposite side of the stone-and-mortar wall, the prostitutes of rue Blondel plied theirs.

* * *

"Bonjour, Rory." Although we'd never met in person, I recognized the big smile from her Instagram profile.

"Madeleine! Bonjour!"

Madeleine welcomed me outside the Barbès–Rochechouart Métro station in La Goutte d'Or neighborhood. We exchanged *la bise*, an air-kiss on each cheek, as two soldiers with FAMAS assault rifles slung across their chests walked by.

The army patrol, one of several I'd noticed since arriving yesterday, was part of France's ongoing national emergency declaration and military-led anti-terrorism campaign called Opération Sentinelle, which sent 10,000 combat-ready soldiers into the streets of major French cities.

"I made it. Your guinea pig has arrived." I bowed, and we laughed.

Madeleine was skinny with big, round eyes and long eyelashes that almost touched her red lips and sharp cheekbones. She wore intricate hair braids and a blue-and-white striped dress covering her from neck to ankles. Twenty years ago, at six, she and her mother left their native Cameroon for Paris. They've returned precisely once, to fetch grandma.

We met a year ago when she submitted an article for the website where I work. We'd never met in person, but she continued writing and I continued editing her work. She was starting a tour company focusing on African diaspora communities, beginning in her hometown. I eagerly offered my services as a test dummy.

"Oui, Rory. Bienvenue à La Goutte d'Or!"

La Goutte d'Or, or Drop of Gold, is not postcard Paris even though it sits due east of postcard-aplenty Montmartre. It's poor, working-class Paris and has been for hundreds of years. West and North African immigrants now predominate, many of whom are first- or second-generation residents.

"Everybody has a concept of Paris like it's a fairy tale or movie. Maybe that's true for tourists because the Paris of their dreams is the only Paris they see. Eiffel Tower, the Louvre, fancy hotels and restaurants. For my people, African people, immigrants, La Goutte d'Or is our one and only Paris. I want more tourists to experience it, dream new dreams of Paris."

She looked up and smiled at vendors stuffing produce into bags, shoppers chatting, laughing and haggling while passersby waved, "I think you will love it, Rory. We start here at the market."

Indeed, where else could we start? Barbes Market, a shoulder-to-shoulder cacophony, overflowed into the Métro station. The instant I hit the pavement, I felt like I'd inadvertently day-tripped to Africa as I snaked behind shoppers. Anyone feeling jaded by European travel, like my dinner hosts back home who questioned whether it still constituted "real" travel, should take a stroll through Barbes Market. Suddenly, I was transported to Morocco, Algeria, Cameroon, Lebanon.

Shoppers jostled over vast piles of olives, oranges, lemons, stacks of eggs, baguettes and *boules*, whole uncooked and golden-rotisserie chickens, fish, shrimp, lamb (no pork!) sausages, avocados, strawberries, tangerines, tomatoes, cabbage, root vegetables of various origin, purple carrots, rainbows of chili peppers, garlic, chocolate bars, jars of whole-bean coffee.

And that was just the first three stalls.

I put away my notebook, gave up trying to record everything and just absorbed the scene. Nigerian hip-hop blared from a silver stereo under a clothing merchant's table intermingling with shoppers shouting rapid-fire French mixed with African patois. Gorgeous aromas pulled me from stall to stall, a pinball game cranked to expert level. From fragrant North African oranges to festering, over-ripe chèvre and fresh-caught fish. Barbes bombarded my senses.

Two hours later, we met her Senegalese boyfriend, Mamadou, for lunch at a Rastafarian-colored restaurant on a side street off rue de la Goutte d'Or. They hugged and exchanged cheek kisses with every employee. I was advised, urged, implored to order the peanut butter-sauced chicken *mafe* served over fluffy jasmine rice.

Mamadou, a painter-carpenter-artist specializing in shop facades, asked, "Tell me, Rory, what do you think of our Paris?" He smiled at Madeleine.

"Your Paris is wonderful. Exciting, vibrant. Really, my head is spinning." We chuckled. "I'm ashamed it's my first time here." I looked at the table. Several Paris trips spanning two decades and never once had I set foot in this neighborhood. "Thank you, Madeleine, for taking me around this morning. Thank you," I looked them in the eyes, "for sharing your Paris."

"You're welcome, Rory. And I hope one day you can show us your Colorado," she replied.

After hoovering the rich and buttery mafe, while nursing a muddy Ethiopian coffee, I showed them photos of my family. The waiters and cooks gathered behind me as I swiped through pictures of my wife and son, hiking, fishing, traveling, skiing. The snow impressed them. "Like the Alps," a chef remarked.

One woman, who stuck her right hip to my left shoulder, sighed and dabbed her eyes with a white tea towel.

"I have a son the same age," she said in singsong English. "But he is in Mali."

She slung the white tea towel over her right shoulder and hunched her back when I asked how long she'd been in Paris.

"Two years," she said. Then, as if expecting my next question, said, "I will go back for him soon. I must save more money...Find a better apartment..." She trailed off and returned to wiping the tables clean.

I turned to Madeleine and Mamadou and confessed, "I don't know much, anything really, about French colonialism and the connection to your Africa. Where can I learn more?"

"Well, Rory, you start with the best place," replied Mamadou. They laughed as their eyes narrowed, searching for the right answers.

"We have good African art museums. And we also have many artists, ateliers elsewhere in the city. I will give you a list of them. But I will say..." She braced for disapproval from Mamadou. "I will recommend, maybe controversial, the Museum of Immigration."

Mamadou rolled his eyes so hard I heard them.

"Then you go to the Museum of Hunting and Nature." She paused. "Be sure to see the new special exhibit," she added.

"Pfft, why? Why go to those places? They are museums made by White French people to make themselves feel better," Mamadou protested.

Madeline stared through him, and explained, while never taking her eyes off Mamadou, "Rory is a journalist." She stretched that word's definition. "He should see the other side. Today, we saw how French immigrants live, how we maintain our culture in France, where we raise families and do business. This is more than our neighborhood we share; this is our truth. Tomorrow, Rory will see the French truth."

"But understand something, Rory." Mamadou leaned over the table, stopping inches from my nose. In a calm voice, he asserted, "French people don't want immigrants; they want more French people. African, Arab, Caribbean, Asian...," He pointed at an imaginary map. "You are expected to forget it and become only French."

He reclined and exhaled. I sensed he could have continued.

Madeleine rubbed his back and said, "This is a country, remember, that denied citizenship to Pablo Picasso."

I didn't remember because I never knew. Picasso moved to Paris in his early 20s, and I had just assumed he was an adopted son. Plus, he was rich, famous and, you know, White.

"If Picasso cannot become French," she threw up her hands, "what chance do we have?"

"One last question," I said as we bid adieu on rue Caplat. "It's so damn hot." Paris had surpassed 95 degrees today, the first week of September. "I hope to go swimming tomorrow. Can you recommend somewhere?"

"Bien sûr, Rory! Piscine Edouard Pailleron—," My eyes glazed over at her staccato pronunciation. Pool what? "—in the 19th...by Buttes-Chaumont. It's close to here. I'll write it down." She scribbled the name on a cocktail napkin. "It is très Art Deco," she emphasized, "and positively gorgeous. You will love it, Rory."

* * *

I drank a champagne apéritif at a café on rue de Trévise, near Uzbek and Uyghur restaurants. The Picasso thing gnawing at me, I Googled for the truth. Turned out to be true, but several articles cited Picasso's membership in the communist party as the reason, not his immigration status. Still, I saw Madeleine's point. In tenuous postwar De Gaulle years, authorities considered being communist the same as being anti-French.

From rue de Trévise, it was a short stroll to Bouillon Chartier, where I queued for dinner. The working-class *bouillon* serves hearty French favorites, meals fit for kings but served to peasants. After all, bouillon means broth, and it doesn't get more peasant than broth. But it's *elevated* broth. I think of them as the French equivalent of American diners—home-cooked food served cheap and fast by no-nonsense waitstaff. The food is usually mediocre, occasionally good, never superb, always filling. Food arrives promptly, and they keep a casual atmosphere. Most importantly, they're cheap, and I was compensating for the 12-euro champagne with a 12-euro dinner.

But cheap doesn't mean plastic. Bouillon Chartier, like its bouillon brothers, featured lush Art Deco interiors honoring their founding era—the jubilant Belle Époque (which I learned today was built on the backs of colonialism, so jubilant for the privileged I guess!). Ten-foot-tall mirrors with intricate moldings and bright mosaics covered the walls, while tuxedo-clad waiters shuffled past ornate brass light fixtures topped with huge glass globes. I was mesmerized. In no other Parisian restaurants would living this large cost so little.

The tender vinaigrette leeks tasted delicately tart, setting up the herb-crusted roasted chicken and salty fries. I'm proud to report the Parisian bouillon endures.

Back on Blondel, I again fumbled with an overabundance of keys under the prostitutes' unwavering gazes. A couple new gals prowled the strip tonight, maybe eight total. The one standing across from my door had a prominent Adam's apple and unusually broad shoulders.

* * *

"France," explained the wrinkled, silver-haired man standing in front of me at the bakery, "is a boulangerie country." He wore a tweed hat and blue scarf as an empty pipe dangled from his thin lips. He could have stepped out of a souvenir-shop postcard. The morning line at Boulangerie Leroy Monti maintained a steady pace, and 10 minutes later I strolled Avenue Daumesnil with a *pain au chocolat* and latte en route to the National Museum of the History of Immigration.

The National Museum of the History of Immigration...Oh boy, how ambitious! The name alone sounds like they're pole vaulting with Pogo sticks. Sure enough, controversy has followed this museum since, well, before it even opened. And, of course, even the opening caused contention, which we'll cover. Grab your popcorn. Get comfortable.

Paris in 1931 teemed with life; over a half-million residents, including the first waves of immigration from French colonies, flooded into the city after the Great War's conclusion. The Continent was recovering from World War I, and the European powers sensed they should impose optimism...or distraction. Look, these were precarious times, the Great Depression raged and a curiously mustachioed lunatic named Hitler was banging pots next door. But the economy was growing, and Europe had learned its lesson about the destructiveness of modern warfare just a decade ago. The 1930s, as everyone knew in their hearts, would bring the turnaround Europe needed. And colonial pillaging of natural resources, labor and land would provide the foundation.

Paris threw a parade of colonial booty called the Colonial Exposition. It would not be repeated. The Paris Colonial Exposition was like a world's fair, but a breathtakingly racist one.

Colonial "artifacts," academia's euphemism for stolen property, were displayed by the Netherlands, Belgium, Italy, Japan, Portugal, the United Kingdom and even the United States, who had leapfrogged from being a colony to establishing colonies in just 100 years. Food, art, cultural loot, they even imported native people for the six-month soirée celebrating everything subjugation, I mean, colonialism. The exposition's not-so-hidden agenda sought to show the mutually beneficial aspects of colonialism. It introduced Europeans to foreign cultures (Asian cuisine quickly became a sensation) as over seven million people toured the exhibits.

But colonialism's stated purpose was to make the world [insert your favorite colonial power here] and grow rich, an end by which colonial powers justified any means. Instead, the exposition painted colonialism as a reciprocal cultural exchange, trading bananas for Christ, an idealized, colonizer-centric view of colonialism.

The building housing the immigration museum, Palais de la Porte Dorée, was the center of the exposition's universe. When the exposition wrapped, a string of colonial and ethnic-art museums followed. In 1989, Algerian immigrant and professional soccer player Zaïr

Kedadouche proposed building an immigration museum. Great idea, everyone said. So, guess who they put in charge of creating the museum? A naturalized immigrant?

Nope, instead of finding one of millions of actual immigrants or children of immigrants, the museum's creation was given to...an old White guy! But not just any old White guy. President Jacques Chirac tasked his fellow right-wing buddy, Jacques Toubon, with fulfilling the museum's stated mission of contributing "to the recognition of the integration of immigrants into French society." It became abundantly obvious that if this museum was to happen, then it would happen on conservative-French terms.

This Toubon fellow must have held an open-minded worldview, even for a conservative, right? Nope! Toubon's crowning political achievement up to this point came in 1994 when, as Minister of Culture, he rammed through a law mandating French be used in all public documents, publications, advertisements, offices, contracts, schools, pretty much all non-private entities. That's the guy chosen to lead the immigration museum, Mr. We All Speak French Here And So Will You.

In 2007, almost 20 years after its initial conception, the National Museum of the History of Immigration opened to much fanfare and significant public and political support. Just kidding! It hardly even opened. The French president, Nicolas Sarkozy, refused to inaugurate the museum. Sarkozy is also a conservative, and a museum celebrating minorities did not fit his agenda. Naturally, Sarkozy's father immigrated from Hungary, hence the blatantly non-French surname. Nice guy, huh?

(For fans of karmic retribution, Sarkozy lost reelection, got implicated in the Panama Papers scandal and was mired in revolving criminal trials and court appearances. He's best remembered as the only former French president to be held in police custody. Quite the career accomplishment. Congratulations Nicky! Toubon and Chirac also enjoyed frequent brushes with the law.)

It wasn't until 2014 with Socialist François Hollande in power that the museum received a proper inauguration. Of course, I didn't know its sordid history before entering. Madeleine left me blissfully unaware. I went in with an open mind. But before I stepped through the front door, everything I thought I knew about France was shattered.

The museum lives on the western edge of the Bois de Vincennes in the ghastly Palais de la Porte Dorée. Yes, ghastly. Paris has few architectural atrocities, but the Porte Dorée is undoubtedly one. Three architects, led by Albert Laprade, fused two competing styles—jubilant Art Deco with refined classical French—to disappointing results. The creative tug-of-war shows. I'm no fan of Laprade's work (though his designs suit industrial applications—dams, factories, etc.), but this, being his chef-d'œuvre, is particularly rubbish. The horrid design screams ego and meddling bureaucracy as if the message it's meant to convey supersedes aesthetic value.

First, I stood in the portico, examining the columns. What happened here? Were they never finished? They looked like stacked cinder blocks awaiting a marble veneer or Roman ruins after locals pillaged the cut stones. The many horizontal seams clashed with the busy facade (which, oh, we'll get to). I've seen better cinder-block work under double-wide trailers. They were also disproportionate, far too skinny to complement the girthy edifice. The columns stopped at an almost-Italianate roof cornice that had an alternating brown and beige brick trim that looked like dentil molding.

While the columns were ugly, at least they were not blatantly bigoted like the facade. Completed by Alfred Janniot over two years, it raised eyebrows even in 1931. I stepped backward to grasp the full scope and almost tumbled over in horror. The facade's carved bas-relief frieze was impressive though incongruous. And it was huge, covering the entire facade, over 1,200 square feet of three-dimensional imperial propaganda. One scene depicted wild animals dashing around as European ships conquered ferocious seas and scantily clad, doughy-eyed natives looked longingly at their White saviors. My eyes roved over natives acting subservient; their comic proportions, chunky lips and misshapen breasts froze me in place. The White guys looked triumphant, beautiful and in total control. It is Paris' Robert E. Lee statue.

The looted culture, shoot, I did it again...I mean, the "rescued artifacts" that once sat in variously named Porte Dorée institutions were moved to the ethnographic Quai Branly Museum. This cleared the way for the Palais de la Porte Dorée to host the immigration museum. (Well, almost. A wonderful aquarium, whose relocation proved too burdensome, remained in the basement, a head-scratching contrast—immigration and tropical marine life.)

Through the lobby, its walls plastered with frescoes depicting half-naked Africans doing manual labor for the French Empire's enrichment, I dove into the permanent exhibits. And you know what? The museum itself is harmless. It's fine. It's okay. Really okay! The exhibits tell lovely stories and contain actual facts that don't (always) support the French-White savior narrative.

But something was missing. As I went from exhibit to exhibit, I noticed the focus placed on generic immigration, not colonialism or even colonial immigration. Stories spanned from an Italian migrant grape-picker to Spanish shepherds to West African textile workers. But I found few mentions of colonialism, and never once did the museum distinguish immigrants from the colonies and immigrants from everywhere else. Here, the struggle of a rich, educated and famous Pablo Picasso did not differ from an illiterate agricultural laborer from Algeria who fled a colonial French landowner. This museum dodged the hard conversation.

It's a strange case of cognitive dissonance. Paris is Europe's most multicultural capital, with over 20% of residents born outside France. After France, Parisians' top five countries of birth are Algeria, Portugal, Morocco, Tunisia and Guadeloupe. All but Portugal are former French colonies. Guadeloupe still is, though it now carries the more palatable label of "overseas department." Yet, the country won't acknowledge its multiculturalism stems from colonialism's horrors. France's hijacking of native economies, societies and cultures drove waves of immigrants to l'Hexagone.

While departing, I looked again at the bas-relief, and couldn't shake the feeling someone should tear down the entire edifice and chuck it in history's scrap heap next to America's Confederate monuments. We'll never reconcile the sins of our fathers if we continue lionizing their exploits. Plus, it's not just racist; it's racist and ugly. That should seal its fate. I know, I know. The Palais de la Porte Dorée is a protected historic monument of supposed cultural import, but so is the whorehouse near my Airbnb.

The experience left an uneasy question brewing in my mind: Can colonial "subjects" ever be compatriots? True equals? Or was it an intentionally impossible task, dangled like a carrot to induce assimilation?

From the immigration disaster's location on Boulevard Pé-riphérique's eastern edge (the eight-lane roadway encompassing downtown Paris), I traveled into central Paris past Gare du Lyon train station, looking for this alleged hunting museum. A hunting museum in Paris? Yeah, right.

If the immigration museum is making a belated and flailing attempt at atoning for past sins (arguable), then the Museum of Hunting and Nature couldn't care less. It celebrates the plundering of the world's wildlife by European hunters with an idiosyncratic joy that's simultaneously off-putting and charming. The collection is cloaked with environmental awareness, a love for nature, and simplifies the tenuous relationship between hunting and conservation. After all, nothing says "I love nature" quite like a trophy room overflowing with the mounts of extinct and endangered species from around the world (but mostly Africa!).

Housed in an 18th-century mansion on rue des Archives in the 3rd arrondissement, the museum was dead quiet when I entered after consuming an unremarkable chicken-stuffed baguette en route. A short, bald security guard, wearing a simple gray, bellhop-like uniform and round eyeglasses pushed against the bridge of his nose, leaned on the admission counter chatting with the female ticket seller. He looked concerned and greeted me with a hearty, "Bienvenue!"

Clearly, my French had miraculously improved because as soon as I replied, "Merci. Bonjour, monsieur," he clipped my ticket and led me upstairs.

In rapid-fire French, he ushered me from curio cabinet to curio cabinet, explaining the hunting guns, falconry accessories (no actual living falcons), fur traps, clothing, furniture and art. At least, I think he was explaining it. My French hadn't improved, especially in the vocabulary of hunting and naturing. The art was engrossing, though. Owl feathers covered one room's ceiling in an installation called "The Night of Diana." Curators kitted out one room like a 19th-century hunting cabin in the Vosges Mountains.

In a hallway, a tabletop, um, "piece" caught my eye, and I couldn't contain my awe. Da Vinci's Mona Lisa, Monet's water lilies, Rodin's Thinker...What I now stared at deserved its rightful place among those Parisian masterpieces. How had I lived over 30 years and never seen it before? Why hadn't Madeleine sung its praises?

It was mind-boggling.

It was tantalizing.

It was two porcelain chihuahuas dripping in gemstones, glass-bead flowers and costume jewelry.

I had to tell Madeline on WhatsApp:

Have you seen the fooking chihuahuas?

This is why I'm here, right?

...

Focus, Rory. One reason I told you to go there

...

Is because I know you love nature. Look beyond.

...

special exhibit

The passionate security guard, Michel, continued leading me around, explaining things in French. I did not know what he was saying, but I sure pretended I did. Luckily, he did the talking. I loved his enthusiasm and didn't want him to stop. Plus, well, I'd been alone all morning, and I enjoyed his company. His passion bordered on obsession; he may have been somewhere on the autism spectrum.

On the third floor, we approached his Valhalla, the Trophy Room. The Trophy Room contains the mounted heads and taxidermied bodies of hundreds of animals eviscerated from Europe, Africa, Asia and America (but mostly Africa!). Polar bears, lions, leopards, things with pointy horns, things with curly horns, if it roamed this Earth, then it was probably dead in this room (humans and elephants excepted). Michel held court, pointing and reciting the name of every stuffed animal as we walked clockwise. Every inch of wall space held a mount, and the glass cabinets were packed with smaller prey.

Michel stopped back at the door, chest puffed with pride beside an albino boar head. A fearsome, white-haired wild boar with a head two feet in circumference, he bared three-inch fangs. I stepped closer.

"Le Souillot," Michel said.

"Le Souillot," I repeated and moved inches from its snout. "It's remarkable."

Suddenly, it came alive, screamed and tried to bite me. I jumped backward, almost destroying a glass case containing an entire continent's massacred land mammals. My heart rate jumped as I hunched over, trying to catch my breath, Michel laughing his ass off.

He had turned on the boar. Not sexually. He literally turned it on with a wall switch because the damn thing was animatronic. It talked, moved its mouth and eyes and snapped at unsuspecting tourists. It was a Parisian Big Mouth Billy Bass. Except goddamn terrifying.

Its eyes scanned the room, then dropped its jaw and exclaimed in French something like, "They're coming! They're coming!"

As we stood outside the Trophy Room, it dawned on Michel that he wasn't a tour guide, but a security guard. He halted at the staircase, turned and asked me a question that I couldn't answer because I do not speak French.

Was he offering me the chihuahuas? Awfully nice of him, but I doubted they would fit in my carry-on.

He repeated the question. His eyes remained fixed on me as his glasses crept down his nose.

"Je ne parle pas français," I replied and threw up my hands. He raised his eyebrows, adjusted his spectacles, then descended the stairwell.

"Merci, Michel," I called after him.

At this point, I was charmed by Michel, but bewildered by this place. Did they have a writer's residency? Sure, it's the product of rich 1800s-era White guys, but the collection was eccentric and bizarre, sometimes exquisite. A talking albino boar head. Bedazzled chihuahuas. There was much to ponder.

Then, as instructed, I toured the special exhibit, and the blood rushed from my face. I couldn't believe my eyes. A dozen black canvases hung across the L-shaped room depicting cartoonish hunting scenes. Two triumphant White hunters and a meek Black laborer stood beside fresh jungle kills, marched through thatched-roof villages and rummaged through crates and crates of hunting kit. The black canvases implied the action happened on the "Dark Continent," a term dubbed by Welsh explorer Henry Morton Stanley that helped Europeans justify their eventual dehumanization of African people and culture. The "Dark Continent" tag gave license to European explorers to treat Africa as a zoo rather than an actual civilization.

I thought they were ironic, shocking people into understanding what colonial big-game hunting did to native societies and environments. But I couldn't be sure. I gathered myself and examined one more closely.

The Black porter/guide, I realized, didn't possess oversized lips, misshapen limbs or comical proportions. He was a normal human being, not a breed apart, as the Palais de la Porte Dorée had depicted Black people. He was in the two White hunters' employ, but he wasn't actually working. Instead, the porter, clothed in native wear, appeared to be counseling the hunters with gentle statements. Upon further inspection, the White hunters wore bamboozled looks. They stood triumphantly over kills and beside villagers, but their poses and facial expressions conveyed confusion and uncertainty. These were not White saviors, I realized. The color returned to my face.

Then I noticed the paintings' name plates contained a line of dialogue, in French, that emanated from the porter. I could summon travel superpowers, or I could pull up Google Translate. I shelved my superpowers for another day.

Painting #1 (White hunters stand by dead elephant): "I'm sure his family won't mind."

Painting #2 (White hunters carry slain lion through native village): "Don't expect a hero's welcome."

Painting #3 (White hunters survey skins of various kills): "This shouldn't have long-term ecological consequences."

Painting #4 (Wooden crates of hunting equipment surround the White hunters): "My ancestral village will survive your rampant materialism."

And so forth. Not exactly a Comedy Store-worthy "tight 15," but I chuckled at the sardonic translations. The exhibit was a fox in the hen house. The subversive art flipped the whole museum's original raison d'être upside down.

But was it sincere? Was the anonymous artist genuine? Madeleine and I discussed over WhatsApp as I rode the Métro to Edouard Pailleron pool. We both agreed, if nothing else, it was surprising.

* * *

Opened in 1933, the Edouard Pailleron pool's architecture succeeded where Palais Dorée failed. My eyes followed the seductive brick exterior, a geometric honeycomb with cloud lifts and clean, straight lines. I paused under the subtle and graceful half-circle covered entryway, an Art Deco calling card found at every movie theater built during the era. It was unassuming; after passing through the simple lobby, a three-story behemoth revealed a bustling 108-foot lap pool, gym and workout space, spa and sauna area, lounge pool for families and rectangular hot tub.

One of many pools built during Paris' public-pool building spree in the early 1900s, it was indisputably Art Deco. Two styles didn't compete or vie for space, and it projected no propaganda like the Palais Dorée mishmash. It was big, airy and bright, employing a yellow and light-blue color scheme on the walls, doors and tiles. Windows were legion; the solarium-sun roof had so many it felt open to the sky. The ceiling cleverly employed metal louvers to soften direct sunlight.

The coed changing areas buzzed with the healthy after-work crowd. I showered and walked to the pool, planning on swimming a few laps before sunbathing. So many swimmers clogged the lap lanes, I could've walked across the pool without getting my feet wet.

As I waited for a lane opening, I was gripped by embarrassment. My bathing suit was so skimpy, with a five-inch inseam that fell halfway down my pasty white thighs. Oh, what I would've given for a pair of knee-length board shorts. I felt eyes fixed on me, no doubt shocked at my swim attire. At least in Amsterdam, everyone was naked at the spa. Somehow, that was more reassuring.

At the apex of my embarrassment, cheeks flushed red as I nervously toed the pool's tiled edge waiting for a lap lane, a nearby male lifeguard blew his whistle as though the force alone could save a drowning swimmer. It was ear-splitting, and I recoiled. My goodness, what intensity! Had someone dragged a dead body into the pool? Whoever, whatever happened, I was glad the lifeguard's fury wasn't directed at me. For a brief moment.

He angrily pointed, then beelined straight for me. Turns out, I *was* on the receiving end of his fury. But what had I done? I hadn't even gotten into the pool yet.

"This," he pointed at my swim shorts, "is not possible." He spoke English straightaway, before I could ask or protest my innocence in kindergartner French.

I didn't understand. Not possible? Are my bleached thighs so embarrassing that they won't let me in the pool?

"Not possible," he muttered again, shaking his head. He pointed to the lobby. "You must go."

I hadn't touched water yet and already I was being kicked out. But what had I done? Or what had my shorts done to raise such ire?

Men, women, children all were enjoying the pool, swimming and playing. What did they have or do that I didn't? I paid three euros, the same as everyone else. I showered with soap and shampoo before entering the pool area. I wore a dedicated swimsuit.

I scanned the pool, piecing together what faux pas I'd committed. As I approached the locker room, and people came streaming out, showered and ready to swim, I realized it: The men wore clingy Lycra or "Speedo"-style bathing suits. My "baggy" gray bathing suit violated their swimwear regulations because it had pockets and didn't coddle my nether regions. My ultra-revealing bathing suit didn't reveal enough.

I'd been to enough French beaches (one) to understand their preference for skimpy, butt-hugging, skin-clinging bathing attire. Men either wore Speedo-style swim briefs Americans associate with swim racers or retro-looking, skin-tight square-leg suits that covered slightly more than swim briefs. Slightly. I figured the French penchant for immodest men's swimwear was just that—a preference, not a requirement. Turns out, that was true on beaches; lifeguards-cum-fashion police won't whistle you off the *plage*. In vast ocean waters, where dilution was the solution, contamination from dirty swimwear wasn't a concern.

However, here in France's public pools, as I would soon discover, authorities strictly regulated men's swimwear to prevent dirt, debris and, apparently, male pride from entering the pool. France's public pools limited their use of chlorine and other chemicals. (In fact, according to a multipanel display in the lobby, Piscine Pailleron used an ozone cleaner instead.) So, authorities limited contamination by requiring a thorough shower before swimming and outlawing any suits that could be worn on the street. Certainly nothing with pockets. These rules were codified into law in 1903 just as public pools proliferated across Paris and greater France. Since then, French pools have been board short- and swim trunk-free.

A lobby attendant, who heard the whistle-borne commotion, intercepted me just outside the pool area. She looked in distress, dreadfully anticipating our conversation.

"You must have...," she searched for the English word, then gave up, "...a slip de bain." She pointed at a sign near the reception desk that I'd overlooked upon arrival, lost in appreciating the beautiful lobby.

The sign had a big red "X" over a man wearing a baggy bathing suit like mine and a big green check mark over a man proudly displaying his banana hammock.

"Right. But I don't have a, uh, slip de bain. Non slip de bain," I pleaded, throwing up my hands and setting the stage for my eventual three-euro refund.

But no refund was coming.

She insisted that a solution sat against the lobby's far wall, where she pointed with her right hand and waved her left hand for me to follow. She walked toward the vending machines.

This was no time for a beverage! I wasn't thirsty or hungry, I tried telling her, but ever-obstinate, the attendant motioned me to follow her until we stood in front of three vending machines. One machine dispensed sodas and juice. Another offered sandwiches and snacks. The third one sold...bathing suits! Utterly revealing, butt-clenching, testicle-swaddling men's bathing suits (and kid's and women's).

The triumphant attendant spun on her left heel and returned to the reception desk as I perused the offerings of "Swind"-brand bathing suits. The machine also doled out ear plugs, soap, shampoo, bathing caps and goggles. Ten euros later, I strutted poolside in a navy-and-white vending-machine Speedo, ready to swim laps like a debonair Frenchman and introduce my upper thighs to something they'd never experienced: sunlight.

* * *

Three hours of swimming and sunbathing later, I sat at Little Breizh, an authentic, family-run galette joint a couple blocks off the Left Bank's buzzy boulevard Saint-Germain. The sunburned thighs started making their itchy, fiery presence known as I hunched over the restaurant's signature dish, a hearty "super complete" buckwheat galette stuffed with bacon, ham, *comté* cheese, leeks and crème fraîche and topped with a fried egg. I devoured it in five bites along with a mixed-green side salad, washed it down with hard cider and ordered a sweet Nutella *flambée* crepe for dessert.

The noble galette differs from a crepe in several ways. First, chefs spin galettes from buckwheat batter while crepes use straight wheat flour. This makes galettes thicker, healthier and more filling. They're served differently, too. A crepe is folded into a triangle, similar to a quesadilla, so it's easier to eat while walking. A galette comes folded in a square with a small opening in the middle, thus necessitating a fork and knife.

Both the crepe and galette originated from Brittany, but even there the terms are used interchangeably or may mean something entirely different: Some Bretons use galette when referring to blini-type pancakes. Either way, they're a Breton specialty that has conquered France and spread worldwide. In Little Breizh, the proud Breton chef stood under a black-and-white-striped Breton flag.

My eyes drooped as I cut into the flambée galette; hours of walking museums and lap swimming had drained me. But I had to persevere and figure out where I'd go next. I had made no plans after Paris. Foolishly, I was hoping fate would intervene. Instead, I was now spinning around a France map while checking train timetables.

Provence? The Dordogne? Burgundy? The Alps?

I stared at the Breton flag hanging over the chef as he cranked out savory galettes to eager, happy diners. I'd never set foot in Brittany...

Brittany?

My phone buzzed, and picking it up required summoning all my remaining energy. My vision blurred at the blue-light glare before it focused on the green notification. It was a WhatsApp message from my boss, the travel website's head-honcho editor:

whatsup mate, hey ru in france?

...

Hey man. Yup France. Got something?

...

Quick dday van tour in bayeux? 750 words, 4 photos. Udwn?

Oh, yes, I was down, er, "dwn," I assured him. That settled it. I accepted the assignment, even though it meant tagging along on a group tour, albeit a small group. With Brittany on my mind (and in my mouth) and a paid assignment in Normandy, a plan crystallized: I was going west, first to Bayeux in Normandy and then somewhere in Brittany, Normandy's western neighbor. Why not? It made sense. I'd figure out the details later—like where I'd go in Brittany. I solidified my decision over a swig of cider, an Airbnb search and a quick reference of the train timetables.

After dinner, I waddled west along the Seine and crossed the pedestrian Léopold-Sédar-Senghor bridge to Tuileries Garden. Several groups of gray-haired men played *boules* in the park, relishing every last glimpse of daylight. The summer amusement park in Tuileries' east end blared music as the neon-lit Ferris wheel spun.

A block from the park, happy conversation emanated from a modest café. I pounced on an open bar stool at Au Petit Bar, a 50-year-old café so lost in time it's a miracle they know when to open. Amid expensive museum-district restaurants, luxury hotels and stuffy antique shops, Au Petit Bar somehow remained family owned—dad and one son worked the back while mom and the other son ran the front. It was authentic to its core, with unheard-of prices for central Paris. They served beer, wine, coffee and classic French appetizers, omelets and a rotating plat du jour.

Pushing eight o'clock, the summer heat had relented and the cool breeze through the open front door made for a comfortable nightcap. I ordered a seven-euro Bordeaux that would cost 10 euros anywhere else around here. It was a merlot-cabernet franc blend from Saint-Émilion, a grape-growing town that traces its wine-making history to the 2nd century when Romans planted the area's first vines.

It was roast beef and lentils night, so patrons buzzed around the bar. I almost regretted my galettes. Almost. Plates flew out of the kitchen as beer and wine glasses slid across the counter. It was far too busy to strike up conversation, so I removed my elbows from the Formica countertop, reclined with my wine glass and relished the scene.

The narrow, shotgun-style establishment held 20 tables and a five-seat countertop bar. The stainless steel draft beer station, the bar's hardest-working piece of equipment, dispensed three beer types through its dark-wood handles. In front of it, a 1960s-era candy dispenser held salty bar snacks for 25 euro cents. Occasionally, one family member dashed behind the counter to answer the phone, a brown-and-green corded relic with a rotary dial.

I wrote and read my paperback until the only English conversation in the whole café caught my attention. The two well-dressed women spoke in hushed tones, tempering thick British accents.

"Oh, yes, I saw it on the telly tonight. They tried to bomb Notre-Dame. I think in a car. Just yesterday. Can you imagine?" the female voice said. "What if they had succeeded?"

Her companion's mouth dropped in shock as her eyes bulged. "Tragic. No, I didn't hear about it." She sipped her wine. "I can't imagine."

Bayeux

L ison is not Bayeux, where I should have been. It's not terribly far, just two stops down the train line or about 18 miles off target. But in Lison I stood, knocking on the train station manager's office, anxious that my document holder—containing passport, money, credit cards, my entire life—was somewhere on the other side of that hollow-core white door.

That morning on the train, I slid into the aisle seat next to a solitary gray-haired woman. When I pulled out my Eurail, she slid her Interrail Pass, the Eurail-style pass for Europeans, on the seat-back tray. We exchanged grins, brothers-in-rail-passes.

"Vee might be zee oldest people with rail passes on zee train," she said, laughing and nodding at my Eurail. Her thick German accent converted every "W" into a "V" and "Th" into "Z."

"We might be the only passes on this train," I added, craning my neck to survey the carriage.

An indispensable tool for backpacking Europe in the '70s and '80s, the celebrated Eurail has been fending off a protracted death for ages. The rigid rail pass squandered its appeal as travelers shifted to last-minute, one-way mobile bookings. Modern backpackers maximize their itineraries and budgets with high-speed routes, cut-rate flights, and dirt-cheap buses not covered by Eurail. These forces, and that they didn't offer a phone version until 2020, have conspired to kill the

126

once-almighty Eurail Pass.

"My parents, zay gave me Interrail for my birthday at 18 years. Zat was 1974, many years ago. I think, ja, Interrail had only just started, perhaps two, three years earlier, and vas very popular vith my friends." Her eyes twinkled in memory. "Vee travel all through Europe. I buy one every year since. Every year." She wagged her right index finger. "I buy zee senior pass now, of course. Some years I go east. Some years I go vest," she said.

"You are very lucky," I said as I leaned toward her. "In America, if we are lucky, we take one, maybe two Eurail trips in our lifetimes."

"Ja, I know zis. Is zis your first Eurail?"

"Second, actually. But the first was..." I looked at my hands. "Like 15 years ago." We both lost ourselves in memories for a second.

"What are your favorite routes or trips?" I asked.

"So many vunderful trips. I prefer zee country railways. Vee have many in Germany." She looked up, her many train journeys replaying in her mind. "Ja, I zink Bohemia is very nice for train travel. Zere are many small train lines zere...in zee country. Zee Harz line in Germany as vell."

She scratched her head. "In Hungary, zee Carpathians. Oostria and Switzerland, of course. I like Portugal very much. So many vunderful trips, vunderful memories." She reclined.

I scribbled her recommendations, and we chatted about our families. The train bumped and rattled, slowing as it approached Caen, her destination. I helped lower her roller bag down from the overhead storage. We said goodbye, and she strode toward the door before stopping and looking over her left shoulder.

"I have one question for you, Rory. Vill Donald Trump vin zee election?"

"Ha! No," I shook my head, astonished she'd ask. It was the first time in weeks I'd thought about the political circus underway on that side of the Atlantic. "Of course not," I assured her.

I slid into the window seat, and soon I was enraptured by the scenery. Tidy rectangular green fields abutted golden ones, late-season grains awaiting their last cut. Dairy cows roamed pastures and rows upon rows of apple trees filled orchards stretching to the English Channel.

* * *

No one answered my knock at the Lison train station door, though muffled French jazz music emanated from the office. Before entering, I briefly forgot my predicament and admired the handsome country station. A standing-seam gray-metal roof covered the two-floor main hall. Each window featured a graceful Norman arch trimmed in white stone with matching white wooden shutters. It was quiet and graceful. I imagined how locals must beam with pride every time they pass their humble, yet elegant pastoral gateway.

My cheeks flushed as I wondered how this day could get worse. Distracted by the Normandy scenery, I'd left all my valuables on a train a couple of hours ago. The Bayeux station manager assured me they'd located the document holder in Lison, two stops west of Bayeux. At least, I think that's what he said. But was anyone even here? Had I misunderstood the Bayeux station manager's broken English? Had I even gone to the right town?

Just as I raised my fist to knock again, a squat middle-aged man wearing an unbuttoned white collared shirt opened the door, wiping his mouth with a napkin, a half-eaten *jambon-beurre* sandwich sat on his desk atop a Jackson Pollock mess of paperwork. Lison's station manager spoke no English, but expected my arrival, and waved me inside his 6'x8' office in the quaint country depot. I pulled up an Internet photo of my blue Victorinox document holder and showed it to him. He nodded, and handed me a bulging manila envelope from his black-metal desk.

Was that it? Really it? I didn't have to prove it belonged to me? No song and dance. No need to prove who I was? No forms or blood tests? In Paris, I'd be filling out a bible's worth of forms, submitting a DNA test and having my mother fax a sworn affidavit. Not in dinky Lison. He didn't even compare the passport photo to my face, let alone ask for proof.

The station manager returned to his very important paperwork. Just kidding! He resumed eating his sandwich and turned up the radio as I walked out with the envelope. Not a single question asked, in neither French nor English. It was easy. Countryside easy. I was no longer in Paris' human fermentation vat, and was now exploring a land where people, apparently, trusted each other.

The next train to Bayeux left in a couple hours, so I wandered the sleepy farming village. A rusted-white Peugeot puttered down main street, but otherwise Lison was a ghost town. Inspired by the station manager, I scored a bakery's last jambon-beurre baguette before they shut for lunch. I then walked down a narrow, shoulder-less country road past pasture and farms looking for a bench or grassy field. Ten minutes outside town, I stumbled upon a frying pan-shaped pond among a sea of rolling green farm fields. A dirt trail led from a gravel parking lot.

Weeping beech trees surrounded the pond's edge, while yews fought for space a few feet back from its shores. Birds chirped and shuttled between the swaddling beeches. Two mallards, sporting brown, green and white plumage, paddled across the pond, sending gentle ripples toward the grassy shore.

Refreshing unfiltered sunshine beamed while a gentle breeze shook the bulbous beech branches and punctuated Normandy's mild mid-70s temperature, the first daytime temps under 90 degrees since Copenhagen. I nibbled the baguette, its crunchy crust revealing a chewy, airy middle enveloping smoky ham and salty, earthy butter. Picnicking beside a Monet pond, like I'd stumbled into my own living Impressionist painting, lifted my spirits.

I scratched my stubble beard, again reminded myself to find a razor, and lifted my chin to the sunshine. As I removed my notebook and pen, I realized losing my valuables had led me to this pond-side picnic. It was perhaps the best thing that could've happened today.

* * *

"Bonjour Rory!" said the late middle-aged woman with dirty blonde hair. She wore black-framed glasses, a beige business skirt with matching sport coat, white-collared shirt and white loafers. Her big smile led me forward.

She held open the gray arched door, made from thick vertical planks, and hung inside a matching white-stone Norman-arched entrance. All the windows had matching arches and neat gray shutters, swung open. Floral wrought-iron spanners ran the width of the second-story windows. The stark, Neo-Romanesque facade sat on a two-foot-tall, white-granite foundation that matched the door and window stones. Only the graceful Norman arches overlooking the doors and windows served as ornamentation. Buildings running down the street looked similar, distinguished only by different colored shutters and doors. A white porcelain tile bearing the number "15" adorned the doorway's keystone.

"Bonjour Christine!" I stepped inside.

"I apologize, my English," she smiled broadly and wagged her right hand, "is not good."

"Fine, no problem. Your English is better than my French," I replied, annunciating and slowing my conversational pace while raising my eyebrows. "I promise."

The doorway arch matched the entryway's barrel-vault ceiling. Every wall and ceiling held a fresh coat of thick white plaster. I followed Christine into a t-junction foyer with a kitchen on the right and family room on the left. In the family room, Christine's oldest son rose from the couch and extended his hand, so tall he needed only a step to close the distance between us.

"My son, Clement. He speaks English! Better than me!" She erupted in laughter as Clement and I shook hands.

"I'm learning," he said while pinching his left thumb and index finger together.

"Nice to meet you, Clement. How old are you?" I asked.

"I'm 17, in my last year before university," he said, ready for that last year to hurry up and end already.

"He's youngest," Christine said while draping her hands across his shoulders. "His brother, sister are..." She threw up her hands and waved goodbye.

"They are gone," finished Clement. "My brother at university and my sister works in Paris." He spoke with confidence, a young man ready to experience the world.

Pascal entered the foyer from the courtyard, wearing all-white painter's clothes spattered with blue, yellow and orange. Tall and lean like his son with a narrow face and prominent nose, he extended his right hand.

"This is Rory. Rory, Pascal, mon husband," said Christine, kissing Pascal on the left cheek as he embraced her.

Pascal and I exchanged greetings, then he placed his right hand over his heart and apologized for his English. He was nice, if standoffish, perhaps nervous about speaking English.

"Are you from Bayeux originally?" I asked them.

"Oui, me, my whole life. Pascal is from a small town nearby, Lison. Maybe you don't know it."

I didn't have the energy to explain that not only did I know of Lison, but I had just spent all afternoon in Lison.

"And for work?" I asked.

"I work at the school," she pointed vaguely out toward the street. "It is close."

"I'm a painter," Pascal stated. He held Christine close as she leaned against him.

"What do you paint?" I asked.

"I paint the canvas for gallery...for sell. Um, and I'm painting sometimes walls and fresco...for house and commercial," he replied, stretching his nervous English to its limit.

"Ah I see. Not a house painter, but art? Art on the walls and the canvas."

"Oui, correct. I paint only this house!" he said, slapping the wall closest to him.

"Ah, right. So, tell me about this beautiful house!" I exclaimed. "How old is it?"

"The maison is from beginning 18th century," Christine said, leading me through the living room, kitchen and into the garden courtyard as Pascal and Clement went about their business. The house was L-shaped—the neighboring house, a stone wall and built-in dovecote enclosed the courtyard.

"This was a grand mansion. This whole," she twirled her right index finger searching for the correct word, "area? Um...pâté de maisons."

"City block?" I offered.

"Oui! This city block, one house. Three years ago, they sell the mansion and," she made a chopping motion, "divide into five maisons." That explained why every house on the block looked identical.

"We buy one, and we, um, fix, rénovation, rénovation complète," she said and scanned the ceiling, no doubt wondering if they'd missed a spot.

"Well, it's beautiful. Really beautiful. Très belle," I emphasized.

The scrubbed doorways featured the same graceful Norman arches as the exterior. The windows were tall and narrow, just like the building's inhabitants, with thin muntins dividing each one into two-over-four panes. Simple white baseboard and case trim covered the door jambs and walls. Other than Pascal's bright, playful canvases featuring googly eyed fish and smiling bullfrogs, everything was white and flat, an updated and Scandinavian-inspired take on classic Romanesque.

Christine showed me my clean, white, bright room. Evening light poured through the skinny windows. The room's only color came from a vibrant Pascal canvas and the bed's red, green, blue and yellow comforter. Christine explained the toilet was next door, but the shower and sink were on the top floor, past Clement's room. No problem, I assured her, silently commiserating with the challenge of plumbing 300-year-old homes.

Propped against the glossy-white headboard, I called home, checked email, where my confirmation for tomorrow's D-Day tour was waiting, and freshened up before leaving to explore Bayeux. As I crossed the foyer toward the front door, I said thank you and goodbye to Christine, who was now wearing an apron in the kitchen. The countertop radio played instrumental music.

"Ciao Christine," I waved while striding for the door.

"Au revoir, Rory," she replied, then dropped her copper pan, shouted, "Rory!" and scurried to intercept me at the front door.

She opened her mouth, but nothing came out.

"Uh..." she thought, sifting through her English vocabulary. "You must...um, the lumières."

The lights?

"Lumières," I repeated.

"Oui!" she smiled, "Les lumières!" She pointed toward the center of town and grinned. "C'est magnifique," my Norman host added with such conviction I almost understood her.

"Sure! Sure. Loo-me-air, oui." I had no clue what she was saying. Something about watching for the lights, so I vowed to turn off the lights when I returned that night. She was passionate about lights, and my turning them off would be magnificent. Obviously.

Of traveling Europe's many pleasures, kicking around small towns at nightfall has to be among the most pleasant. As the sun set, I walked to Parc Michel Ornano, then followed the River Aure past the café where I almost ate lunch today to the medieval Bayeux Mill, a stone building with a working water wheel and low-head dam. Bright bougainvillea and electric-green moss crawled along the dry-stone walls while pink and red geraniums bursted from window boxes. The Aure dove under rue Saint-Jean, Bayeux's major pedestrian thoroughfare, where white-granite restaurants and shops lined the walkway.

Even with 13,000 inhabitants, Bayeux felt like a small town, especially after Paris, Amsterdam and Copenhagen. I leaned against a stone building and read about the town's history from a brochure I had hastily fetched from the tourist office earlier that afternoon. In the 1st-century BCE, the Romans established a garrison on the Aure River's west bank, stationing a legion here to protect inland trade routes and defend the English Channel coast. (Of course, back then, it was just the "coast.") The Romans called the settlement Augustodurum, which never stood a chance of sticking around with that many "U"s, and they later changed it to the much-worse Noemagus Biducassium. Compared to its previous designations, pronouncing Bayeux (Bay-yew) is a cakewalk.

The Middle Ages brought a destruction-and-revival cycle. After Viking raids destroyed the town, successive Norman dukes, themselves descendants of Viking raiders, rebuilt Bayeux and made it an important commercial and political center. For a time, Bayeux jostled for prominence with Normandy's biggest cities, nearby Caen and farther-afield Rouen. Post-Middle Ages, however, trade and influence shifted toward those cities, both of which thrived while Bayeux slumbered. Thrust onto the world stage during WWII, Bayeux became the first French city liberated by the western Allies following the D-Day invasion. Miraculously, Bayeux survived the Normandy landings unscathed as German resistance centered on Caen, which was mostly demolished by Allied bombing. Playing second fiddle to Caen saved Bayeux.

I tacked left onto rue de Bienvenu, completing a horseshoe loop at Bayeux Cathedral, the town's landmark Gothic-Norman-Romanesque monument. Consecrated in 1077, a date so ancient William the Conqueror had already ruled England for a decade, the church received a Gothic face-lift over the Norman-Romanesque edifice in the 12th century.

Gothic towers anchored the front's left and right sides, perfectly framing the massive crossing tower with its green-dome roof. The main doors, 15-feet tall and painted red, bisected the front, while secondary doors sat under the facade towers. Much like Normans themselves, the cathedral was tall, narrow and imposing. The Gothic face-lift couldn't obscure the building's Norman-Romanesque roots.

Always traveling, the Normans developed a style of Romanesque architecture that drew influences from across Europe, North Africa and even the Middle East. This makes Norman architecture perhaps influenced by more cultures than any other European form. The geographic distribution of Norman architecture is as diverse as its influences; Norman churches, monasteries and castles are found throughout Europe from London's Westminster Abbey to the Cathedral of Palermo in Sicily.

I stepped through the door on the right and felt the rib-vaulted ceilings towering over me. No amount of Gothic tinkering could hide the distinctive, imposing Norman arch running the cathedral's length from nave to transept to chancel. This semicircular grand archway, like the entry at my Airbnb, is Norman architecture's calling card, whose principal purpose, it seems, was to impose awe amongst us mere mortals. And, my mouth agape, I felt awestruck, but the feeling didn't last long as I snapped to attention.

Before I could appreciate all the Norman-ness, I faced a choir concert, several audience members narrowing their eyes at me as I stood there acting like this performance didn't surprise me in the least. But it most definitely did. I did not hear a note from outside.

I faced a snap decision: Should I backpedal the way I came or sit and pretend like I was perfectly expecting the concert?

The choir's voices filled the cathedral, dripping in candles now that the night had grown inky black. I tiptoed down the nave and sat on a wooden folding chair three rows in front of the adult choir.

Standing at the crossing (where the nave meets the transept) instead of the actual choir area, the choristers faced the seated audience while the conductor stood inconspicuously to the choir's left. The 20-strong group neither held music books nor looked to the conductor as they sang old Christian hymns, taking only a few seconds' breather between songs. I discerned, through melody, because they sang in French, "O Bread of Heaven" and "Agnus Dei."

It didn't matter what they sang, only that they were singing, and I was one of the lucky couple of dozen people in attendance. The colossal arched ceiling carried their voices, each one distinguishable yet in harmony, to the rafters and higher, perhaps into the heavens themselves. Goosebumps ran down my neck and arms. I couldn't believe my fortune, and closed my eyes, letting the lilting songs carry me away.

What separates a daydream from a meditation? If you're daydreaming in a church, does that count as meditation? I ruminated about my loved ones back in the States, letting my mind wander through memories of my son's childhood, the day I met my wife and, of course, what I could do to make my parents proud of me.

Soon, though, my musings, I mean, my very spiritual meditations, turned to the trip. Was I fulfilling my stated mission? Have I been experiencing things worth writing about? Would I return home to find the locks changed? Would I ever grasp basic French?

Maybe 30 minutes later, still lost in daydreams, but reaching my limit of Catholic hymns, I resolved to leave as the choir sang on. Except I had fixed my gaze on that Norman arch ceiling, so many rib vaults, so tall and narrow, and I wasn't paying attention. I figured I'd sneak out the way I arrived and activated my tourist-ninja superpower.

It couldn't have been less stealthy unless I was riding a dirt bike.

Eyes glued to those sexy rib vaults, I stood up at the exact moment the choir marched the nave's central aisle, presumably to exit the premises as a unified, sacred procession. But since I hadn't been watching, only listening, and the choir never skipped a beat as they paraded out of the cathedral, I inadvertently merged into the procession.

I was now part of the procession with everyone's eyes fixed on me, the unsuspecting interloper. I looked over my left shoulder at the conductor, whose eyes bulged as he looked ready to fly across the aisle and tackle me. The choir kept walking and singing, so I marched in lockstep. I summoned a new travel superpower, impersonating a French choirboy. Calmness washed over me as I blended into the choir and mouthed along to songs I'd never heard in a language I didn't understand. But I did it all in perfect harmony like a walking metronome as the procession cleared the nave. They turned right and I ducked left out the front door.

Moments after escaping the cathedral cavalcade, another river of humanity swept me up on Passage Flachat, a pedestrian corridor running parallel to the cathedral. Crowds of people followed multicolored lights and blaring orchestra music coming from the cathedral's east end.

The cobblestone Passage Flachat led to Place de la Liberté, a sandy stretch encircling a gigantic burled maple tree, known as Arbre de la Liberté or Tree of Liberty. Psychedelic lights of every color bathed the tree in stripes, then geometric shapes, before morphing again into waves and famous historic scenes, all set to swooping classical music interspersed with famous speeches in English and French. From Martin Luther King, Jr., and the Normandy landings to celebrating nature and seasons, the Tree of Liberty told stories of freedom and the human spirit. The 360-degree light show came from six, eight-foot tall projectors that looked like sci-fi robots girdling captives with space rays. Additional colored lights illuminated the cathedral's windows and arches, and liberty was translated into eight languages and projected in yellow against the cathedral's outside wall.

Inspired by the American revolutionaries, the First French Republic, after ceremoniously guillotining Louis XVI and so many other people, planted Liberty Trees across the country as symbols of the people's newfound power. But as the prefix "first" implies, the republic didn't last, and counterrevolutionaries laid waste to dastardly Liberty Trees.

Subsequent revolutions never replanted, at least not with such zeal as the first go; I think everyone was tired from all that revolting. They weren't all chopped down, though, as Bayeux's Tree of Liberty attests, having occupied its perch in Place de la Liberté since 1797 (that explained the gnarly burls protruding like tumors from its trunk and the tangled web of limbs). It's one of the few remaining Liberty Trees not just in Normandy but all of France, in a town spared D-Day's ravages.

Bayeux's a damn lucky place is what I'm saying. It's Normandy's four-leaf clover.

And fortunate Bayeux celebrates by throwing this psychedelic party a few nights a week every summer. In fact, this was the last week it was playing. Imagine my luck.

Then it hit me: lumières! Christine was trying to tell me about this light show when I departed, telling me to watch the lumières tonight. Despite my best efforts, I had followed what turned out to be Christine's sound advice.

Everyone was entranced, and soon I was, too. Stories of the triumphant human spirit, told through snippets of speeches, classical music, sound effects and twirling, whirling swaths of lightsabers shot from sci-fi robots, brought actual tears to my eyes. I blinked them away and slyly looked left and right to ensure no one saw. Soon, I couldn't contain them and tears streaked down my cheeks. Brahms' "Tragic Overture" brought the prismatic presentation to climax, as American civil rights activists marched, seedlings time-lapsed into flower blossoms and our father's fathers stormed the D-Day beaches, all of it unfolding against a 300-year-old maple tree.

* * *

I awoke early, ensuring time for coffee and croissants before meeting my tour at 8 a.m. Christine was already prepping dinner in her apron when I tiptoed down the stairs, the rising morning sunlight flooded the space, bouncing off the bright-white plaster.

"Christine, bonjour!" I said, eager to discuss the whole lumières thing.

"Bonjour Rory!" she replied, this morning's smile as wide, warm and welcoming as yesterday's. I pondered asking if she'd be my French mom.

"Christine, I saw the light show last night. Les lumières! On the tree by the cathedral. Thank you, merci!" I gushed.

"Oh, voilà! Magnifique, oui?" Her eyes lit up as brightly as the morning sun outside and her bonny personality filled the space between us.

"So, so magnifique, Christine. Thank you, thank you."

"Oui, I become, um, a little," she flapped her right hand at the wrist and dabbed her eyes, "... émotive."

"Oh, really? Huh," I feigned surprise, hoping she wouldn't see through my bluff. But it didn't matter because she had already returned to wrapping pliable pastry dough around an eight-pound seared filet of beef, dripping in goose fat and duxelles paste, an aromatic mixture of mushrooms, onions, herbs and black pepper.

She finished wrapping the *boeuf en croûte,* or Beef Wellington as they say 20 miles across the Channel, and withdrew the beautiful creation to the oven top before I could salivate all over it. She double-checked the temperature, then opened the oven door and just as she slid the pastry-beef off the gas burners, she lost control. Her right hand lost grip and her left hand pushed the beef directly toward the floor.

Without thinking, from around the corner, I dove for it, arms fully outstretched. My knuckles grazed the oak floor as I just barely cradled the beef before it landed. I laid on my stomach and gently held the beef. Never in my life have I moved so fast and so decisively.

"Merde!" Christine shouted before leaning over the counter and seeing I'd caught it. "Rory, thank you!" She slammed the oven door shut, caught her composure by fanning herself and then lifted the boeuf en croûte from my trembling hands.

After inspecting for injury and swabbing with butter, she slid it into the oven.

"Rory, you saved dinner. You must join us tonight, oui?" Her smile never wavering, she looked expectantly.

Join them for dinner? Did she understand what she was saying?

I looked around for Clement. Surely, he'd talk some sense into his mother, in French, bien sûr. He was still sleeping. Pascal was nowhere to be found, not that he'd be much help.

"Um, dinner?" I asked. Did she mean I could pick leftovers from the garbage?

Was she inviting me, a virtual stranger, to a meal that required prepping at 7:30 a.m.? Did...did she run this by her other guests?

"Oui. My friends come. You will join us."

"With you...eating that." I pointed at the oven door, my mouth watering just thinking about what laid behind it.

"Oui," she laughed, "Rory, you will come? Possibly, about...vingt?" She said while cleaning the utensils in soapy hot water.

"Yes, yes, of course. Bien sûr! Double bien sûr! Merci Christine! May I help you?" I opened my hands, palms facing the ceiling. "Put me to work."

"No, no, you go. Go! Au revoir Rory," she insisted.

* * *

I waited inside the tour office, eating my second pain au chocolat and sipping a latte. Tearing apart the puff pastry filled with a silky chocolate ribbon felt like I had set the airy delicacy free after a long confinement. The receptionist promised the guide would arrive shortly. Indeed, I was a few minutes early. Outside the office window a bald man smoked cigarettes. He downed the cigarette with vigor and wore an expression that wavered between "Not this again" and "I'm so hungover." Without a doubt, this was our tour guide.

I knew the look well, having led tours for a few years before finding a full-time journalist job. He'd done the same tour countless times, just this summer alone. A guide his age working an overview-style tour like this had peaked in his profession. His mastery of English and moderate knowledge of WWII would only lift him so far. He knew it; this was it and the repetition was driving him into the ground. He lit another cigarette. It was 8:03 a.m.

Perhaps I, like last night's sci-fi robots, was projecting a bit. Maybe this would be an insightful day and he'd possess an encyclopedic knowledge of D-Day. I accepted the van tour because, yes, I needed the money, but also because small tours bring rail travelers to far-flung sights. Since D-Day planners didn't take rail-pass holders into account, the invasion beaches are one such sight.

But before I could pay homage to my countrymen's sacrifices, I needed the tour guide to extinguish his butt. And we'd likely need some other tourists, as I was still the only one in the office. As if on cue, two fair-skinned middle-aged couples, wearing hats, sunglasses and matching white, Wimbledon-ready outfits, walked past the smoker into the office.

They spoke a sing-song English dialect, expressing utter contempt for the holy diphthong union and trading in supreme vowel confusion where "A"s were now "E"s, "E"s turned into "I"s, and "I"s became "U"s. These two men and two women, in their starched-white, mid-thigh tennis shorts, bleached knee-length socks and impeccable ivory sneakers, hailed, without a doubt, from a far-off land where people speak New Zenglish. Yes, they were Kiwi.

"Is that the price, then?" asked the redhead, the group's apparent spokesperson, pointing to a folded brochure he'd produced from his pocket.

"Yes," replied the receptionist.

The redhead's brunette wife whispered into his right ear. He looked concerned. "Well, that's what she says," he whispered back. "Are you certain we're in the right place?"

"So, so," the redhead said, and leaned against the reception counter. Cripes, it's always the ginger, I thought, wishing I had brought a hat to hide my crimson hair.

"So, the beaches are nee-ah are they?" He continued, "Close by to hee-ah? And the guide, he speaks English?"

"Yes, close to here, a few minutes by car. Your guide will explain the route...in English," replied the woman, her hair pulled back tight, stressing her expressionless face. She spoke perfect English.

"Really?" He looked stunned, and his comrades stayed quiet, yet also wore doubtful expressions. A few more participants arrived, strode to the counter, and the Kiwis shuffled next to me.

"Wayne," said the redhead's freckled brunette wife while tugging his left bicep. She then whispered in his ear again, something I couldn't hear.

"Well, that's what she says," he muttered, flabbergasted. His tone rose in inflection to a mouse squeak, and threw up his hands before stuffing them into his pockets, defeated.

"Good morning, bienvenue," said the sidewalk smoker to the nine of us gathered in the office, never altering his "not-this-again" face. His lackluster, perfunctory pronunciation of bienvenue made me cringe.

"Ah, I'm so sorry," Wayne blurted upon hearing "bienvenue." He grabbed his only non-white article of clothing, a navy blue Member's Only jacket, and turned to his friends. "Let's go. Must be a mistake. I knew it."

He stepped to the exit before apologizing again to our Eeyore tour guide. "I'm sorry. We were told this tour was in English."

"It is, it is. In fact," the bald tour guide corralled the fleeing Kiwis, putting himself between them and the door. "I'm English...from England."

"Really?" asked Wayne, ever dubious, clutching his blue jacket. His wife whispered in his ear. "Well, that's what he says," Wayne replied in a hushed tone, his gaze fixed on the supposed Englishman.

The drive to Pointe du Hoc started in silence, our guide doing his best unguiding act, so Wayne's friend Mark (Maaahk) took it upon himself to point out pickup trucks ("utes"). All of them.

"Ah, choice ute, ay?" We passed a parked silver pickup.

"A bloody rugged ute right there," he said after a white Toyota Hilux overtook us on the N13.

"Oy, Wayne, have a look at that ute!" Wayne nodded, studying the green truck idling beside us.

The sweeping dunes encompassing Pointe du Hoc gave way to the Channel horizon, a geographic crush of sand, saltwater and chalky cliffs. We followed a white-sand trail through knee-high grasses bowing to the unrelenting onshore wind. Craters pockmarked the point. Eeyore Richard, the guide, herded us onto a wooden platform a few hundred feet from the cliff's edge. Three concrete-domed bunkers with mangled rebar twisting skyward faced the sea.

Richard propped himself against the platform's 2x4 railing, leaning against his left elbow, and faced us, barely concealing his disinterest. He opened a blue, three-ring binder containing photographs of Pointe du Hoc before the invasion, bristling with artillery guns and German infantry.

"At 7:10 a.m. on June 6, 1944...D-Day," he paused and leveled his eyes, "approximately 250 U.S. Army Rangers, after losing half the initial force to rough seas and enemy guns, landed on the beach below us. They scaled the cliff using ladders, ladders provided by the London Fire Brigade. Here, entrenched elements of the German 352nd Infantry Division waited for them." He pointed at the ruined fortifications.

"For months, the Germans fortified Pointe du Hoc as part of the Atlantic Wall, Hitler's scheme to stop an Allied invasion. They built casemates and gun positions for coastal artillery cannons and anti-aircraft guns. As you can see from up here, this is an ideal spot to direct those guns against the landing forces. Allied planners had to neutralize Pointe du Hoc."

He spoke precise words, on script, yet lacked any genuine conviction or emotion. His words rang hollow, and he looked tired. Richard struggled to hold his own weight, perpetually leaning against something, let alone add gravitas to a story we all knew from *Saving Private Ryan*.

His chronological recount droned on as I scanned the landscape behind him.

What I had thought were dunes interspersed with craters were actually craters interspersed with more craters. The Allies lit this place up with naval guns and aircraft bombardment until they'd created a lunarscape, scars that may never heal. Trenches and overgrown earthworks intersected sprawling trails leading to concrete bunkers and circular gun emplacements. I tuned out Richard and plugged into the moment. I could almost feel, almost here, the battle, valiant Rangers hurrah-ing over the cliff top and into enemy positions. Surprised Germans shouting orders, firing and retreating through Pointe du Hoc's complex maze.

I shifted my hips, ready to slip past Richard and plunge into this laboratory of history. Wayne and his wife conspired in muzzled tones and raised eyebrows, unable to conceal their bewilderment, as Eeyore Richard reached his verbal crescendo:

"But the Rangers never found what they came for," said Richard. He stared at us, holding the binder, teasing a page-turn. After a few seconds, he flipped the page, revealing more black-and-white war photos. This time Rangers stood guard over surrendered German troops huddling in Pointe du Hoc's trenches.

"Notice something in these photos?" Richard asked. "Or rather," he flipped to the previous page, "do you notice anything in these photos... ," he stuck out the binder, displaying the German photos, then returned to the Ranger photos, "that you don't see in these?"

"The guns." Four of us replied in unison, shaking Richard from his self-induced spell.

Enough of the binder, Richard! We're standing in history's backyard; let us roam through it instead of you droning on about it.

"Yes, exactly. Very keen." He almost smiled.

Were we? Or had we just seen *Saving Private Ryan* one too many times?

"The cannons and anti-air guns were gone. The Germans had removed them days, even weeks before the assault began," Richard concluded and released us to explore the battlefield.

"For 20 minutes. We meet at the van," he warned, tapping his leather-strapped wristwatch. We cascaded toward the fortifications as Richard lit a cigarette and fled to the parking lot.

"No guns? Really?" asked Wayne's wife in his right ear.

"Maybe, I couldn't see," Wayne whispered as I skipped past them. "That's what he says," he added while stuffing his hands inside his pockets.

Few other tourists tromped about Pointe du Hoc, and soon I was by myself. A thick, stamped-bronze memorial plaque emblazoned with the 2nd Battalion Ranger tab hung in the main outpost, a semicircular bunker overlooking the English Channel. It listed the 81 Rangers killed in the assault and associated actions on Omaha Beach from June 6–8, most of whom died during determined German counterattacks after the successful cliff-side assault. That's not even a rounding error in a war that took the lives of over 20 million soldiers. But still. Eighty-one lives cut short. War is futility defined in masculine form.

I arrived last to the van, having slightly exceeded my 20-minute allotment. The passenger seat was empty, so I jumped into shotgun, hoping to milk Richard's backstory. But I couldn't help eavesdropping on the frazzled Kiwis piled into the row behind me.

"Uff, I'm knackered, darling," complained Wayne's wife after she collapsed onto the gray-cloth bench seats.

"I think my ute would handle these dunes a treat," Mark informed us.

Wayne and his wife conspired in hushed tones while nervously scanning the van.

"Well, I don't know. If we're to believe him," said Wayne, his every statement sounding like a question as his tone inflected and doubt invaded. His wife murmured an unintelligible response.

"Oh, that ute's a stunner, ay," said Mark, gazing outside as the van passed tidy green farm fields and pulled onto the D514, heading eastbound to the Normandy American Cemetery.

Mark's wife mumbled some unknown intrigue to Wayne's wife. "Exactly," Wayne's wife confirmed. She then passed the information to Wayne.

"That's brilliant," Wayne replied, his eyes widening before lowering his voice. "Maybe they were never even there."

"Have a look at that ute, Wayne."

If I heard them, then Richard heard them. But he never spoke, never defended history's honor. He kept his eyes on the road and his mind on the cheap French wine waiting for him at the tour's conclusion. I, however, was ready to burst. I'd heard of Holocaust deniers, but were Wayne and his wife (and Mark's wife) World War II deniers?

"Well, go ahead then, have a go," urged Wayne's wife, elbowing her husband and nodding at Richard.

"Richard?" Wayne leaned in, then looked back at his wife for reassurance. "Question."

"Sure, Wayne, have at it," replied Richard. He'd regret letting Wayne have at it.

"Well, the missus and I couldn't help but notice...Well, is that story true? About the guns and Rangers. It seems like...they'd know the guns were gone. They had binoculars, ay?" Wayne laid out his bulletproof case.

Richard pulled the van over beside a wheat field, unable to grasp the question while driving, or, more likely, to prevent himself from plunging the 15-passenger van into the goddamned English Channel.

Richard explained how Allied intelligence had seen the guns go missing, but worried the Germans were hiding them from aerial bombardment and might wheel them out during the landings.

"Does that make sense?" implored Richard.

"Yeah-nah," replied Wayne, thoroughly unconvinced.

"Well, uh, any other questions, Wayne?" asked Richard, no doubt hoping Wayne had no more questions.

"Nah mate, good as gold. Carry on," said Wayne, who returned to whispering conspiracies with his wife and Mark's wife.

"Blue ute," observed Mark.

Rows of white headstones, 9,386 total, mostly crosses with a smattering of Stars of David, marked the last resting places of the young American men who died in the Normandy operations. They fought and died in a land where they couldn't speak the language, understand the food or wrap their heads around its complicated history. Few could have even found France on a globe.

With no ancestors buried at the Normandy American Cemetery, I delivered flowers to the one namesake in the cemetery directory, Vermont-born William A. Moulton Jr., resting in plot B, row 14, grave 27. William, according to the burial database, was a captain serving in the U.S. Army's 314th Infantry Regiment, 79th Infantry Division. In civilian life, William was a 24-year-old accountant called to active duty from the Vermont National Guard, which he'd joined in 1939. He died on June 23, 1944, 10 days after the 79th landed on Utah beach and just four days after entering frontline combat.

The 79th would become entangled in fierce street fighting, taking over 15,000 battle casualties by war's end. They fought through northern France and Haguenau before joining the assault on Germany's defensive Siegfried Line and vicious battles in the Ruhr pocket. But poor William Moulton, Jr., never left Normandy, his war lasting barely a week.

All these years later, I intended to honor his sacrifice. I leaned a mini-tulip bouquet against his tombstone and took a wax-paper transfer of his name, which I folded and tucked inside my notebook's back cover.

"What a sticky-tar day," said Wayne's wife, who, along with Wayne, Mark and Mark's wife, stood in the sun outside the van waiting for me, the last arrival. Again. It was maybe 85 degrees, with a steady breeze under a cloud-free sky.

I decided I couldn't endure another van ride. Richard was off smoking a cigarette by the oak tree-studded bocage surrounding the parking lot. I saw my opening and strode over to him. He stubbed out his smoke as I approached.

"Richard, yeah, so I'm leaving the tour here. I'm out, man," I said. His mouth opened, but nothing came out. "I'll hang here a bit then walk to Bayeux."

"Walk? To Bayeux? It's probably," he scratched his forehead, "10, 15 miles from here. And what about Omaha Beach?"

"That's okay. I like walking, and it's such a lovely day. I'll swing by Omaha Beach. Then I'll catch a bus or something. I'll figure it out." I passed a five-euro bill in my handshake. "I know you're supposed to, you know, return with the same number of people you left with, but I just can't get back in that van. Thank you so much, Richard. It was splendid."

Wayne stuck his head out the sliding door and yelled, "Oy, Richard. What's the hold up, mate?" He checked his watch, not waiting for a response, before establishing his true motivation. "Lunch is included, right?"

* * *

France has a nationwide network of hiking trails called "GR" trails, short for Grande Randonnée or "Long Hike," with which I'd recently become familiar while researching another trip. Once I recognized the trail blazes—white-over-red horizontal stripes—I noticed them everywhere, on light posts, electrical poles, stone fountains and traffic signs. Everywhere. While strolling the cemetery, I saw the ubiquitous waymarks pointing down a sandy trail. Pointe du Hoc had whetted my appetite for sea, sand and fresh air, so I scampered down to Omaha Beach, then picked up the GR 223 heading east, somewhat toward Bayeux. The trail cut through grassy coastal promontories, affording endless views of the English Channel, tidy villages and rolling green farmland.

Armed with a stuffed curry baguette from a bakery in Aure sur Mer, I departed the GR trail for a beach picnic. I strolled the rather promisingly named rue de la Mer to a small coastal village called Les Bateaux. An information board on the town's outskirts detailed its history as a filming location for the 1962 D-Day epic, *The Longest Day*. I followed signs pointing to Plage de Saint-Honorine des Pertes. The street descended a cut in the cliffy coastline, and soon I was lazing about a pebble beach, nibbling my baguette, writing and enjoying the sunshine on my face.

I swam in my black skivvies, having forgotten both my vending machine and store-bought bathing suits. The water was frigid, and the breeze made getting out and air-drying painful. But it was a refreshing prelude to exploring the teeny cove. I found a small waterfall pouring over the cliff onto the beach. I dropped my backpack and stuck my head under the stream of water, rinsing the saltwater from my face and hair. The cliffs were imposing and the inlet looked too treacherous to attempt by sea. Allied invaders avoided this terrain trap, which is why I was the only tourist here.

Back on the GR 223, I turned inland, then entered a "holloway" dividing two farm fields. A holloway, as I learned from reading Robert Macfarlane's book *Landmarks*, is a footpath sunken from centuries of use to the point it feels like a tunnel, especially if, as was the case with this holloway, trees towered over the track. The fields I bisected in the holloway sat three feet above the ancient path. How many feet pounded this path three feet below grade? How long had humans used it? Shortly, the holloway opened to the ruins of Saint-Nicolas Church of Villiers-sur-Port near the trail's junction with the D206 roadway.

The Saint-Nicolas Church of Villiers-sur-Port ruins are emblematic of France's secular embrace. Although 60% of French people say they're still Catholic, only about 15% practice and do Catholic things (involving candles), while less than 5% attend Sunday Mass (more candles). That disinterest in Catholicism equals a lot of empty churches, like Saint-Nicolas Church of Villiers-sur-Port. Parishioners abandoned this 12th-century chapel in the late 1800s when they joined the church in Huppain, one village over. They stripped the church of all furniture and art, then let it return to earth. Of all the ways she could have been destroyed, from the countless wars waged in this region to simple, everyday accidents like fires, it was disinterest that did her in.

It was now an elegant wreck beckoning me closer. Its stone crossing steeple overlooked a caved-in roof and buckling walls. Green and gray vines swarmed every nook and cranny, sheathing what was once the front facade. I wandered the ruins, ignoring the *"Privée"* signs and plopped onto a granite plinth—perhaps it once supported the pedestal holding the holy water font. With my notebook on my thigh, I sat atop it and wrote as golden hour bathed me and the crumbling stone walls in yolky sunlight.

Wrapped in solitude, I sensed ghosts roaming this storied land. Maybe Norman, Frankish or Roman soldiers camped here while on military campaign. Perchance ancient Celtic families farmed these fields. I imagined American soldiers, fighting their way through Normandy, resting here during a lull in battle, huddling around G.I. pocket stoves, reading letters from home and opening cans of Spam. Maybe even William Moulton, Jr. took pause here.

The sun had hit the western horizon when I sprang to my feet.

"Crap! Dinner!"

I checked my watch: 7:57 p.m. In three minutes! Bayeux was calling, but the GPS app confirmed I was only halfway. I couldn't walk the remaining distance in time. I stuck out my thumb as I trudged the shoulder-less D206.

"Bayeux?" I asked the driver who sported a gray stubble beard.

"Bayeux," he confirmed. I climbed into his rusty-white four-door Citroën, its diesel engine spewed sweet-smelling exhaust as we puttered toward Christine's boeuf en croûte salvation.

* * *

I tore through Christine's front door, stumbling under the Norman archway. Sweat dripped down my face after sprinting the few long blocks from the florist. I'd held the pink-posy-and-yellow-garden-rose bouquet like the Olympic torch as I dashed through Bayeux. Luckily, my driver knew the local florist and had kindly dropped me at their door.

Christine danced through the kitchen as blues music played low on the indoor-outdoor speakers. The door to the courtyard was open, revealing the patio table set and plated for five under the amber glow of string lights suspended in a Z-pattern from the second-floor window sills. I checked my watch: 8:21 p.m. No sign of Pascal or the other couple.

"Bonjo—. Bonsoir Christine! I'm so sorry I'm late," I said, wiping the sweat from my brow.

"Ah, bonjour Rory! No, not late. Pascal gets the wine and soon my friends come," Christine radiated joy, which I returned as my shoulders loosened in relief. I ran upstairs to freshen up just as the doorbell rang.

"Rory is our Airbnb guest from Colorado in America," said Christine as I extended my hand and she clarified further in rapid-fire French. I adored how she pronounced Colorado.

Her dinner guests, Jean and Marie, shook my hand and smiled, cooing as they repeated, "Colorado."

"Le ski, oui?" Jean confirmed while wiggling his hips and pretending to plant ski poles in the limestone-tile floor.

Jean could've been Pascal's professorial brother: Tall, lean and balding, with a narrow face and long nose holding up thin wire-frame glasses. He wore a navy blue v-neck sweater over white collared shirt, taught beige khakis and leather ankle boots. But unlike contemplative Pascal (artists!), Jean instilled his presence throughout the house from the moment he stepped inside. With solid English, he also served as the night's de facto translator.

Marie wore black closed-toe heels, tight jeans cut just above her ankles, a gray tweed waistcoat and light-blue blouse, the unbuttoned cuffs of which jutted through the coat's arms and flailed as she talked. Her dark-brown hair featured silver streaks emanating from her elegant crow's feet.

"Rory saved dinner," Christine explained.

"Nah, I just, no." I demurred.

"A national hero!" Jean shouted, raising my right arm like the winning prize fighter.

Pascal's face appeared in reflection on Jean's eyeglass, and I spun around to greet him. His massive hands and long fingers clutched two bottles of cabernet-based Bordeaux and two white Muscadets from the Loire Valley. He bowed his head but kept his distance from me before embracing Jean and Marie with air-kisses on each cheek. Double air kisses, no less! Jean slapped Pascal's back as we instinctively moved to the patio for wine and appetizers.

Christine placed the posy-rosy bouquet in a crystal vase and set it in the table's center, surrounded by five place settings, two wine glasses and three plates per person. A platter of leeks and smoked herring, sliced razor-thin, sat beside the flower vase. Pascal opened the Muscadet first, signaled by the herring, as conversation erupted in French. I sat back with my wine, observing how the conversation flowed. They laughed and talked nonstop, but never interrupted each other. Between animated discussions, they sipped white wine and nibbled herring shavings. Occasionally, Jean translated something, a funny anecdote or local legend, then returned to the conversation.

The two couples had known each other for over 20 years, raising families and building careers together. Marie and Christine worked as school administrators at the same school. Jean was an architect specializing in renovations, and Normandy's preponderance of aged dwellings ensured a continuous client stream.

After the Muscadet ran dry and the final herring slice disappeared, Pascal slipped away to the kitchen. Here we go, I thought, he'd return any second with what had occupied my mind all day, what currently sent my taste buds aflutter just thinking about it...the boeuf en croûte. Oh, the anticipation!

Maybe Pascal needed help carrying it, but just as I stood up, Pascal returned to the string light-lit courtyard bearing a stout, green-labeled bottle of Calvados brandy. This was not a beef filet wrapped in pastry dough, and I could barely hide my disappointment. But at least it was booze, and a booze I'd never tried. Pascal poured a shot for everyone, then spit a barrage of French at Jean while cutting his eyes back and forth between Jean and me.

"Rory," Jean said, turning to me. "This is special Normandy brandy, a very typical brandy." I studied the label Calvados Domfrontais AOC - Vieux Réserve. "This brandy must sit in oak barrels at least three years. We take it, typically, between courses, part of a tradition we call trou Normand." His enraptured audience awaited my tasting.

"Yes, we use it to...rinse the mouth..." He thought for a moment, scratching his head and sniffing the brandy, then continued, "Le palais...Clean the palate! Oui. And prepare the stomach," he said, rubbing his belly.

"Très typical," added Jean, the first words he uttered in my direction all night. His Franglais elicited laughter from Christine, whose face miraculously showed no signs of distress after smiling for two straight days. In fact, her smile seemed bigger than ever tonight.

Jean continued: "We prefer to pour the brandy over apple sorbet. But tonight...," he searched for the English words, "the feast is too grand for sorbet between the plates. We must save our appetites."

We raised the shot glasses to a chorus of *santé*, and I swigged the brandy. This caused my dinner mates to laugh as they cautiously sipped theirs. The sweet liquor flushed my cheeks red, and I shook my head as my eyes bulged and my body shivered.

"Wow! Phew. Good, good," I said, "Très bon. I like it."

The brandy and shot glasses stayed on the table as both Marie and Christine walked arm-in-arm into the kitchen. Okay, now with palates properly cleansed and stomachs primed, it was time for the main event. I smelled the puff-pastry ensconced beef before I saw it. Jean uncorked the Bordeaux as Christine entered, holding the brioche-wrapped tenderloin on a silver platter at eye level like she carried the royal crown. To me, anyway, this was much more exciting than a ruby-studded crown.

The pastry had four delicate openings cut into its rounded top. Steam unfurled from the 18-inch-long concoction. I'll never forget the aroma. Even outside, the earthy redolence of mushrooms, duck fat, baked dough and seasoned beef overwhelmed the fresh air and sent my taste buds singing. I licked my lips. If haute living needed a symbolic bouquet, it wouldn't be fancy perfumes or whatever luxury yachts smell like; no sir, it'd be freshly baked beef in brioche.

Whoever Christened the dish—a fiercely contested matter pitting British versus French—was building on an illustrious European tradition of wrapping meat in dough. Cornish hand pies. Spanish croquettes.

155

Italian *porchetta*. Europeans had been doing it for centuries. But the *filet de boeuf en croûte* raised the bar. It entailed a full beef filet, preferably the juicy tenderloin, smothered in some combination of foie gras, pâté, truffles, duxelles paste and goose or liver fat before encasing it in a sweet brioche pastry dough.

The recipe doesn't appear in French or British cookbooks pre-1900s, lending skepticism to both arguments. It's unlikely to have originated from a single "voilà!" moment, and evolved in both Britain and France over centuries of culinary indulgence and cultural exchange between the two rival nations. The common English honorific, "Beef Wellington," comes from Napoleon's Anglo-Saxon vanquisher and is, therefore, British. Yet, the critical ingredients, especially pâté, foie gras, duxelles and truffles, are continental to their core.

In sum, who cares if it's British or French? Let's eat.

As Pascal plunged his chef's knife, the released scent caused me to blurt out, "Oh, my god," which generated snickers at the table. Jean closed his eyes and nodded in agreement as if to say, oh my god, indeed. Everyone laughed, except Pascal, who remained committed to carving the beef. Each beefy stroke dropped juicy salmon-colored, pastry-encrusted meat against its predecessor piece. The artful contrast of medium-rare pink against the black duxelles paste and golden brown puff pastry mesmerized. I watched each slice fall, glued to the partitioning that released the sweet smells of oven-fresh dough, succulent beefsteak and tender mushrooms.

Christine fetched a boat of sauce *colbert*, a beef-bouillon-based, bearnaise-like brown sauce, while Pascal delivered slices, flat on the bottom with a rounded top. I tested the flaky pastry with my fork, while pouring colbert sauce. Not too much, though, or I'd mask the full taste. I cut a vertical piece, ensuring all three layers made it onto one fork. Steam rose from the meat as I lifted it to my mouth.

"Oh my god," I said, stuffing down another forkful. "It's so fu—." I caught myself. Swearing at the dinner table? How uncouth.

"It's so good, Christine. It's so, so good. I can't...," I consumed another bite, "I can't put enough of it in my mouth at once."

Jean chortled, translated my reaction, and everyone laughed. Everyone except Pascal, of course, who dug into his meal with a zeal matched only by his indifference toward me. It'd become obvious, as I strained to tell stories about my family and life, that Pascal didn't like me, didn't care to know me and didn't want me at dinner. It could've been his English, which he was self-conscious about. Or maybe he just didn't like Americans—not the first time I would've encountered that sentiment while traveling.

Maybe, I realized, swallowing my first bite, it was something altogether simpler. Perhaps Pascal played me off because I was eating his leftovers, tomorrow's lunch. That's understandable and unforgivable, but I'd long since crossed the Rubicon.

The buttery tenderloin surrendered, falling apart in my mouth. The roasted herbaceous flesh escaped from under the sweet pastry, both of which were accentuated by the mushrooms and duck fat. Salty, savory, sweet, smoky—the meal delivered every mouth-watering sensation layered in each bite. I washed down the tender morsels with healthy gulps of murky Bordeaux.

"Rory, you like it, oui?" asked a coy Christine, her permanent grin now a mischievous smirk.

"I love it," I replied, devouring another forkful and hoping Christine had a second secretly stashed in her kitchen. I'd have been willing to eat it in my room.

We reclined as a collective, patting our bellies and licking our lips, as Pascal poured another brandy round. A pattern emerged: food, brandy, food, brandy, food.

"Bravo, Christine," said Jean, who struck up conversation about music, the night's first all-English discussion. We circled the table divulging our favorite artists, songs and genres.

"Oui, jazz, blues, Motown, um, classic rock. I don't care for rap or reggae. And I don't like the American pop music, non," said Pascal, waving his right hand, his English improving with each wine glass and brandy dose.

At that, Pascal leapt up and returned carrying his iPhone, which was still connected to the speakers. He and Jean debated the playlist, while Christine unveiled a cheese plate with a creamy heart-shaped Neufchâtel and a round buttery Camembert, two of Normandy's four AOC-designated cheeses. I managed only two small slices before begging off further offers.

After another sipped brandy and more English discussion of music, Marie produced the coup de grâce, *tarte Normande* stuffed with creamy custard and sliced apples. I slumped into my chair, happily defeated. For good measure, Christine added two fluted porcelain ramekins of Caramels d'Isigny, their twisted white wrappers covered in burgundy type.

"Please, only a little slice," I beseeched Christine. She obliged, then dolloped crème fraîche beside it.

"I like the American alt rock," said Jean. "I enjoy the guitars."

"Non, I don't like," said Pascal. "The instruments..." he rubbed his hands, "sound together. I can't hear guitar. It's one loud sound. No, I don't care for this."

"I like most music, except country," I shuddered. Everyone nodded. No country music for us, please.

"Except Johnny Cash," said Jean. Pascal tilted his head, readying an argument, but I'd have none of it.

"Bien sûr! Except Johnny Cash," I blurted. "Everybody loves Johnny Cash."

Pascal smiled and made eye contact with me for the first time. Bemused, the interrogation started.

"Rory, what do you and your family like to do in Colorado? For fun, diversion?" asked Pascal, the accidental linguist.

I would've fallen off my chair in surprise, had my midsection not been anchored by beef, cheese, cream, pastry, brandy, wine, mushrooms, herring, tarte, and, okay, yes, one caramel. Was he talking to me? In English? Pretty good English, no less. Roused from my food coma (who knew I'd have to speak again?), I gathered my composure.

"Well, we love the outdoors. Camp, hike, bike, fi—" I didn't even finish the "F" word, and his eyes lit up.

I'd seen the look before. The publisher at my first newspaper job had passed my desk, the new cub reporter, for my first two months on the job without saying a word. Then, at the company Christmas party, I mentioned the "F" word in a group conversation and the publisher's eyes, like Pascal's eyes, leapt from their sockets as he opened a 45-minute conversation with, "Why, I didn't know you fished."

"You...you fish?" Pascal asked. He sat upright and leaned over the table, maintaining direct eye contact.

"Yes!" I affirmed. I hooked him. "I fly-fish, mostly. Do you fish?" Of course, I knew the answer.

Christine, Jean and Marie cackled. "He loves fishing," Christine clarified before Pascal could answer. "More than painting. Maybe more than me!" She huffed and reclined, but smiled ever onward.

"What kind of fishing? Where? What do you catch?" I asked.

Pascal unleashed a smile and scooted his chair next to mine. "I fish with reel," he made a spinning sound effect, "in the river, lac, in the ocean. I did not know you fish, Rory." He leaned back and sipped his brandy. "We catch salmon, trout, pike, um..."

He even knew all the English names. Sly bastard.

"Um, maquereau."

Well, almost.

"Sometimes big fish!" he exclaimed.

"Haha, yes, those are the best fish," I concurred.

Pascal reached for his phone, but since it didn't stretch all the way, Christine disconnected it from the speakers, and the music ceased, but Pascal didn't care. He sat beside me and swiped through his trophy collection filled with, as promised, sometimes very big fish. I lauded his fish-catching abilities.

"Rory," Christine interjected. Something told me she'd seen the photos once or twice before. "Would you like to pick the music? You have your phone, oui?"

"Yes, yes, I have my phone." I was now treading back into dangerous waters. Choosing the wrong music could completely negate all the capital I'd built with Pascal after outing myself as a bona-fide angler.

"Um, oh, I don't know. I only have English music," I laughed.

"S'il vous plaît," she insisted, holding up the forsaken aux cable.

"Yes, yes, of course. Excuse me, Pascal." I stood up, took one-half step and promptly stumbled into Pascal's lap (so much wine and brandy). He coughed laughter as I dusted off his shoulders, gathered my balance and skipped to Christine's side. I noticed Pascal almost made an effort to help me up.

Jean laughed. "This is a fateful choice, Rory. America is the world's leader of culture."

"Yeah, sorry about that," I murmured as I spun through my song downloads.

It was a fateful choice, as Jean couldn't resist pointing out. My playlist bristled with everything Pascal despised—alt rock, reggae, '90s hip-hop and, oh no, reggaeton, the offspring of both hip-hop and reggae. I considered pleading my case for Bob Marley. Who doesn't like Bob Marley? But this was no time for me, a Millennial (by a year!), to teach these 50-somethings about the joy of reggae's one drop, let alone reggaeton's seductive dembow rhythm. I required divine intervention and summoned my travel superpowers, with extreme discretion, for aid guiding my hand to glory.

My index finger landed on Redbone's "Come and Get Your Love."

Whoever bestows travel superpowers is a benevolent and righteous god.

Now, when Redbone plays, you'll want to start dancing because no human being can resist shimmying their hips to his masterpiece. I helped Christine to her feet, she twirled and Pascal, Jean and Marie soon joined us, all smiles. We danced across the ancient courtyard's patio, the couples traipsing in each other's arms while I shadowboxed the amber string lights.

For optimal effect, I suggest following Redbone with Sam Cooke's "Good Times," then let Percy Sledge bring the heat on "You Really Got a Hold on Me." By the time you slide Otis Redding's "That's How Strong My Love Is" into the mix, the couples will forget you exist as their bodies mesh, and you can slink away to your little Airbnb room up above the amber string lights.

Dinan

The four-hour slow train arrived in Dinan after crossing into France's largest peninsula, Brittany, at the Couesnon River somewhere around Mont Saint-Michel, the island fortress-abbey that's a hopelessly majestic tourist trap. Normandy's gentle green hills gave way to steeper broken terrain. The aerodynamic, single-deck TER regional train traversed the Armorican uplands, home to interior Brittany's plunging gorges, limestone pillars and misty forests.

Unlike a couple days ago, I paid attention to the passing stops and gathered and organized my belongings before making an orderly disembarkation from the train. While packing, I found the receipt from the pastries and flowers I had brought Christine that morning. They were under no obligation to treat me so well, like family, and I couldn't return the favor, always a traveler's regret when accepting the kindness of strangers.

I hoped the gift went some small way to expressing my gratitude because my lousy attempt at speaking French that morning certainly didn't do it. Christine hugged me after smelling the flowers, her smile never wavering. Pascal met me at the door and shook my hand, saying goodbye as well. He smiled and held Christine by the shoulder as they stood in the foyer. The remnants of last night's dinner party, which they refused my help to clear, sat spread across the courtyard dining table.

"Someday we will fish together," I promised Pascal. I stood under the Norman arch doorway, thanked them again and departed the old maison on rue Poterie forever.

* * *

So, why was I in Dinan? In fact, why was I standing in a town almost as far away from Barcelona as I could go without leaving France? Unlike Hamburg, this had nothing to do with a misdirected superpower, resulting in a linguistic misunderstanding.

My revelation at the Breton Parisian *crêperie* was only partly to blame. They serve persuasively delicious crepes, true, but Brittany's proximity to Normandy (they're next-door neighbors), and that I'd never been there, drove my somewhat spontaneous decision to hop aboard the Dinan-bound slow train.

Admittedly, I hankered for another multinational slice of French pie. Why stop at Normandy and the Goutte d'Or? As I laid in my bed last night, digesting a small farm's worth of production, the question of what, exactly, is a Frenchman or Frenchwoman rippled through my brandy-addled mind. France is tremendously diverse, I realized, and not just from immigration. It's really a collection of little nations, and Paris represents but a microcosm, or a sun around which its planetary nations orbit.

That's true throughout Europe, the most tightly packed, multinational continent on Earth. For comparison, Europe has 43 countries and Asia 47, yet Asia has 4.5 times the landmass. To understand France, I'd have to scour her corners, her least-French nooks. Turning south, I therefore determined, was a problem for another day.

The concept of France is relatively modern. In the pre-petroleum era, when mobility between cultures and communities was treacherous and downright exhausting, France's rugged, varied terrain bred characteristic, disconnected communities distinguished by their local geography, agriculture, social mores and language. Present-day France has seen armies, empires and bandits pillage, plunder and, sometimes, settle her lands, incubating distinctive cultures like an ethnic petri dish.

France is Europe's mutt, seeded by Gauls and Romans, then spliced with nearly every imaginable European variety: Germans, Franks, Visigoths, Suebi, Burgundians and so on. That splicing, mind you, comes atop all the native inhabitants who called France home sometimes eons before the Gauls and Romans arrived: Bretons and Celts in Brittany, Occitans in Occitania, Basques in Basque Country, Greeks in Provence, Catalans in Catalonia and Flemings in Flanders.

Is there a single France? Is Paris all that counts as France? As long as the City of Light remains the gravitational center, does anything else matter?

The idea, therefore, of a unified France boggles the mind. Like any good American or Brit with a superiority complex, I enjoy criticizing French bureaucracy. In reality, keeping this country united is an incomprehensible task. How it forged a national identity that thrives to this day is utterly inconceivable.

Le Tricolore flies over a complicated country. There's no right or wrong place to start, so let's just use Brittany as an example. Okay, then, for starters, Brittany is perhaps more British than Britain. Let me explain.

Britons are the original, Celtic inhabitants of the greater British Isles who fought Roman and Saxon incursions. They forged a Celtic-British identity. Now, it's probable, given the English Channel's short span, that Britons emigrated to the Brittany peninsula in the 4th century or earlier. The unstable Roman Empire faced a decline from which it would never fully recover, and they were fast losing their grip on Britain. So, it makes sense, Romanized Britons would seek safer, greener pastures in areas under nominal imperial control.

What those first settlers found, well, reminded them of home. The massive Brittany peninsula, clocking in at over 13,000 square miles, juts into the Atlantic Ocean where it's kissed by the same Gulf Stream that blesses Britain with ample rain and mild temperatures. There are geological similarities to the British Isles as well, especially England's Cornwall region, since they were attached before continental drift split the peninsula from the Isles once and forever.

Brittany proved an abundant, albeit isolated place, to foster Briton communities. Soon, a trans-channel Celtic nation formed within the Roman Empire. After the fall of the Western Roman Empire, Britons flooded into Brittany, earning the region its predecessor name, Britannia. Britannia connected with other thriving Celtic communities along the Atlantic seaboard in Spain's northern Galicia region, Wales and Cornwall, Ireland and Scotland, all linked by sea routes.

The maritime Celtic nations, pushed to Europe's westernmost fringes, soon ran up against new continental powers, with Brittany facing down the burgeoning Frankish Empire, whom they defeated to become an independent kingdom in the 9th century. Then the Vikings came and subjugated the Bretons. To kick out the Vikings, Bretons partnered with the English and French, alliances that would end Viking overlordship but also Brittany's independence. It was a "new boss, same as the old boss" situation.

Rebellions followed, though none maintained Brittany's independence for any substantial period. The back and forth, will they or won't they, ended for good in 1789, when Brittany was formally annexed during the French Revolution.

So, there you have it: A British outpost in France that's more British (genetically) than Britain itself. Residents with Breton heritage are shorter and paler than their countrymen and have Celtic surnames as opposed to Frankish ones, more MacArthurs than Pepins. Brittany experienced a cultural revival in the 1960s. Proud Bretons cultivated interest and understanding of their ancestry. Bilingual schools were opened, folk singers wrote songs in Breton, and a renewed interest in Brittonic natural heritage spurred a progressive political and environmental movement that persists today.

At least, that's what I had read on the train. But now here I was, standing inside Dinan's whimsical train station. The two-story lobby felt like a medieval great hall. Intricate mosaics adorned the yellow walls. One detailed the Bretagne railways; the other displayed a Dinan town grid. I stood dead center, alternating between the two gorgeous maps. The whimsy continued outside, where an art nouveau clock tower jutted from beside the triple-peaked roof.

Armed with a tenuous understanding of Brittany's history, I trudged uphill from Gare de Dinan into Dinan's fairy-tale old town, where half-timbered buildings from the Middle Ages swayed over cobblestone streets. I strolled the well-preserved medieval ramparts secured by a 14th-century fortified tower called Donjon de la Duchesse Anne, or Keep of the Duchess Anne.

The 15th-century Duchess Anne lived quite a tumultuous life. As the oldest daughter and heiress to the Duchy of Brittany, her family betrothed her no less than eight times to French, English, Austrian and Burgundian royalty. Her life as Europe's most rag-dolled pawn perfectly encapsulates Brittany's history of pitting its more powerful neighbors against each other through shrewd and material diplomacy.

The afternoon heat arrived as I finished my ramparts amble and navigated Dinan's maze for my Airbnb. The redheaded middle-aged host answered the door seconds after ringing the bell, as if she'd been lurking. She was also named Anne, though no relation to the whip-lashed Duchess. She stood with her left side behind the door and right side covering the gap left by the quarter-opened door.

"Bonjour. Anne?" I asked. I double-checked the address, which was where I stood, but Anne, or whoever was standing at the door, eyed me with suspicion.

"Um, yes?" she said, closing the door another inch. She spoke with an English accent.

"Hi, it's Rory, your Airbnb guest." You know, the fella whose reservation you confirmed this morning?

"Ah, right, Rory," she held fast her defensive position in the door gap. "I'll be right back." She closed the door as her flip-flops slapped against the hardwood floor.

I stood in the cobblestone rue Haute Voie, admiring the medieval buildings. Rue Haute Voie turned into rue Michel a block from the 14th-century Porte du Jerzual, which straddled a street that looked like a downhill ski run. It led to Dinan's port and promenade on the Rance River. The old town sat atop the hill overlooking the port with Rance River views for miles. I wanted to go appreciate the views, but my Airbnb host plodded through check-in.

The Airbnb's exterior stonework had fresh, bleached-lime mortar pointed between the irregular brown, beige and red stones. The stones were rough-cut quarried, not dressed with flat faces and right angles like buildings in Normandy. These walls looked ancient. The three-story home's windows were tall and narrow, with horizontal granite lintels over every rectangular door and window. Anne returned and hid behind a brand-new, brown mahogany door with 10 inset panels and a gigantic brass door knob in the dead-center.

"The flat's just been fully renovated," said Anne, back in her protective position between the entryway's wall and front door. What was she hiding? She handed me a nine-inch brass key dangling from a purple carabiner. "They finished a couple weeks ago. I hope you enjoy it. Let me know if anything's wrong. You never know with Irish plumbers!"

Irish plumbers? Baffled, I tried ginning up the conversation.

"Hey, I like your red hair, like mine," I said, switching subjects with a big grin.

"Red?" She inched the door toward the jamb. "My hair is blonde."

It was red. Unlike my father, I am not color blind. I'm cursed with red hair, and I know it when I see it.

Anne remained stuck to the door jamb, staring at me, wondering what else she could do to make my stay more comfortable that didn't require leaving her home. Breakfast would be brought to my room at 8 a.m., she added, before forcing a smile and pushing shut the door.

In the same building 20 feet away, a matching mahogany door marked my room's entrance. The house appeared to be two buildings stitched together, though the facade's fresh stonework hid any patches. I stepped to the door. The original inhabitants of these buildings entertained customers in their first-floor shopfronts, while living in the second and third floors. Now, opening the door, I discovered the room was a stunning, renovated private room with an enormous bathroom. The shower's frying-pan head was the size of a basketball hoop. A travertine tile floor ran throughout the flat. The smooth walls were painted peach, and fine upholstered chairs and a round wooden table filled the sitting area. A fireplace with slate surround and queen bed sat against the farthest wall. Irish plumbers apparently do great work. Not bad for 60 euros a night, I decided.

After washing my face and calling home, I stepped onto rue Haute Voie, then went right on rue du Rempart toward the Jardin Anglais, a park built atop the ramparts overlooking the Rance. A group of teenagers smoked cigarettes while I sat and wrote on a park bench. The yellow-orange golden-hour sun illuminated couples embracing and kids passing a soccer ball. I kicked about town for a few hours before dinner, admiring the heaving buildings, colorful storefronts and narrow passages. I wrote and took photographs as the fading daylight allowed.

I found a snug café-bistro serving a full dinner menu, displayed out front on a chalkboard. Inside, massive oak ceiling beams bowed under the second floor's weight, accented by red walls, 10-inch wide plank floors and a smart, dark-wood bar with six barstools. I climbed aboard an open stool next to an old-timer reading a book, nursing an ale and nibbling delicate forkfuls from a grilled sole filet. The bartender was also the hostess, busser and chef's close confidante, so I ordered two draft beers, blondes from Brasserie Coreff, France's original microbrewery.

France produces some terrible, watered-down beers (looking at you, 1776) just like the States (Budweiser), Canada (Molson) and even Germany (Warsteiner). But a common misconception, perpetuated by lazy travel writers and cultural stereotypes, is that France only makes bad beer. Besides spirits like Normandy's cider and brandy, beer, top-notch beer, abounds. Sours. West Coast IPAs. Biscuity pilsners. If it can be fermented from hops and barley, then France's small-batch brew houses are making it.

Craft breweries produce smashing beer from Provence to Bordeaux, Brest to Paris. This isn't a recent development; France's beer revolution has been brewing for decades, fermenting at a similar rate to America's. Brasserie Coreff led the way, opening in 1985, around the same time microbreweries sprouted up in the States following the success of Anchor Steam and Boston Beer Company.

Just one sip of Coreff's flagship blonde confirmed this, malty and light with a sticky foam head, a satisfying French beer. My *coquilles St.-Jacques* arrived, juicy scallops shipped fresh this morning from St.-Brieuc and baked with cream, white wine, cheese and breadcrumbs. The old timer sitting on the barstool next to me folded his book closed and said, "Good choice," nodding at the three scallops sitting on a red cast-iron skillet.

My first bite confirmed his hunch. The breadcrumbs crunched, and the scallop exploded, its briny juice assaulted the initial creamy tang.

"Oui, very good," I said. "How is the fish?" I asked, aiming my fork at his plate.

He wore a dark-blue wool Breton cap, turned a few degrees left aloft his bushy reddish-brown hair, and spoke the queen's English. Curls flecked with gray spilled out from underneath his hat. His unkempt beard matched his hair and his mustache curled at either end. His brown leather shoes dangled from the barstool. Thick, freckled forearms and calloused hands signaled a lifetime of hard work. He kept a notepad in the breast pocket of his short-sleeved plaid shirt and an assortment of pens and a putty knife in the leg pocket of his scruffy, paint-speckled canvas work pants.

"Bon," he said, tipping his pint before quaffing a generous gulp. "You are American?" he asked, forking into his fish.

"Yes. I'm traveling through France on my way to Barcelona," I said.

"You are far from Barcelona. I'm afraid you're traveling in the wrong direction," he snorted. "So, why Brittany? Why are you in Dinan?"

He spoke fluent English with perfect sentence construction. Here was a Breton who felt duty-bound to refine his mother tongue.

"I'm traveling by slow train, kinda planning my route as I go." My thesis poured forth. I told the old-timer about my friends who didn't consider Europe "real travel" and the crowds and joylessness of following the modern tourist trail. "I'm trying to break out, experience less-touristy places, smaller towns, and places I've never been, moving at a slower pace on my rail pass." I tapped my pocket even though my rail pass was back in the Airbnb.

"And meeting people like you instead of other tourists!" We smiled as I received my walnut, cured beef and Gorgonzola galette. The briny buckwheat conferred hints of minerals.

"But why Dinan?"

"I arrived today from Normandy. I stayed with a charming family in

Bayeux. They were so warm and welcoming that I figured I'd continue on to another part of France's, ah, non-French areas. I mean, I know they're all French, but places like Brittany and Normandy have different histories and distinct cultures. But are part of modern France." Oh lord was I out of my depth. Was I offending his Frenchness? I recalculated. "I like experiencing these subcultures and nations within a nation. Since Brittany is so close to Normandy, voilà, here I am. Plus," I looked outside the window, "wow, it's gorgeous, a perfect medieval town. The half-timber, cobblestones, ramparts, Dinan is a fairy tale."

He laughed, "You Americans love old things." He laughed again before continuing. "Ah, but now you interest me. I'm also a student of these subcultures: Basque, Catalan, Breton, of course. My mum and father also. They taught me that Brittany would always be part of larger nations, France and the greater Celtic lands, yet always keep a unique position in both nations. You've made a good choice coming here." He knocked on the straight-grained wood bar top.

"Much sets Brittany apart—history, ancestry, even the weather is quite different in Brittany. We have much better beer, too," We both knocked back a healthy gulp of grog in agreement. "But make no mistake, Brittany is very French, but few other regions have such strong ties to an outside nation like Brittany has with England, Cornwall, really. It's not so far!" He chortled and looked up.

"But the atmosphere, lifestyle here is French, not English. Or maybe somewhere in between. It's more relaxed, more focused on happiness, love, food and living life to the fullest. Let me put it this way: I don't know any Bretons who wished they were Britons. But I know heaps of Britons who wished they were Bretons." He cracked himself up again and polished off his beer with gusto.

"Even if it's not the Provençal sun that so many Brits seek, it's still France. Besides," he looked left, right, then lowered his voice to a whisper, "there are parts of Brittany that get as much sunshine as

Provence, but without the, uff, deadly heat of the south." He rattled off a few names south of here that I scribbled into my notebook as he put on his blue duffel coat. With his Breton cap, he was now ready to board an 18th-century whaling ship bound for Newfoundland.

"Well, thank you for the chat. I only have a few more days in France, and I must turn south after Dinan. Where do you recommend I go?" I asked.

"The Pays Basque will also interest you." He snugged his cap over his nest of curls. "It may be the oldest civilization in France. Yes, the Basques. You should look, maybe, around Biarritz or Bayonne, then you can cross into Spain at Hendaye. Yes," he contemplated. "I've made that run by train several times myself. Bon voyage."

I thanked him, noting the recommendations. As he turned to the door, I called, "I'm sorry. I forgot to ask. What part of Brittany are you from?"

"Falmouth," he said in his most kitsch, most pirate-like West Country accent. He winked and smiled, before lashing his coat closed and exiting the medieval tavern.

After drinking another two beers, I walked the Promenade Duchess Anne to La Tour Sainte-Catherine scenic overlook. Car headlights snaked across the D795's Romanesque Dinan Viaduct, while down below pedestrians strolled the triple-arched Vieux Pont, a stone bridge spanning the languid Rance. Stars appeared overhead as flickering port lights illuminated the Rance River until it bent out of sight and emptied into the English Channel at Saint-Malo.

* * *

With temps expected to exceed 90 degrees, it was another scorcher, especially by Brittany's standards. So, I paced outside the TI until it opened, ready to dig into Dinan history early. The freckled clerk at

Dinan's tourist center slapped a map on the shiny desk and robotically circled sights and drew walking routes with her black Bic pen as she'd done a million times.

The gleaming glass-and-metal TI sat next to the Château de Dinan, a monolithic 14th-century stone fortification built not to protect Dinan but to subdue it. From its hilltop perch, strategic Dinan straddled communication and trade lines from Brest to Normandy and controlled north–south movement on the Rance between Rennes and Saint-Malo. It was wealthy and important and, unfortunately, had chosen the wrong side in the Breton War of Succession (1341–65).

The "Black Pearl," as Dinan was then known, threw its weight behind French-backed Charles Blois against the English-backed John Montfort. This was a rare example of Breton disunity since the nation had handled succession disputes quietly, quickly and internally. However, as is often the case, as royal trees grow longer and heavier with ambitious branches, it takes but a small breeze to uproot the whole tree. And so it happened in Brittany.

A seesaw war ensued in which both sides struggled to gain and maintain the upper hand until Montfort's English forces routed Blois, thereby merging control of Brittany under the House Montfort, who now owed Brittany's allegiance to England. Montfort, in France's worst example of a midlife crisis, built a mammoth stone fort so bristling with defensive measures, gargantuan walls and an impenetrable tower, that he even made the King of France, Charles V, jealous. In a fit of castle envy, Charles V built the monstrous Château de Vincennes east of Paris. Dinan's castle proved so impregnable that even 200 years later, 100 soldiers (British soldiers, long story...) resisted over 3,000 besiegers for six weeks.

Forsaken in the 17th century, the city government gave the chateau an immaculate renovation with a museum, fine period furnishings and whitewashed walls in the 1990s. Given Dinan's homespun charm, I was a little disappointed at just how spiffy the castle appeared nowadays. What, no blood splatter? Boiled tar stains?

If Montfort's castle represented English hegemony in Brittany, then a church across town holds the heart of Brittany's unyoking from her English overlords. And I'm not writing metaphorically: A Breton hero's literal heart is buried in the floor of Basilique Saint-Sauveur across town. To get there, I hoofed it from the castle into the warren of rambling streets marking Dinan's old center. Rue de Lehon turned into the 10-foot-wide rue de l'Horloge. It was packed with shops selling souvenirs, clothing, art, books, gourmet food, and oh god what's that pie-looking thing in the window?

Morgane, a happy shop clerk with Mediterranean sunset hair, fair skin and a starched-white apron, introduced herself after we exchanged bonjour.

"I like your hair," she said.

"I like yours, too. It's beautiful," I replied. She blushed and laughed, twirling a red strand that dangled by her yellow-frame glasses.

"How can I help you?" she smiled, tilting her head.

I explained my pressing dilemma: This humble, hungry traveler wanted picnic fare, something Breton-authentic, but I hadn't a clue where to start. And the edibles needed to survive my backpack for another two hours. She thought for a nanosecond before grabbing a wicker basket.

"Follow me," she said.

She presented a jar of Henaff pork rillette. "From here, Bretagne," she confirmed. "Very local. All ingredients come from farms in Brittany. It's excellent rillette," she promised, dropping the white-lidded jar into our wicker basket.

I love simple rillette: pork (shoulder, belly, whatever) cooked low and slow and processed one step less than pâté so that it's more a schmear than a spread (bagel enthusiasts know what I'm talking about). It's then jarred with fat and sea salt. Done. Morgane was one-for-one. Morgane waved me forward to the next shelf for pickles. That's two in a row. She then picked out a baguette. "Of course," she said, dropping it in the basket.

"You care for something sweet?" she asked. I nodded and affirmed that the wicker basket looked awfully lonely without something sweet. She led me to the pies that had first drawn me inside.

"This is kween-uh-man," she said, pronouncing the name so I could write it down, which was nice of her, but I asked her how to spell it, anyway. She held up a muffin-shaped pastry that resembled a caramelized croissant. "It is very traditional from Finistère, the preferred cake of Brittany." She placed a mini-cake in my basket. "They bake with one-third sugar, one-third butter and one-third dough."

"Ah, perfect, my three favorite things," I smiled. "But what is this name?" I looked at the sign hawking her kouign-amann cakes. "Can you pronounce it once more?"

"Kween...uh...man. Kween-uh-man."

"Kween-uh-man," I practiced.

"In Breton, kouign means 'cake' and amann means 'butter.' Butter cake!" she announced. We added a sea-blue bottle of sparkling water, carrots, apples, and I was on my way, outfitted for a lunchtime fête for one.

The Basilique Saint-Sauveur, first raised in the 12th century by returning Crusaders but rebuilt in the 15th century, sat behind the English Garden that overlooks the River Rance. The triple-arched Romanesque facade pulled me closer as I appreciated the stepped surrounds. The center arch, flanked by Doric pilasters, contained the main entryway, but I paused to first walk a lap around the old house of worship. Back at the entry, I noticed the Gothic gable featured sculptures of menacing beasts and wild creatures, no doubt meant to frighten the residual paganism out of early churchgoers.

After entering, the interior unsurprisingly followed the traditional Latin cross plan, but, oddly, it was asymmetric. With a one-euro donation, I grabbed a pamphlet describing the church's construction. The asymmetry was not planned. Builders added an aisle to the nave's north side but not the south, saving that installation for another day, leaving the rib-vaulted ambulatory and choir in-line with the central aisle. But the semicircular apse, with five radiating chapels, rested askew, awaiting a southern aisle that will never arrive.

I ambled through the nave, then went right around the choir. I roamed the apse and its five chapels counterclockwise before returning by the northern aisle, where I discovered the hero's heart in a large niche. Inside the granite tomb, a bronze plaque commemorated Dinan's hero, Bertrand Du Guesclin. Almost 50 years before Joan of Arc was born, Du Guesclin's actions saved France from total annihilation during the Hundred Years War and concurrent Breton War of Succession.

Du Guesclin, a minor noble of the Lords of Dinan branch, led Dinan's defense during the Breton War of Succession. According to legend, Du Guesclin won a single-combat duel against an English knight selected by the English general, the Duke of Lancaster. Lancaster lifted the siege and released Du Guesclin's POW brother. Everybody needs a hero, especially when armed men wait to kill and plunder you, and the residents of Dinan had theirs.

There's just one problem though. Like so many legends, it's impossible to verify and likely only partially true, if at all.

The historical record grows fuzzier than an Amazon corporate tax return: Either after or, more likely, before the Dinan battle, Lancaster's men had laid siege to Rennes, about 30 miles to the southeast. They arrived outside its walls in October 1356 and invested the city until May, June or perhaps even July 1357. Or maybe it ended in February. We don't know! The siege of Rennes is well-documented, yet historians can't determine when or even how the siege ended. Regardless, Du Guesclin's spirited defense of Rennes is credited with convincing Lancaster to accept a ransom and drop the blockade.

At some point, Lancaster set his sights on Dinan, but little evidence of the Dinan siege exists beyond the oral legend. It seems unlikely Lancaster would charge farther into Brittany, away from his power base in Normandy following Rennes. It seems especially unlikely that he'd spend dwindling resources besieging another fortified town. However, if Lancaster had received a ransom from Rennes, then he may have sought the same hefty reward in Dinan.

And this is where I questioned the legend. Assuming Lancaster besieged Dinan and Du Guesclin defended it, then why wouldn't the Duke of Lancaster demand a ransom before leaving? Du Guesclin is said to have won several duels at Rennes, yet Lancaster maintained the siege. Plus, Lancaster held Du Guesclin's brother hostage, which would have increased the ransom. It sounded to me like the legend was a face-saving measure. Maybe Du Guesclin won a duel or several duels at Dinan, but I bet Dinan, acting on Du Guesclin's orders, paid Lancaster to leave. But that ending is none too legendary, so the historical record conveniently forgets it.

That's not to say Du Guesclin didn't win his fair share of battles. As mentioned, he rallied French forces, paving the way for Joan of Arc's leadership a half-century later. Du Guesclin almost single-handedly reorganized and reinvigorated French resistance after the country's catastrophic loss to England at the Battle of Poitiers, where Edward the Black Prince captured King John II of France. The loss sowed demoralization and chaos among French forces. He then regrouped and led successful raids and crushed English armies in pitched battles.

Du Guesclin's actions didn't prevent the England-backed House of Montfort from winning the Breton War of Succession. However, it marked a symbolic turn away from England and toward France, and it happened thanks to Dinan's most famous son. (Also: He wasn't from Dinan proper but 15 miles away in Broons.) By that time, he'd risen through the ranks as Constable of France and led successful expeditions against the English until he died in 1380, doing what he loved best, fighting the English.

That tangled history led to where I now stood, at his memorial in Basilique Saint-Sauveur. The gold-colored shrine held his heart, but nothing else. So, where's the rest of him? Even though he wished to be interred in Dinan, he was such a national hero by his death, French King Charles V insisted his remains receive the royal treatment—dismemberment. Puy received his entrails, Montferrand his flesh and French royals interred his skeleton at Paris' Saint-Denis in the tomb of the Kings of France. His heart, however, arrived in Dinan, where it sits today behind the golden plaque.

Some Breton nationalists consider Du Guesclin a traitor for siding with France rather than fighting for an independent Brittany. During World War II, pro-Nazi Breton nationalists destroyed his statue in Rennes. History supports him, though, since Brittany is inextricably French. Besides, anybody capable of raising Nazi ire from the grave deserves our admiration.

Upon exiting the church, I sipped cappuccino at an outdoor café table near Place des Merciers and wrote a few pages. That's when I heard them approaching. Voices in several languages called out, while sun hats and tour flags appeared on the horizon and the clatter of Birkenstocks and Reeboks bouncing off cobblestones reverberated through the timber-framed town.

Just like in Du Guesclin's time, outsiders besieged little Dinan, unleashing the Waddling of the Pensioners. The horde thronged old town, tour guides shouted instructions, while gray-hair couples argued about directions. Café waiters smelled blood in the water. Springing into action, they poured wine, cider and coffee down wrinkled gullets. Guided tour groups wore earpieces like woefully out-of-shape secret-service agents as their guides narrated into flight-control headsets. They bumped and barreled through the old town, eating, souveniring and photographing.

I ducked the cavalcade on rue de la Poissonnerie, and escaped the stampede through the Jerzual medieval gate where it becomes the cobblestone ski run, rue du Petit Fort.

Until the Dinan Viaduct connected the modern D795, rue du Petit Fort was Dinan's primary entry point. Standing on those hallowed cobblestones, I imagined a frenzy as boats offloaded passengers and products in the port, who then hauled themselves and their goods up, up and away into the hill town while passing under Porte Jerzual. During sieges, frightened townsfolk frantically latched shut Jerzual's six-inch-thick oak doors.

Wattle and daub timber-framed homes, their exposed lumber so sun-worn they appeared fossilized, crowded the street. Some tilted precariously over rue du Petit Fort and looked one firm push away from tipping over. Every balcony displayed wooden flower boxes, pink geraniums reached for the sun, and blossoming bougainvillea climbed to elegantly flared slate roofs.

I peeked inside bustling restaurants and cozy boutique shops. Cafés sat between shopkeepers with cottage industry displays—painters, sculptors, engravers, bookbinders, glassblowers—next to a smattering of postcard and souvenir shops. Between the restored cobblestones, stone walls and timber-framed relics, it felt like I was traipsing through someone's private garden, a very vertical garden. The scene was so perfect as to feel contrived like the postwar replicas seen across Germany, but these buildings were the real deal, original to the Middle Ages, with some dating from the early 1200s. A remarkable street, perhaps the most picturesque passage in Europe, I postulated.

Both because of its precipitous pitch, the street plunged over 300 feet in less than a quarter-mile, and also because its well-preserved medieval dwellings distracted me from the descent at-hand, I stumbled, then caught myself, nearly tumbling down the scarped thoroughfare.

I settled upon a riverside bench with beefy oak-plank slats bolted to stone legs, where the cobblestones spilled into the Rance River. The spot afforded stunning views of ancient Vieux Pont bridge and its contemporary replacement, Dinan Viaduct. The 15th-century Vieux Pont remained in exquisite condition. A graceful center arch spanned two-thirds of the river, and was flanked by smaller, complementary arches. Nowadays, it seemed primarily responsible for shuttling blissful walkers and cyclists.

The Rance River view was enchanting, but my attention quickly shifted to the imposing viaduct looming above me. A soaring, early industrial bridge with graceful arches built from sleek gray granite, the Dinan Viaduct changed Dinan and the Lanvalley area forever. No longer would Dinan rely on river traffic and neither would horse and foot travelers have to ascend and descend Dinan's hilltop perch. Instead, the viaduct opened a serviceable land route, integrating the town with Rennes and Saint-Malo and flattening the area's fickle transportation landscape. Designed to complement the Vieux Pont, I counted 10 graceful arches supporting a 131-foot-high, two-lane deck.

Opened in 1852 by Napoleon III, notorious Napoleon I's nephew, whose disastrous foreign policy tarnished his legacy as France's great builder of roads and railways, the viaduct not only whisked passengers through undulating geography, it served a political purpose. The viaduct was one of the first critical, non-military infrastructure upgrades built in Brittany since France absorbed the realm in the First Republic. The viaduct had little military utility; it wasn't meant to repel an English invasion or check the Bretons. Its construction was symbolic of Brittany's undeniable Frenchness, an act of solidarity binding two nations 70 years after their forced union.

I studied the bridges and stone dwellings lining the riverside promenade while I spread the toothsome pork rillette over baguette chunks and wrote in my notebook. I wolfed down silky, briny mouthfuls using baguette pieces to wipe clean the glass jar. I ate a pickle between every bite. I pulled the caramelized kouign-amann cake from my backpack and inspected it. This curious, unpronounceable pastry perplexed me. It was so heavy and durable. The first bite's saccharine goodness coursed through my veins. It tasted heavenly, chewy and moist thickened caramel. Licking my fingertips and smacking my lips, I gobbled every gooey morsel.

Then, money belts, sun umbrellas and telephoto lenses rustled from on high. I stood and turned around to see the cobblestone clatter coming from the daytripper crowd cresting the top of rue du Jerzual and beginning a perilous, sunscreen-fueled descent right toward me.

They were closing in, and I was trapped, my back pinned to the river. I had two options. To my left lay the atmospheric stone port, where the daytrippers would invade next for its picturesque Vieux Pont bridge and pricey seafood restaurants. It was just too damn Instagrammable (or, judging from this crowd, slideshow-worthy). Right led, according to a sign I stood under, toward somewhere called Lehon. I contemplated a third option: jumping in the river. Maybe I could swim the 20 river miles to Saint-Malo? (The glossy vending-machine Speedo sat stashed in my daypack.) An ivory-gravel towpath paralleling the river meandered toward this alleged Lehon, and I followed it, making tracks up the Rance River as German, Japanese, Chinese and British package tourists swarmed my once-angelic riverside perch.

The defunct towpath snaked along a riverbank, bursting with flowers, plants and trees. Birds chirped, bees transported pollen, and I strolled the level trail into a meandering river bend occupied by Lehon, an official "small town of character," according to its town sign. Lehon traces its history to Roman times, when it was a garrisoned fording site for crossing the Rance River, making it older than Dinan. With the Dinan Viaduct's completion, road and river traffic through Lehon plummeted, and the town has slumbered ever since.

Post-Roman Lehon owes its existence to God. Dramatic, right? In the mid-800s, Nominoë, the first Duke of Brittany (otherwise known as King of the Bretons), gifted the abandoned Roman ford and adjacent land along the river bend to six Welsh monks who started the Saint-Magloire Abbey. Rue Le Bourg's mossy cobblestones led from the towpath to the abbey's front door. The monks enjoyed an idyllic life on the banks of the Rance; I contemplated their simple pastoral existence as I watched a farmer rake the riverside hay field, neatly trimmed after the summer's final cut.

Then, as was their wont, Vikings arrived at this God- and sun-kissed land sometime prior to 900 CE and shattered the peace.

With Vikings rampaging the countryside, the monks grabbed their relics, treasures and, presumably, their bibles and fled to Paris, where they founded a new abbey. Once those simple country monks tasted Parisian life, however, they never returned to Lehon. The abandoned Lehon outpost never regained its monastic stature, but the Catholic Church didn't become Europe's largest landowner by giving up its properties. Several renovations led to the consecrated Catholic church's hodgepodge of architectural staples I tried unwinding standing before it.

Rebuilt in the 14th century around the original Romanesque portal, an entryway featuring a six-stepped arch surround on Corinthian pilasters, the abbey began its second life as a Catholic church. I touched the pilasters, then stepped back to study the subsequent Gothic renovation, which added flying buttresses, rib vaults and drip moldings.

Once inside, I was struck by the elongated nave, claustrophobically narrow with only a central aisle. It's divided into four bays with carved wooden stalls lining the north and south sides. I'm certain it appeared almost Nordic in its simplicity and dearth of decoration. Thirteenth-century stained-glass windows adorned the sacristy, capturing my curiosity and depicting crucifixion, cherubs, Saint Peter, Saint Paul, the Virgin with the Child across five translucent panels.

Outside, I meandered the cloister, grounds and monastic buildings. The sense of an agrarian utopia pervaded the air; I felt and smelled the pastoral life gone by. Those poppy fields, blooming gardens and riverside hayfield kicked off airborne dander, happy bees and a sense of a world unto itself. I shut my eyes and imagined those happy monks reaping hay and God's sweet graces, not a care in the world. When out of the blue, blood- and booty-thirsty Northmen landed on their halcyon shores.

A humid afternoon enveloped Lehon. I found shade under an evergreen in the front courtyard and wrote in my notebook when I heard splashing and playing in water. I followed the clamor past Lehon's "city" hall through a parking lot, where I discovered the source of aquatic gratification, the Piscine des Pommiers. A few minutes later, I pulled on my vending-machine Speedo in a coed changing booth, worrying it had somehow gotten smaller. The front desk attendant gave me a metal basket, which I returned with my clothes and daypack, awkwardly adjusting my briefs while she stared. She tucked the basket into a closet behind her and went back to her paperback without saying a word.

Children lined up to ride a double-dip water slide while their parents swam and sunbathed. The 80-foot-long main pool was deliciously inviting on this 90-degree day as I strutted around the patio. My white thighs blinded innocent sunbathers as parents scrambled to cover their children's eyes and muttered, "L'horreur." After weeks of beer, sausage, cheese, pasta, pastries and various fried ephemera, my physical appearance resembled an amorphic, pregnant Steve Buscemi after a bon-bon bender. I slipped into the alleviating waters before my pudgy-pasty appearance induced mass panic.

I swam laps, then floated on my back under the watchful gaze of Abbaye de Lehon, wondering how many outdoor pools come with views of 9th-century abbeys. Few, I wagered. I counted clouds and my dumb luck at stumbling upon this oasis. It was large and modern, not dripping in Art Deco like Piscine Edouard Pailleron in Paris. But the "Pool of Apples" was clean, well-run and, best of all, outdoors. Plus, that view: the abbey on one side and verdant Rance riverbank on the other. After a few laps and a hot shower, I retraced the one—and-a-half mile towpath to Dinan as the sun dropped low.

* * *

Restaurant Le Colibri turned me away for lacking a reservation, something I'm surprised hadn't happened yet. Well-regarded French restaurants get booked out even on weekday nights like tonight. From the looks of it, Le Colibri was well-regarded.

I didn't care. The more I traversed Dinan, the more I fell in love with it. The daytrippers had departed and the old town sat quietly, whispering legends to anyone who listened. Bedraggled Dinan was striking at night, a rustic beauty. Right angles didn't exist. Nothing was plumb and vines grew wild across stonework. Shadows played on the lily-white daub. Soon, I was posted up at Le Cantorbery after studying the chalkboard menu posted outside. The lime mortar-and-stone walls accented with matte-painted woodwork created a cozy atmosphere. I was warmly received and ushered to an empty two-top.

I ordered a Kir Breton, Brittany's take on France's iconic apéritif. The bartender-hostess-server poured Calvados and *crème de cassis* into a champagne flute, then trickled in cider as the concoction grew frothy.

The first sip tasted sweet and refreshing with berry after-notes thanks to the cassis.

The old-timer at the bar last night had suggested Basque Country. I could then reach Barcelona by cutting east across the Pyrenees' southern flanks. That seemed reasonable. I researched towns, needing somewhere affordable, interesting and, obviously, on the train line. Biarritz looked too fancy and Bayonne too urban. San Sebastián's luxurious reputation preceded itself, plus I wanted to wring another couple of days out of France. I'd rather avoid a pure beach resort, so I Googled "basque fishing villages."

Guéthary looked lovely and even had a surf break at which I could thoroughly embarrass myself. Other than a few lux digs exceeding my budget, the beach town was completely booked. After seeing mentions in a couple articles and confirming with a Google image search, I pinned Saint-Jean-de-Luz, a resort town, yes, but one with a commercial fishing fleet and dashing past. (Pirates! Whalers! Smugglers!)

The server brought a carafe of red house wine and crispy rabbit with vegetables and mesclun salad. (Or "*croquant de lapin aux petits légumes et mesclun de salades.*" For those of you scoring at home, yes, I sheepishly pointed at it rather than attempting to say it.) Chefs prepared the crispy rabbit meat like a spring roll, wrapped in a thin layer of dough and fried. I devoured the delicate crisp; the minced rabbit harbored earthy notes. I know many Americans don't share the French affinity for eating rabbit, but I come from a rather long, distinguished line of rabbiteers. Except, my family didn't eat them, either.

My grandfather was an award-winning breeder of Checkered Giants and Swiss Giants. Here was a man of average height raising giant rabbits. As a child on visits, I'd help in the hutch. Those early morning memories are redolent with the stench of rabbit shit. Opening the door in the crackling dawn light, the combined napalm of 30 rabbits' overnight deposits would cause me to reel backward. We'd spend the next hour scooping out that shit, only to then feed the Giants so we'd have to repeat the process at 6 a.m. the next morning.

To my grandparents, they were commodities like show dogs—their value defined by blue ribbons granted by discerning bunny judges throughout the Northeast and upper Mid-Atlantic. Their only valuable product besides blue ribbons was their byproduct—copious rabbit shit—that my grandmother chucked into her overflowing garden compost. When the rabbits outlived their show-worthiness, grandma sold them to the "Eye-talians" from the other side of town who, of course, ate them.

Since Airbnb returned no options, I spent the time between courses nailing down a hotel room in Saint-Jean-de-Luz (which henceforth I shall refer to as SJDL). Not a simple task on less than 24 hours' notice, but a family-run boutique joint two blocks off the beach with an unpronounceable Basque name had an opening, and I reserved it just as my entrée arrived, grilled cod in butter and balsamic. The cod fell apart just looking at it. The butter-balsamic was so tangy and sweet, I licked it straight off the plate after looking both directions to ensure no one was watching. And when I finished the cod, I polished the plate with baguette slices.

With clafoutis—black cherry-infused flan—en route for dessert, I took my red wine for a walk around the block, assuring the restaurant staff I'd return in 10 minutes. "No problem," the hostess-bartender-server said. Dinan was seductive at night. With daytime crowds a faint memory, the storybook came to life. Locals and French tourists held hands as they walked, basking in the medieval afterglow. There's something mysterious and intriguing in this land called Brittany, like they're jealously guarding a secret or unknown truth.

A refilled carafe and a personal clafoutis awaited my return. After a few spoonfuls, I went back to planning my Pays Basque foray. It soon became apparent, after sorting the timetables, that while one can, technically, make SJDL from Dinan in a day, it's not recommended. It was fixing to be a long day, about 10 hours with five connections. But I had little choice. I was threading the Eurail needle, and after bullying my way west into Brittany, I knew a reckoning was coming, a grueling and unavoidable transit day. But even with 10 hours' travel time, I'd make SJDL by dinner, and do it on all regional trains, maintaining my goal of not paying the high-speed toll.

It'd be a helluva long day. Leave at 6 a.m. and arrive in SJDL at 4 p.m. If all goes according to the timetables.

Ten hours, five connections...

I love trains, but, wow, 10 hours with five connections would surely test my devotion. And that was assuming everything ran smoothly, and I didn't encounter any trouble.

Saint-Jean-de-Luz

T rouble began in Rennes.

The journey's second leg, after switching in Dol-de-Bretagne, should've swept me from Rennes to Nantes to Bordeaux and to my destination, Saint-Jean-de-Luz. As I stood on platform two in Rennes station, with a spare minute until departure, no train occupied the tracks. The route to Nantes originated in Rennes. The train should've been idling and loading passengers at least 10 minutes ago. Yet, here we were, standing on platform two with no locomotive in sight. The crowd grew fussy.

Trains, planes or boats, travel days, especially ones with multiple connections, can go sideways fast. What looks like a long, but straight-forward jaunt down France's Atlantic Coast can devolve into an all-day epic that crisscrosses almost the entire country from west to east.

It started innocently enough when I overheard muted murmuring about a train running late. Yeah, no kidding, I thought. My terrible French did me no favors, but the concerned looks on fellow passengers' faces while their eyes darted between wristwatches and departures board said everything.

Then the murmuring became growling as rumors of a cancellation spread. Uttered "annulé," "terminé," and, of course, "merde" rippled through the anxious crowd. Then an announcement from a far-too chipper station attendant, who, judging by sound quality, must've been broadcasting from the ocean floor, confirmed the rumor. Anger and arguing between railway workers and passengers commenced.

People alighted the platform, but I dawdled, having only understood the announcement's cancellation bit, not the directions for where to go next. Then a train worker shooed me off the platform, explaining in rapid French why I mustn't linger a second longer. Confused, I followed the dejected crowd, plunging into the station's underbelly.

On the stairs, I overheard a senior couple speaking with British accents. At the landing, I slowed down and paced beside them before asking, "Excuse me, I'm also on the canceled train. Did you understand where we've been rerouted?"

They laughed and admitted they were a smidge bewildered, too. "And I speak French," the woman added with a guffaw.

"We think we're being sent to platform four," the man said.

"Yes, certainly platform four. But what awaits us there, I can't say!" said the jolly woman.

"Hopefully a train," I said. The old guy nodded while his wife chuckled.

Both my fellow prisoners, I mean, passengers lugged vinyl wheelie suitcases behind them and carried small shoulder packs. They wore staid clothing, him a short-sleeved dark-blue collared shirt with khakis, and beige pleated slacks and light-blue blouse for her. They had neat, close-cropped brown hair.

I found a departures board, but gave up searching for a slow train connection among the myriad canceled and delayed listings and rejoined my British friends. Besides, no one was checking tickets, so I wouldn't need a reservation.

We boarded a Le Mans-bound high-speed train heading due east. By boarded, however, what I mean is they packed us like a teenager stuffing three loads of laundry into one machine. We did not look forward to the spin cycle. The Le Mans train was already full, every single seat was taken, and we conducted a fruitless walk of shame carriage by carriage. Besides having their train invaded by another entire train's worth of passengers, we were delaying the Le Mans departure. We encountered many vexed faces, as if we wanted or were somehow responsible for this.

My new British friends and I stopped in the vestibule before the last car. I poked my head through the door and confirmed it was standing room only—full-grown adults huddled on neighbors' laps while a dozen or more passengers stood in the aisle.

"I think we'd better just stay here," I said, scanning the open hallway with a restroom and luggage storage.

The train lurched forward as the connecting corridor between the two rail cars filled with more passengers who had completed their own unsuccessful walk of shame. Before long, 20 of us squeezed asses to ankles in the luggage bay, on the vestibule floor and even in the restroom. Twenty people and their luggage. On top of the luggage from the train's original occupants.

I doubt you ever have and hope you never will ride in a train carriage's vestibule for six minutes let alone for 60 minutes like my downtrodden fellow prisoners, crap, passengers and I did on our journey to Le Mans. Let the record reflect I don't recommend it. However, you will receive a lesson in just how bumpy and tortuous train travel is without cushioned seats and climate-controlled carriages. Train tracks sure look smooth and flat, and they even feel that way from the comfort of a rail car. The rutted reality is very different, at least when stuck on the floor of the rail car's stiflingly hot vestibule.

Eventually, after about 10 minutes of pissed-off silence, someone in a heavy French accent declared in English, "French efficiency." We all bursted into laughter, the British woman dabbing her eyes as she sat folded in half on her husband's lap, who himself was stored securely atop his roll-aboard in the luggage closet.

At Le Mans, the good-natured British couple and I parted ways. The departures board had cleared a bit and slow trains were once again an option. I hopped aboard a train to Paris...wait, what? That's right, to reach SJDL today (which, just to reiterate, lay due south) by slow train, I backtracked all the way to Paris Montparnasse Station. Departing Dinan that fine morning, my circuitous route looked like:

1. Dinan to Dol-de-Bretagne: 20 minutes (Layover: 12 minutes)
2. Dol-de-Bretagne to Rennes: 45 minutes
3. Rennes to Nantes: Canceled
4. Rennes to Le Mans: 45 minutes
5. Le Mans to Paris Montparnasse: 60 minutes
6. Métro to Paris Austerlitz: 20 minutes
7. Paris Austerlitz to Chateaudun: 100 minutes (Layover: 5 minutes)
8. Chateaudun to Tours: 140 minutes
9. Tours to Nantes: 100 minutes (Layover: 10 minutes)
10. Nantes to Bordeaux: 260 minutes (Layover: 10 minutes)
11. Bordeaux to St.-Jean-de-Luz: 150 minutes

A determined traveler could hardly plan a more roundabout journey from Brittany to Pays Basque. Trust me, I've tried. In the end, I traveled for 16 hours on nine trains, two of which went the wrong direction, and one subway. If I hadn't departed Dinan on the 6 a.m. train, then I would have never reached SJDL.

At every stop, I discovered a station in chaos and a rail network verging on total meltdown. Everything was such a harried mess. Cancellations and delays littered departure boards. Rail employees threw up their hands and stopped checking tickets, stopped doing anything. The French rail network had devolved into a free for all. Where would you like to go? It doesn't matter! Just jump on a train and go somewhere! Hey, maybe you'd like to drive this train!

Every train I boarded departed late and had no open seats. Over 12 hours into my journey, I sat in an actual, honest-to-god seat on the last leg, Bordeaux to SJDL. By that time, I'd nearly exhausted my travel superpower to remain an uncompromising Zen sea stack amid thrashing seas.

I reached SJDL long after the sun sank behind an orange-hued Atlantic Ocean. My back was twisted into a pretzel and the train coma left me delirious. The flamboyant Basque station, adorned in resplendent white-stone trim, red brick and and red iron trusses, hardly caught my attention as I staggered through its arched doorway.

I'd survived railway purgatory, I realized, as I plodded SJDL's brown-sand beach toward the gently lapping waves. I didn't stop, didn't think, didn't take my eyes off the sea or take notice of anything happening around me. I just walked toward the ocean, dropping my big backpack and daypack in the sand, and peeling off articles of clothing until a trail of my belongings stretched from SJDL's bustling promenade to the high-tide line. I reached the surf zone in my black boxer briefs (Speedo be damned) and plunged headlong into the Atlantic Ocean.

I swam a hundred yards out in the Bay of Biscay, then returned halfway, floated on my back and let the nighttime stars envelope me. A Portuguese man o' war could have wrapped its venomous tentacles around me, and I wouldn't have flinched. A small crowd gathered on the promenade watching the crazy ginger who had discarded his backpacks and hat, stripped to his underwear and staggered into the ocean. A few people lucky enough to capture the full spectacle clapped when I returned to my trail of littered belongings. I bowed, then got dressed.

My little stubble beard had started looking and feeling (itchy!) like a real beard. Maybe I'll just let it grow until Barcelona, I thought. My back ached, and I was sandy, salty, wet and smelly, but at least I was not on a train.

* * *

My interpretation, "Saint Jean by the Light," based on the Spanish-sounding word "*luz*," didn't pass muster with these two longtime visitors. I ate another fluffy forkful of sheep-cheese omelet. "Non, no," said the woman, wagging her right forefinger while her dyed blonde hair rustled in the gentle breeze. We ate breakfast alfresco at adjoining café tables on Place Louis XIV.

"Oh? What does it mean," I asked the middle-aged couple from Lyon, vacationing for two weeks in SJDL.

"Rather, the opposite of light, actually. It comes from the Basque Euskara language," she explained in flawless, unaccented English, wiping the corners of her mouth with a napkin. Her husband focused on his *petit déjeuner* and foamy latte.

"Luz comes from lohitz. It means 'marsh.' It's a...," she thought for a moment, "broken translation, changed over time. So, it means Saint John by the Marsh. It comes from the time before they drained the swamps on the River Nivelle."

"Do you speak Basque, er, Euskara?" I asked.

"Eww-skare-aah," she corrected me. "Non, only a few words. But it's fascinating." Her husband fixated on his pastry and coffee. "Euskara is an isolated language with no relation to Latin. No connection to Spanish. No connection to French. Perhaps the oldest spoken language in Europe, or even the entire world."

"Do you know how to say hello?" I asked.

"Oui! That is one word I know. 'Hello' is kaixo, kai-show. Kai, like 'pie,' and show." She spoke clearly and maintained eye contact, exuding a fascination with the Basques that was infecting me as well.

France's Basque community is tiny, about a quarter-million strong, but it offered my first glimpse into this ancient nation. Their origins have stoked debate for centuries. Confident historians and scientists swung for the fences when postulating Basque origins. Some thought Basques were direct descendants of Paleolithic Cro-Magnon, "living fossils" of the earliest humans in Europe.

Then along came DNA, the great destroyer of baseless theories.

Deep genetic sequencing in Iberia showed Basques share 70% of the same DNA as other Iberians. They probably originated from an Iron Age farming population, possibly even a late Stone Age group. So, Basques are really old but not Paleolithic old. Most importantly, they lived in isolation starting around 1000 BCE, preserving their unique DNA and language, which predates Indo-European languages. Other Iberian peoples mixed with central European (Celtic), eastern Mediterranean (Greek, Carthaginian) and northern African populations over millennia of migration, but not the picky Basques. At least not much.

Basque historians aren't the only ones having their theories upended by modern science. In Italy, DNA studies have revealed the Etruscans, once thought to have descended from Greeks or postulated by Roman chronicler Herodotus as a "mysterious people from a faraway land" (enter sunken city of Atlantis conjecture), were original inhabitants of the Italian peninsula, probably having arrived from the Eurasian steppe like other Indo-European groups. Much like the Basques, the Etruscans' unique language and culture survived for a long time, prompting widespread modern speculation of their ancient origins. Also like the Basques, DNA has disproved language-based postulations. Genetics, it would appear, trumps language.

But I digress to the Basques. By Rome's arrival in the 1st century BCE, Basques had organized as the Vascones tribe with shared ancestry and distinct cultural, linguistic and social characteristics. Tribes and peoples would pass through their territory and into history for eons, but the Basques remained the immovable Basques against which other ethnic waves crashed and receded.

* * *

SJDL's commercial fishing port, the settlement's original raison d'être, sat within eyesight of my metal café table as I paid the bill. It begged for a closer look. The port has enriched SJDL as courageous Basque sailors hunted whales and netted fish as far away as North America. Every year, Basque fishing boats offload some 10,000 tons of fish in the port. Two marinas occupied the port, one for commercial fishing vessels and the other for pleasure craft. I strolled the waterfront, scoping fishing vessels, when I saw four gray-haired men sitting and smoking on a trawler's open stern. I hopped the dock's locked gate and headed toward them.

"Kai...show," I said, perhaps having overdone my sole Basque word's pronunciation. So, I repeated and waved, "Kaixo!"

Cigarettes dangled from their mouths as they waved back and replied, "Kaixo!"

The 16-foot white boat had a blue-and-gray stripe running down the hull's length. White coolers sat in shallow puddles on the deck. The four fishermen appeared at least 60 years old and wore orange and yellow waterproof bibs over buttoned-up, long-sleeve shirts. Two had on navy-blue berets. They were squat men with broad shoulders, stubble beards and wrinkled faces. All four had their sleeves rolled up, revealing tattooed forearms as thick as Louisville Sluggers.

"Right-o, great, so...parlez-vous anglais?" I asked, ignoring the faux pas of switching from Basque to French without warning. This prompted laughter and muffled chatter from the friendly fishermen. One old-timer sitting farthest from me flicked his butt overboard.

"Yes, I do," said the man nearest me in orange bibs. "Them," he nodded toward his comrades, "not much."

"Ah, great." I rested my right foot on the horn-shaped cleat to which their boat was tied. "So, what type of fish do you catch?"

The fisherman nearest me translated to his friends in what must've been Euskara. They discussed a minute or two when their orange-bibbed spokesman answered.

"We catch many fishes. Tuna, mackerel, sole, sardines, anchovies, hake, cod. Fishes magnifique," he replied, pronouncing each fish's name with great care in heavily accented English. "Do you like these fish?"

"Yes, I like eating all fish. Where in town can I eat the best fish?" I turned and pointed toward old town, which is the only town in SJDL, just so they understood where their hometown was located. Okay, so maybe I was a little nervous. "Which restaurant cooks the best fish? Any recommendations?"

"Maya," they answered in unison. The other three understood English better than they let on.

"Maya?"

"Oui," said the man in yellow bibs. "Chez Maya is best."

"Okay, then, Chez Maya," I confirmed, scrawling the name in my notebook.

We chatted for another few minutes about fishing, which wasn't what it used to be in these parts. In fact, the old-timers said this year would be their smallest catch in recent memory. They asked where I was from and reacted with nods.

"Colorado, yes we hear of it. Colorado has Basques, you know," said the orange-bibbed fisherman.

I did not, in fact, know this. In Reno, Nevada, I'd encountered a fairly substantial Basque community, even once dining on authentic oxtail soup near Reno's minor league baseball stadium. But the Basque diaspora's Colorado outpost was news to me. Turns out there are a couple thousand Basques in Colorado, the seventh largest U.S.-based community.

From the harbor, I traced the Quai de L'Infante leading to the natural harbor on the Bay of Biscay. The town sat in a right-angled bend that defines this windswept corner where the River Nivelle empties into the Atlantic. I walked past stout, well-maintained Basque buildings dating from the 17th century. They exuded subtle yet confident wealth and vibrant charm. The half-timbered buildings employed a colorful rainbow palette, similar to what you'd see in the Caribbean or Bermuda. I strolled rue Mazarin and rue Gambetta, old town's arteries, as the sleepy beach town awoke to a smoky inversion layer. Under clearing skies, I inspected the classic buildings, cobblestone warren and vibrant boutiques. It's a shame, I thought, its glitzier neighbors to the north (Biarritz) and south (San Sebastiàn) outshine this historic Basque community.

Or maybe it's content hiding in their shadows. I sure was.

At the tourist office, I grabbed a self-guided walking map and strolled by timber-framed buildings with white or pastel stucco bays between the heavy sepia posts and beams. The tour pinged locations around town with placards documenting its adventurous past, starting with whaling.

Enterprising Basque fishermen hunted whales in the Bay of Biscay since at least the 7th century, making them the first-known commercial whalers. The industrious Basque seamen delivered whale oil to monasteries as far away as Normandy and Brittany. Back then, coastal lookouts would burn hay or beat drums when they spied spouts, so hunters never ventured beyond the Bay of Biscay. By the 16th century, however, demand for whale oil exploded as Europeans illuminated their streets and homes. SJDL was sending out two-, three-, six-strong whaling fleets to hunt as far afield as Iceland, Greenland and Newfoundland. SJDL grew rich.

But other nations, enviously eyeing those fat whale-oil profits, started whaling, too, causing increased competition and rapid declines in whale stocks. The sailors of SJDL needed a new golden goose, and the French king obliged. The fearless seafaring Basques would make ideal pirates, and were given free rein to hunt France's enemies at sea with the same zeal they caught whales. Basque corsairs—the term given these state-sanctioned privateers—terrorized Spanish and British ships, earning SJDL the nickname "Nest of Vipers." By the 17th century, thanks to whaling, fishing and privateering, SJDL became the region's second largest city after Bayonne.

But the sea giveth and the sea taketh, which is something I'm certain many a crusty sailor has philosophized. The ocean gave SJDL wealth and power, but then the sea snatched it all back. My walk ended at the promenade, which sat on a 20-foot-tall seawall and afforded stunning views of the natural harbor and the massive stone dykes that protect it. As beautiful and calm as the bay looked today, several stories testified to its bipolar tendencies.

Furious storms had long plagued the coast, but as SJDL expanded from its original footprint, filling in swampland, laying cobblestone streets and erecting heftier structures, those storms increased in destruction as storm surges had nowhere left to go. In 1749, rogue waves destroyed seven houses and left another 180 uninhabitable. Nature's fury returned in 1782 when storms laid waste to the port, washed away over 40 buildings and wiped the Là Barre neighborhood off the map. An 1822 storm swept one-quarter of the town into the sea. In 1854, master builder Napoleon III (he of Dinan Viaduct fame) had enough and ordered stone fortifications built to defend the town, the three dykes that now hug the harbor. Two seawalls anchor the left and right spits, while an 800-foot-long freestanding central dyke spans the harbor mouth, leaving thousand-foot-wide openings to either side.

With the Atlantic tamed, well-heeled tourists followed vacationing French and Spanish royals to SJDL in the late 1800s. Tourism now rules the local economy, though international jet setters moved on to glitzier locales. The now-sleepy resort and fishing town enjoyed its obscurity until one fine June day in 1940. During the Fall of France, fishermen and residents spirited the defeated remnants of the Polish, British and French armies to sea and eventual safety in Britain. The evacuation lasted days and involved both military and civilian watercraft; Basque fishermen ferried soldiers from shore to ship. Eventually, the Nazis sent aircraft on strafing and bombing runs.

That was SJDL's ultimate moment in the spotlight. It's remained a listless seaside resort ever since.

Now learned, I located fisherman's favorite Chez Maya restaurant on rue Saint-Jacques. The red-awnings emblazoned with "Restaurant Petit Grill Basque" (not Chez Maya) made me pause and I pressed my face against the window in the gap between the lacy white drapes. A gray-haired woman wearing a red, white and yellow apron wiped down tables, so I knocked.

"Non, not possible. Réservé," she replied to my Frenglish inquiry about a dinner reservation for that night. She went back to wiping a table as I stepped one foot inside the restaurant.

"Impossible?" I pressed. "It's only me. I will sit anywhere and will order a bottle of wine. The fishermen told me this," I pointed downward, "is the best restaurant in town."

To that, she smiled, but didn't relent. "Je suis désolée, monsieur."

She had a doting grandmother's careful demeanor, a coal miner's stiff back, and the stubborn indignation of a French business owner. I was not the first person to attempt a last-minute reservation through a charm offensive. But I offered to sit anywhere, on the floor, kitchen, bathroom, atop the serving buffet, anywhere. However, she didn't care. I needed a new tact with this wily restaurateur and surveyed the space. Kitsch filled the cozy, yellow-walled interior. Two rows of painted porcelain dishes hung on the wall next to black-and-white framed photographs and various bronze fountain pieces. A wood-handled broom sat in the far corner.

Without saying a word, I slipped past the woman, whom I'd soon learn was one of the two female owner-operators in their 60s, and grabbed the broomstick. When she had said, "désolée," my mind raced and landed on an anecdote my neighbor had told me years ago.

He's a professional glassblower who learned the trade in Paris in the early 1990s. Instead of applying for work or an apprenticeship, he strolled into a prominent glass studio, grabbed a broom and cleaned the place top to bottom, in total silence. The bemused studio owner watched and also said nothing. Upon finishing, my neighbor left, but returned the next day, grabbed the same broom and gave the studio another thorough cleaning. This repeated for a week until the glassblower relented and asked what he wanted. From that day and for the next year, my neighbor apprenticed at the studio, learning to blow glass from Europe's top artisans.

If it worked for a yearlong apprenticeship, then surely it'd work for a dinner reservation. I swept the red, yellow and green tile floor, collecting debris into a pile. Before I could ask, the woman handed me a dustpan and pointed out the trash can. After sweeping, I requested her rag and cleaning solution and held open my palm.

"I'll take it from there, madame," I smiled.

She looked at the dripping rag ball in her right hand, then at me.

"D'accord!" she exclaimed, then summoned scant English. "Table at 20, à vingt. Exactement à vingt!" She then shooed me outside and continued prepping the restaurant.

Dinner 8 p.m., sharp. Got it. My cajoling had worked.

After eating a cheese-and-tomato baguette for lunch, I rashly decided to swim from SJDL's main beach, Grand Plage, across the bay to Plage du Fort de Socoa, a 300-foot-wide sandy cove tucked inside the western seawall.

Before long, I realized my cross-bay crawl would require more time and much more energy than I had anticipated. No matter how much I swam, the farther away the destination beach seemed. Was I swimming in place? About halfway, I clung to a buoy just outside the main channel where pleasure craft and fishing boats sliced through the placid sea. As I gasped for breath, I contemplated a few truths: 1.) First, and most urgently, I was not a particularly gifted swimmer and I'd consumed a prodigious amount of cheese the last two weeks. 2.) This crossing was rife with motorboat traffic, and I was about to traverse the bay's busiest channel. 3.) It was way, way longer than I had calculated (by which I mean I'd looked at it and thought, "No problem!"), perhaps a mile or more, and I'd never swum a mile in my life. Maybe cumulatively.

About halfway, however, meant turning back would be just as arduous. So, I gulped a big breath, waited for a gap in the boat traffic and kicked forward, alternating between breaststroke and something resembling a front crawl. A few minutes later, all energy drained from my body and I sunk into survival mode: I had to finish this swim. Drowning didn't scare me, but missing my hard-earned dinner reservation did. 8 p.m. *Sharp!*

Ten minutes later, after mindlessly paddling and flailing my way toward Plage du Fort de Socoa, the beach came within a half-dozen paddle kicks, which was just about what I had left in me. After washing ashore, I collapsed on the grainy sand and rolled onto my back. I had survived.

The 17th-century, circular-tower Fort de Socoa loomed overhead. It stood sentinel, albeit abandoned, over the adjacent small-boat harbor and commanded views across the bay. Inland clouds swirled the knobby summit of La Rhune, a mountain littered with Neolithic monuments and, according to legend, witches. Witch allegations may have provided a convenient cover story, however, as La Rhune was also a key stop on cross-Pyrenees smuggling routes, including those ferrying Spanish Civil War and World War II refugees to SJDL.

Somehow, against the odds and common sense, I'd smuggled myself across the bay. But now I wondered, exhausted and barely able to sit upright, how the hell would I get back?

* * *

I returned to Chez Maya as instructed, ready to feast and, if need be, grab another broom. I informed the two proprietors as much, but the suggestion spurred laughter from the apron-wearing grandmothers. They shooed me toward my table and resumed the hurried business of cooking, seating tables and operating a curious Rube Goldberg-esque ventilation system. A hand crank turned louvers in the ceiling that exposed two belt-and-pulley powered fans feeding an exhaust system. One fan gulped heat from the dining area, and the other replaced it with fresh outdoor air pulled through the opposite side. It was rather ingenious.

I was among the first arrivals, collapsing into a round table abutting the serving buffet and pass-through. My feet ached after walking barefoot for two miles on hot pavement from Plage Socoa.

I surveyed the restaurant's 10 tables covered in white tablecloths, three circular ones against the west wall, and seven rectangular tables jutted from the east wall. This left a narrow middle lane for serving.

Since I was as near the Bordeaux region as I'd get and because my feet throbbed, I ordered a red Bordeaux Supérieur. I was delighted to score a *petit verdot* blend. It's a finicky grape that's fallen from favor among Bordeaux vintners because it ripens quite late, if at all. I ordered the fresh-caught sole meunière and ferreted out an off-menu chocolate soufflé for dessert.

The couple across the serving aisle informed me they were on holiday from Corsica, the Mediterranean island that's sorta-French but more Italian. The husband, in his late 40s and sporting a bronze tan and slicked black hair, reclined in his chair and twisted to face me. With deep conviction and methodical, accented English, he asked, "Do you know how to tell a great restaurant?"

"No, how?" I sipped the juicy Bordeaux.

"If you see Corsicans eating," he roared, exhibiting a united French-Italian pride in local cuisine. I tipped my wine glass, smiled and swigged the red blend, savoring it in my mouth a moment before swallowing.

Chunks of tender sole fell off the in-bone filet. The outside was crispy and light brown, while zesty lemon balanced the decadent meunière sauce, built from white wine and clarified butter, the dish's secret weapon. Clarified butter has all water and milk solids removed, so that only the butterfat remains. It's dairy's Holy Grail.

Because I'd lost a day in transit purgatory, I had given little thought to my next move. Despite yesterday's rather challenging itinerary, I felt the urge to move on, the pull of my Eurail Pass and exploring new places. The traveler's impulse, much like gravity, is irrepressible. I studied the Spanish rail lines radiating from Irun, where I'd cross the border and switch trains tomorrow. With a week left, slashing across the Pyrenees' southern flanks and striking toward Barcelona seemed my only option.

As I studied stops along the latitudinal route, a powdered-sugar-topped miracle of decadence arrived, the chocolate soufflé. Nearby diners dropped their forks and lifted their chins in awe as my Basque grandmother delivered the lofty soufflé. I folded the rail map and slid it inside the timetable and turned my full attention to delicately dismantling the soufflé top before it collapsed. Like a mushroom stuffed into a film canister, the eggy pastry had puffed over the coffee mug's sides, and I scooped chocolate-infused custard after puncturing the cocoa bloat. I reeled back in my chair. The sweet custard illuminated my tongue and taste buds.

Halfway through dessert, I retrieved the map and timetable. Spain, right. One name caught my eye. I'd never visited, but its history ran deep, from Romans and Visigoths to Camino de Santiago pilgrims and the Lost Generation. And were it not for one week in July, tourists would hardly recognize its existence. It was also Basque, and these feisty folk were growing on me, one chocolate soufflé at a time. That's about all I knew as I booked an apartment on Calle Estafeta, Pamplona.

Pamplona

After an early morning saunter across Saint-Jean-de-Luz's deserted cobblestones, I prepped my brain for a new Romance language as the forest-green regional train chugged into Spain at the Bidasoa River. Switching to Spanish requires rewiring my brain and thinking differently, or, rather, not thinking at all. In French, I overthink every word and agonize over pronunciations. Not so much in Spanish.

Spanish is a rhythm apart from its Romance brethren, smoother and more malleable than Italian and more uptempo and casual than French. My colonial Spanish sings to *una buena onda*. I remind myself it's not just a new language, it's a way of life, a worldview I'm adopting. (Listening to Reggaeton helps.) I speak in halting and grammatically incorrect Spanish that's understandable, conversational and instinctual. Sometimes this leads to confusion, but at least it leads somewhere. Trying is what matters.

When my son was seven, we spent a miserable, 105-degree summer day at a Madrid water park. My wife and son had egged me into, for once, skipping the food, museums, parks and shops in favor of something kid-friendly and refreshing. My wife found Aquapolis in a Madrid suburb.

"Are you going to take your wife and son swimming? It's deathly hot out there," asked my wife while she and my son opened their eyes wide.

"Yeah, Dad, are you gonna take us or what?" he chimed in.

We had barely put our towels on the grassy lawn when a Spanish girl about my son's age and her brother pulled him away from us—I'm unsure if they even said hola—and then dragged him around the park all day. They didn't speak English. He doesn't speak Spanish. They didn't care. Every couple hours, he'd return to my wife and me, all grins and laughs. Each time, we'd ask him what they were talking about—the girl jabbered nonstop as she yanked him from waterslide to waterslide. And he always replied, "I have no idea!" before running off with his new friends. (Never lose that childlike wonder, right?)

A simple hello or thank you can unlock cultural doors. Or, as I learned, hiking Peru's Salkantay trail, singing a Justin Bieber song. That time, after dinner with the family who owned the coffee and avocado farm where we stayed, the matriarch and I took turns singing "Despacito" as her youngest child crawled into her arms. We traded verses in Spanish before she took the reins and sang in her native Quechua, a language I'd never heard. I'll never forget her angelic face as she slipped into her indigenous tongue and serenaded us while rocking her 18-month-old.

No amount of language effort, however, can overcome bureaucracy, as I learned after arriving in Irun, Spain. It turns out Spanish railways despise the Eurail Pass. The middle-aged woman working the Renfe ticket counter looked nonplussed as she explained, a second time, that I'd need seat reservations, whether slow or high-speed, throughout Spain. I booked passage and paid 17 euros in fees, cursing the inconvenience imposed by Spanish anti-Eurailers.

I stepped outside the nondescript, open-air train station, buzzing with arrivals and connections. All trains entering or leaving Spain must stop here, not for border or passport controls—the shared Schengen Zone has eliminated those—but because Spain operates its own rail gauge. Iberian tracks are about nine inches wider than standard

European gauge. Those nine inches have caused endless trouble for Spanish railways.

Much speculation surrounds Spain's decision to develop its own railway gauge. Some say they did it to deter French invasions or as a compromise of various Portuguese and Spanish gauges in use. The real reason? Engineering inexperience. In the mid-1800s, Spain tasked two civil engineers, Juan Subercase and Calixto de Santa Cruz, with picking a gauge for Iberia. The problem was, wait for it, neither engineer had much railway experience. They hypothesized that the mountainous and rugged Iberian terrain would require wider tracks to accommodate bigger, more powerful locomotives. But, as the Austrians and Swiss were proving with their wondrous Alpine railways, the complete opposite was true: Craggy terrain prefers narrower track gauge. Long story short: Spain would be just fine had they adopted standard European gauge.

With over two hours until my train departed, I strolled toward a big, green splotch on my map, Parque de Mendibil. The sun shone and a gentle onshore sea breeze kept the afternoon heat at bay. Stone and stucco apartment buildings with balconies off every room lined the narrow streets leading to the park. Roofed in clay tiles, the apartments had graceful rounded corners and seemed to have alternating white, beige and yellow color schemes. Irun's prosperous vibe meant leafy city blocks, bustling shops and immaculate streets in the neighborhood surrounding the train station.

In a café, I purchased a *Catalana bocadillo*, thick slices of manchego cheese with tomato, garlic and olive oil served inside a nine-inch baguette sliced lengthwise, and two sweaty-cold cans of Keler lager. The bocadillo and beers satisfied my belly as I laid against my backpack in the grass at Parque de Mendibil's central rotary, soaking up sunshine and writing in my notebook. I returned just in time to hop aboard a snub-nosed Avila train.

In the early 1990s, Spain laid its first high-speed rail lines, which became their first European-gauge rails. With Franco's Fascist regime long gone, Spain connected with its no longer bellicose neighbors, and the greater European high-speed revolution commenced. Spain built over 2,000 miles of high-speed, European-gauge rail, the most in Europe. Oh, but they still had 7,000 miles of Iberian gauge lines. It sure would be nice to jump the two gauges on medium-distance trips. Manual switching is laborious; it's easier to load passengers on new trains. Then, in 2004, Spain unleashed the Avila, variable gauge electric trains with detachable wheel sets that automatically move closer or farther apart with the gauge break, so trains need only slow to about 30 mph. It's an absolutely terrifying proposition that's worked flawlessly since its adoption.

The train gained a thousand feet as we departed the coast and climbed into the limestone Basque Mountains, dotted with oak, beech and birch trees. After switching to a slow, regional train in Araya, we settled into the Pamplona Basin, a schizophrenic geographic zone of broken plains linking the Pyrenees with the Ebro River Valley. From my window seat, I saw Pamplona's hilly topography, an upland plateau full of ravines and outcrops. Oatmeal-colored fields predominated, between which stood small tracts of scrub-oak forest, while in the distance white wind turbines spun. The Pyrenees filled the background like a fine matte painting as we chugged along the Arga River into Pamplona Station, a beige-and-peach Basque-style blockhouse.

While it's almost 250-feet long and hosts 10 busy tracks, the non-descript facade led me to believe I'd accidentally disembarked at a secondary station outside the city. But, no, the "Pamplona Iruña" sign out front confirmed I had arrived in Pamplona's main station, not some suburban afterthought. The judicious use or, rather, utter lack of decoration shocked me as I tracked the lengthy exterior. Stucco in two colors, white and peachy pink, alternated between simple pilaster columns. The windows were clad in the bare minimum cast-concrete trim. White cornerstones flanked the entrance. Opened in 1860, I chalked up the drab exterior to Spain's crippling economic hardship during the station's last major renovation in 1950. Luckily, the terracotta Spanish tile roof, the key architectural distinction demarcating chilly northern and sunny southern Europe, didn't disappoint, a beautiful, exotic and unequivocal welcome to arid España.

* * *

Paolo managed several Airbnb properties for second-home owners.

"But this one is the best," he said, in staccato Spanish. He unlocked the fifth-floor walkup. "I'll show you why." He wore skinny jeans, retro-style gym sneakers and a garishly tight black t-shirt. We stepped through the modern apartment, an IKEA renovation with flat grays, blacks and whites. We walked across gleaming knotty pine floors to the balcony doors. He hesitated a moment, then swung them wide open.

"See," he said. The balcony overlooked Calle de la Estafeta, a Running of the Bulls corridor, the tile and cobblestone straightaway that comes after the infamous and dangerous Mercaderes curve. There's no escape once the mad dash down Estafeta begins; five-story apartment buildings form a continuous wall from the curve to the outlet near Plaza de Toros.

The sunshine warmed my face, the steady breeze and 1,500-foot elevation checked the rising daytime heat.

"Where do you recommend for tapas?" I asked Paolo before swiftly correcting myself. "I mean pintxos!"

He smiled and spoke in clear Castilian Spanish. "Yes, pintxos. In Pamplona, we call them pintxos. They say tapas in the south...or Barcelona." He rolled his eyes.

"So many great places. Go to Cafe Roch. The croquettes are famous."

I wrote it down as he mulled over further recommendations. "And below us on Estafeta is Bodegón Sarria, very nice. Over on Calle San Nicolas, the other side of Plaza del Castillo, is Bar San Nicolás. But we have many all around the plaza. You can walk it in a circle, go down the side streets and find more delicious pintxos. Pintxos everywhere!"

I wandered Pamplona's oldest old town, Navarrería. Scrubbed tile and cobblestone streets snaked around plumb and skinny stucco and stone buildings. Built on Roman ruins, Navarrería bolstered the feudal Kingdom of Pamplona that grew into the Kingdom of Navarre, an independent Basque nation that once stretched from the Bay of Biscay across the Pyrenees.

Contrary to popular belief, Pamplona exists outside nine days every July when the streets are transformed into conduits for raging bulls and drunken tourists. I considered what a mistake it was to overlook Pamplona outside the San Fermin Festival as I sipped a coffee and flipped open my laptop at Café Iruña on Plaza del Castillo. Wispy clouds floated on the breeze as happy patrons drank beers, cocktails and coffee under late-afternoon sun in Pamplona's premier people-watching destination. The aproned waiter delivered my frothy lager, and I sipped and smiled at nothing in particular, relishing my full beer and empty schedule.

Only such a beautiful day could lure me outside, away from Iruña's elegant interior, unchanged since 1888. Period lamps, gigantic mirrors and ornate Thonet chairs created a privileged warmth. Hemingway drank in the corner where a gaudy bronze bust of Papa Bear sits. Iruña defines Pamplona's café culture, where locals and tourists can imbibe and while away an afternoon. Just take heed of Paolo's advice—avoid its overpriced food.

After writing a few hundred words, I researched options for my next jump, one last stop before Barcelona. Could my Tour de Milk Run be on its last leg already? It seemed like only yesterday I was defeating an

Amsterdam roof-cat invasion.

An arterial railway ending at the base of the Pyrenees had jumped out at me the other night in SJDL after I had booked Pamplona. Connected to Zaragoza through Huesca, it looked remote, and I'd never seen, read or heard about this strange branch line into the Pyrenees foothills. Not that I knew every railway station, but it's hard to miss on a Spanish railway map, a primary line servicing one of Spain's least-populated regions connecting no major cities. I punched the name into Google: Canfranc.

What I found was perplexing, amazing: an architectural gem, a train station fit for Paris, Vienna or Prague tucked into a deserted Pyrenean valley.

And it's mostly abandoned.

The grand Canfranc train station occupies a map smudge of the same name (population: 454). It once served an ambitious but flawed cross-Pyrenees line, a joint venture between Spain and France, and, thus, doomed to failure. And fail it did, in 1970 when France stopped trying, so now Canfranc sits mostly empty. But it's no ordinary depot, but where French trains switched to Iberian gauge and vice versa. Spain gambled this ambitious station could revitalize the entire region. Canfranc was the second largest station in Europe when it opened in 1928, and dripping in Beaux-Arts style so decadent and decorative, it'd make Baroque blush. Built as an international hub, it now welcomes only local hops from Zaragoza, a true milk run.

I knew what I had to do, opening a WhatsApp thread with my boss and uploading a Canfranc image from Google:

Hey, dope abandoned train station in Spain. Going soon, interested in a
story?

...

yass! sick. story + photos. go

I booked an Airbnb in Zaragoza, where I'd base for my jaunt to

Canfranc, and then an apartment in Barcelona's El Born neighborhood. With that, I had now set my trip, the end in sight, the booking, planning, Tetris configurations of timetables and Airbnb reservations now over. The tension in my shoulders released. I leapt to my feet, paid the bill and plodded toward the 16th-century walls, grappling with simultaneous urges of restlessness and disappointment.

Suddenly, three weeks wasn't enough. Could I extend my trip? I was just uncovering my groove, tapping into the *buena onda* and finding my travel flow. I believed as though I could continue forever. If only, of course, my family could join me.

* * *

I gazed over the landscape from Mirador de Caballo Blanco. The plains of Pamplona unfolded below me as the sun slipped from view. Stone restaurants and cafés were built into the city walls. I descended the parapet to a small oak grove growing from a lower wall segment. A group of five or six young people sat in a circle under a hash cloud, laughing, chatting and drinking beers from tall glass bottles.

Returning to my Estafeta abode, I showered, called home and launched my pintxos-not-tapas circumambulation of Plaza del Castillo. The plaza and streets radiating from it teemed with pintxos joints, half-bar, half-restaurants specializing in small plates and drinks taken standing at bars or two-top tables. I strolled the plaza counterclockwise as my pintxos-powered descent into Pamplona's gluttonous belly commenced.

I requested *una caña, por favor*—about half a pint—while I considered the croquettes listed on glossy white poster boards behind Cafe Roch's bar. Of Spain's innumerable sizes of draft beer, including the spindly *tubo* and paunchy *jarra*, the estimable caña is the smallest, ideal for pintxos crawling. The caña allows flexibility, enjoying a cold beer without committing to a full pint because, let's face it, there's always another pintxos joint calling.

Once upon a time, the caña held another advantage: Tapas and pintxos were dispensed for free with drink orders. So, the more beer you drank, the more free food you received. Nowadays, free tapas or pintxos are harder to find than exiled former king Juan Carlos' Swiss bank accounts. Instead, delectable pintxo plates are the principal attraction, worth the one- to three-euro price tag.

Cafe Roch served its first croquette in 1898, and has changed little since. A 1960s renovation introduced a little more metal, vinyl and plastic than you might want, but it's still a cozy, stained-glass mecca for the fried delectable. I arrived early, 8:30 p.m., and had the rear bar to myself. The poster board menus advertised *frito* goodies while simpler pintxos sat under a sneeze guard at the bar. I ordered a caña refill, the sweaty two-and-a-half-inch-tall glass quickly replaced, and three croquettes: pimiento, roquefort and *jamón y queso*.

"We're not the biggest or richest or most famous city in Spain or even the Basque Country," said the bartender and server of sacred croquettes. He wore a red polo shirt and kept a white towel slung over his left shoulder.

The brothy-breadcrumb, three-inch cylinders contained perfectly mixed and melted fillings. The spicy pimiento bounced off tangy cheese, salty jamón kissed its queso partner and the gooey roquefort disappeared in two bites. I chased them with another frigid caña.

"But we have an important history, a beautiful culture. Tell your American friends: Yes! Come to Pamplona before," he rolled his right middle and index fingers, "or after the San Fermin. Experience the real Pamplona."

Two oak Keler barrels flanked the entrance at the long-winded Bar Restaurante San Nicolás La Cocina Vasca. It was about 15 feet wide and thrice as long, with a bar running along the right wall. Another *caña* accompanied two memorable pintxos: mushroom tempura and baked goat cheese. People arrived in droves, couples bellied up to the bar, small groups huddled around the perimeter tables, while extra bartenders appeared. Music played above the conversational din, locals laughing and speaking rapid-fire Spanish in business-casual attire.

Across the plaza, Bar Gaucho occupied the atmospheric corner of Calle Espoz y Mina and an alley of the same name connected to Estafeta. I'd eaten plenty and had only one more stop in me, but I went big with the pork cheek (*carrillera*), foie gras and truffle egg while quaffing perspiring cañas on either side.

Bodegón Sarria, the night's final pintxo palace, operated a chic, exposed-beam atmosphere with numerous outdoor tables, ham hocks hanging from every inch of ceiling space alongside gravity-fed, copper barrels dispensing *kalimotxo*, Pamplona's cola-infused sangria. I was sure this place absolutely pulsates during San Fermin. I closed the crawl with oil-drenched artichoke, fried *patatas bravas* and juicy links of *chistorra*, local chorizo-style sausage, on grilled baguette slices. Washed down with clammy cañas, of course.

Two men, about my age and height, with short, dark hair and dressed in pressed khakis and starched-collared shirts, regaled me with tales from the San Fermin Festival.

"I was running right beside him when the bull got him," said the one wearing glasses. A few years ago, he'd run with an American tourist he'd met en route to the staging area. "He forgot about the curve," he pointed down Estafeta, "and was clobbered by a falling bull. Right, bam," he pounded his right fist into his left hand, "against the wall. Between the bull and the wall. He broke ribs and his ankle."

"Do you still enjoy San Fermin? Is the city crazy during the festival?" I asked in halting Spanish.

The guy without glasses replied to my question. "Yes, we love it. It's crazy, yes. It's very busy, crowded, sometimes difficult. But we love it.

It's our festival, Pamplona's celebration, no matter how many tourists come."

* * *

"Welcome to Navarre!" said Matten, the Pamplona history tour guide. That morning, I hesitated outside the tourist office, debating whether I should join the tour. I'd bailed on the group tour in Normandy, but I knew nothing about Pamplona outside Hemingway, a dangerously unreliable narrator if there ever was one. Plus, the only way to climb Pamplona Cathedral's bell tower was by guided tour. I paid the fee and gathered with six other tourists on Plaza del Castillo.

He blew a long, black curl from his face. A brown leather satchel hung from his right shoulder over a wrinkled, long-sleeve burgundy shirt rolled to mid-forearm. He wore khaki shorts, striped black socks and black skate shoes.

He paced back and forth pensively. "Did, oh no, did you think you were in Spain? Oh, no." He shook his head then spun on his right heel as a grin crept across his face.

"You are in," he cleared his throat, "the Chartered Community of Navarre. In fact, Pamplona, once its own kingdom, is the capital of Navarre, a kingdom within the Kingdom of Spain, none of which is any longer a kingdom." He paused and surveyed the audience. "Raise your hand if you're confused yet. Go ahead, don't be shy." He lifted his hands, palms faced up.

Two young German-speaking professionals raised their hands.

"Okay, we start with Basques," he said. "And, surprise, I'm Basque. There are three popular opinions on Basques: The first is we are mysterious, oooooh. Because our origins are, well, mysterious. We are the oldest surviving inhabitants of Western Europe and we speak a language unrelated to anything else.

"The second popular opinion is that we Basques are a hearty bunch. Every summer we have competitions so manly and tough...I'm growing more chest hair just thinking about them." He looked down at his half-buttoned shirt. "And as you can see, the last thing I need is more chest hair. Anyway, at the Basque Trials of Strength," he flexed again, "we, well, other Basques compete in events such as wood chopping, heavy stone lifting, straw bale lifting and farm-cart lifting. Yes, there's much lifting of heavy objects. And, of course, the most famous Basque invention in the world, *soka-shot* or what you call tug-of-war.

"Third: We are stubborn. Yes, we plead guilty to this one, too. Especially my mother," he murmured from his mouth's left side.

Matten listed the Basque people's many would-be vanquishers: Romans, Carthaginians, Celts, Goths, Franks, Castilians, Vandals, Andalusians, Moors.

He counted his fingers. "Yes, perhaps I missed a few. French and Spanish kings learned what the Romans and Moors learned centuries earlier: Basques are not to be conquered or controlled, but cajoled."

We rounded a corner and smacked into the 13th-century San Cernín Church. Hidden from view, the stark Gothic church postured like a granite fortification. The portico featured Moorish arches extending from a gable end flanked by two medieval towers, key features of old town Pamplona's skyline. We stepped inside, Matten held the door open, to find a wide single nave lined with timeworn wooden benches leading to a polygonal apse and raised choir. The Gothic stillness grabbed me. Ten chapels were fitted between the flying buttresses, most Baroque add-ons, including the opulent Virgen del Camino, which stood where the original cloister once did.

Back outside, Matten led us toward Pamplona Cathedral, while slicing through Pamplona's intriguing history like a broadsword through a melon.

"The Romans and Basques had an understanding, but when the

Romans left, oh wow, things get very bad. The Moors arrive from the south, then the Franks invade from the north. Very messy! The Basque leader, Eneko Arista, played the two powers against each other and, after teaming up with the Moors, defeated the Franks at the second battle of Roncevaux. He was crowned King of Pamplona." Matten strutted across the cobblestones, popping his collar.

With nominal independence, Pamplona flourished, swelling into three distinct neighborhoods called *burgos*. Basques inhabited the Navarrería and Franks lived in San Cernín. San Nicolás hosted a mix, with some Catalans and Moors for good measure. The Franks, looking to avenge their loss at Roncevaux, installed a puppet regime that antagonized the native Basque nobility and sowed ethnic tensions. Soon, the neighborhoods waged war against each other, fighting pitched battles in the streets. The French king had his casus belli and sent the French army to besiege Navarrería's civilians in 1276. They massacred the population and burned every last building to the ground. Navarrería sat uninhabited for over 50 years, a wasteland warning to anyone considering challenging French authority.

Erected atop Roman ruins, the Pamplona Cathedral, or Catedral de Santa María la Real, anchored Pamplona's northeastern quadrant. Whereas San Cernin blended into the neighborhood, ambushing seekers drawn to its towers, Pamplona Cathedral loomed large, dominating this corner of the *casco viejo*. Its grand and sparse Neoclassical design intrigued me, so I lingered out front while the group entered. Could this really be a church? The facade was constructed entirely from dressed rectangular white-granite blocks. It had no fancy marble veneering, minimal window treatments and sparse adornment. The portico's columns held up a simple tetrahedron roof. I could've easily overlooked the cathedral thinking it was a museum, city hall or bank.

Once across the threshold, however, my perception shifted; it felt like recrossing the northern border into France. The narrow and tall

French Gothic style was unmistakable—the stately, concave ceiling bristled with painted rib vaults while an arrow-thin nave completed the cruciform. This curious Basque bastion carried a Spanish name but a French appearance. I caught the group, and we fanned out as Matten told us to regroup below the bell-tower entrance in 10 minutes.

Like the minimalist exterior, the inside featured dressed rectangular stonework, all of uniform length but of varying heights. I crept along the nave, noting the side chapels built along both side aisles, and stood under massive bronze chandeliers suspended from the stone-and-mortar ceiling. A wrought-iron gate surrounded the choir. I closed my eyes, placed my right hand on the ironwork and let the still quiet of the ages wash over me until an unseen hand patted my shoulder.

"Rory," Matten whispered. "We climb the tower now."

On the spiral stone staircase, I slipped past Matten and summited the bell tower first, standing alone for a brief, glorious moment before the group arrived. I took a deep breath and approached the railing. Matten arrived next, followed, one at a time, by the rest of the now-breathless group. A sea of terracotta roofs with bell-tower flourishes unfurled before us, and I leaned over the stone railing, my eye drawn to a terraced hilltop maze in the distance. Matten drew up next to me.

"Matten, que es eso?" I asked, pointing at the earthen spiderweb on the city's northern outskirts.

"That? It's Fort San Cristóbal," he replied. "It sits atop Monte Ezkaba."

"Interesting. Is it open for tourists?" I asked, narrowing my eyes.

"Well, no." He paused, a knowing smirk appeared on his face. "It's closed to the public."

"Really? How closed is it?" I pressed.

"Not very closed." His smirk widened.

Matten launched into his last lecture as we pondered the Monument to the Fueros, a block southwest of Plaza del Castillo, after crossing the third burgo, San Nicolas. He raised his right index finger and faced the monument, "Basque laws were granted special status called fueros, and we held our own parliament in Pamplona Cathedral. But as we say in Spain, we saw the ears of the wolf." Matten made peace-sign ears with his fingers. "Danger was coming. The Basque fueros were curtailed by the Napoleonic Wars, never to return."

After Matten's crescendo, all I could think about was reaching the "not very closed" Fort San Cristóbal. It was just sitting there, a casual 90-minute walk away, beckoning me to hop its rusty gates and explore its mildewy innards. By the tour's conclusion, I shouted "Gracias! Ciao!" and bolted, only to sprint back when I realized I'd forgotten to tip Matten. I found him ambling down a nearby alley, and, after a sweaty apology and five euros slipped inside a handshake, I scampered off once more, pulling up my phone's GPS along the way.

Before my GPS loaded, I spotted white-over-red blazes affixed to a green light pole with a Galician scallop shell pointing west. The conspicuous scallop shell marked the Camino de Santiago pilgrimage route, a long-distance trail running through France and over the Pyrenees to Santiago de Compostela, Spain.

"Hey, I know you." I told the stoic light pole.

Scallop shell stickers, plaques and signs dotted the town, but I hadn't noticed the white-red GR stripes until now. Seeping into Spain, I realized GR trails predated modern borders. Europe's multinational hiker superhighways originated from medieval pilgrimages, trade routes and other footpaths. Of course! If I looked closer, I bet I'd find them all over Western Europe. I could probably walk to Rome! Not today, though. I closed the GPS app and diverged north from the white-and-red stripes wending west. At the base of Monte Ezkaba, a bleached-gravel footpath led up several long switchbacks to Fort San Cristóbal.

I explored serpentine trails leading to the fort's front passageway.

A 20-foot-tall arched steel gate set in a matching concrete entryway protruded a foot from the 50-foot-tall walls. Wild grasses and plants sprouted from earthworks atop the block-and-mortar walls. Blue, black and green graffiti with slogans supporting the Basque terrorist group ETA, anarchist monograms and tags from various artists covered the entryway surround. A sign atop the entrance proclaimed the bastion "Fuerte de Alfonso XII." I gripped the flaking-black gate; it was locked tight. Through the bars, I spied a darkened inner labyrinth.

The fortification peered out from within the mountain like a subterranean submarine, no doubt built to withstand the concussive effects of 20th-century artillery. I walked the perimeter where earth merged with fortress stone, looking for a back door. Around the right side, I scrambled up a grassy incline and found lichen-covered stairs tumbling toward darkness. No one was around, so I cautiously descended. Piercing through the outer walls, I found a three-story stone building with earthen roof surrounded by a grassy perimeter courtyard, a fortress within a fortress within a mountain.

I opened an unlocked gate, turned on my phone's flashlight and entered a dank arched concrete tunnel leading to a staircase. Climbing the staircase, I tiptoed down the first floor corridor, sweeping my flashlight back and forth. Rows and rows of cramped rooms lined each side. Thick steel bars covered tiny square interior windows. Barracks? No, the rooms looked too small. I found more of the same on the second floor before my phone displayed a low-battery warning.

"Damn," I said. My words echoed down the still corridor.

Meticulously picked clean as if authorities expected trespassers, the fortress elicited ominous vibes. I didn't fear getting caught or hurt. I dreaded ghosts more than tetanus. The eerie building coughed silent screams. I'd hear a cackle, flash my light toward the noise only to find more empty hallway or barren room. Cracks in the plaster walls looked like ghostly vines. Only the methodical drip-drip-drip of leaking water filled the void. Every couple minutes, I'd abruptly stop and spin on my heel, certain I was being followed.

Goosebumps rippled down my arms as I re-entered the outer court-yard. I inhaled fresh air, letting my heart rate slow. Late afternoon had turned to evening twilight when my stomach growled. I retraced my steps, toward the stunning view of Pamplona, the dusk light setting its walls aflame. Exiting the fort, however, I came upon a well-worn trail leading to a stony escarpment.

The trail ended at some sort of memorial or statue. Three concrete blocks sat in a row. A split granite block, looking like a broken heart or cleaved circle, was fixed atop the middle block. I ran my fingers across stamped inscriptions in Spanish and Euskara embellishing the larger end pieces. They read:

"For freedom and the republic they gave their lives

22-5-1938

22-5-1988

Escapees from the central prison of San Cristobal. 22-5-1938"

The Spanish Civil War raged in 1938. Judging from the "republic" mention, I surmised the escapees were prisoners of Franco's coup d'état, imprisoned for supporting democracy and killed while trying to escape. A right-quick Google search supplied the details: Almost 800 political prisoners escaped, but the Nationalist army quickly captured then slowly tortured most to death. Some 200 were shot and killed while on the lam. Only a few reached France. The blocks looked beat-up and stained. I inspected the one inscribed in Basque Euskara closer, noticing a scrubbed-away red symbol. Stepping back, I saw the unambiguous outline of a faded swastika.

* * *

Old-town Pamplona is compact and he was a prodigious drinker, so yet another Hemingway haunt, Bar Txoko, sits across Plaza del Castillo from Café Iruña. It's clean, classy and a testament to Hemingway's habitual tendencies. At a patio table, I rested, sipped a few beers and prepped for the Canfranc assignment. After sunset, I embarked on a lightweight pintxos tour, this time daringly working clockwise from Txoko back to Estafeta.

After dinner, at the Airbnb, I discovered some Amsterdam leftovers while packing. I bought a cigar from the tobacco shop around the corner, carefully sliced it open with my Opinel #6 and removed the tobacco. I didn't have quite enough, so I mixed a smidge of the Cuban brown-leaf with the Amsterdam leftovers and poured the mixture into the cigar shell. I licked the top edge and rolled the blunt tight as a top.

I strolled Estafeta north to the walls at Baluarte de Guadalupe. From here, views stretched across Pamplona's northern sprawl, a sea of household lights, to the shadowy farmlands beyond. The beige 16th-century walls of Pamplona reflected dusk's fleeting azure light. The night was still and clear. Stars appeared overhead. There was not a sound, nothing but the ghostly rustle of ancient Basques defending their home turf from invasions in all directions. I heard the pounding hooves of their cavalry, sortieing from the town walls to disrupt siege operations. I smelled the flaming arrows met with the burning tar, setting the town's inhabitants and its besiegers alight. Pamplona's many ghosts sent shivers down my arms.

I descended stone steps to leafy Revellín de los Reyes battlements, where I once again smelled hash. Two young men and two young women, all sporting thick dark hair, sat in a circle. They passed around a joint. One young woman ducked the spliff behind her as I walked up, sorta, kinda, not really trying to hide it.

I saw my opening.

"No problema. No me importa," I said, waving my left hand while pulling the blunt from my left breast pocket.

"Ah," I smiled and turned, waving the blunt like a magic wand. The blue sunset's reflection faded from the Walls of Pamplona. "Actualmente, quieres algo de esto? Es un blunt con ganja de Amsterdam." I absolutely nailed the Spanish-English-Jamaican patois.

They were in their early or mid-twenties, dressed to hipster specifications with requisite oversize graphic tees and ripped skinny jeans.

The woman with round glasses stubbed out their dirty-hash joint. I lit the blunt and took two burly hits, exhaled billowy clouds, then passed it.

"Are you from Pamplona or in university here?"

"We graduated from the University of Pamplona. Two years ago now, well three for you," she pointed at the guy sitting across from her. A couple worked in restaurants, one in an office and the woman I passed the blunt to worked in an art gallery. They shared a three-bedroom in San Nicolas. Three grew up in towns outside Pamplona and one was from Zaragoza.

When I told them I came from America, they gasped and smiled, envious. They professed a desire to see America, maybe even move there, the two women admitted.

"Why?" I asked, pointing to the medieval walls. "Pamplona is magnificent."

They agreed. Pamplona was proving hard to leave. Great food, people, art and climate. But like the rest of Spain, it had one problem for young graduates.

"Few jobs," the young man said, passing the blunt. "Pamplona is better than other places in Spain. We all have jobs. But it's still hard, not the best jobs. We have the Volkswagen factory or tourism. A couple banks. Not many professional jobs for us," he said, meaning young graduates.

Almost half of Spaniards under 30 were unemployed, a staggering statistic that had proved intractable even as 2009's Great Recession waned. I asked why.

"The economy is not competitive enough. The Old Guard protects themselves. The rich people, people with connections, all find jobs, of course. And in Spain, companies can hire young people, new graduates to temporary jobs. They can fire temporary workers whenever," he swiped his right hand.

"It feels like a rigged system," added the young woman in glasses.

The tough job market and entrenched aristocrats coupled with policies biased toward more senior workers all added up to high youth unemployment. I wondered, could there be more?

"What did you study at university?" I asked.

Two said music, one said history and the fourth, the office worker, studied business.

The slow-burning blunt was half-smoked when I took my leave, ready for a nighttime stroll before bed. "Soy bueno." I waved off another round. "Quédatelo, amigas," I closed my hands and brought them to my face in full namaste, "Gracias. Ciao."

"Ciao!" they replied, smiling and waving.

I wandered clockwise outside the walls, going right on Calle Juan de Labrit to Plaza de Toros. A Hemingway bust, chiseled from blistered white granite and depicting the author with his arms folded, sat outside the bullring. Thinking I'd hit on a winning Amsterdam-Cuban combination, a warm, fuzzy feeling washed over me as I studied the statue and its stern appearance.

"Everything you did was worthy of pen and paper, eh?"

I didn't expect an answer as the surrounding trees and bull-ring lights cast shadows on the sidewalk.

"Mate, then what happened? You had everything. Too much money, fame, drink? Man, if I ever have half what you had...which I won't, I'll, uh, I'll..." I smirked at the moon cresting the bullring.

"Yeah, right? I'd push it all to the edge. Like you did."

My cynical laugh rang out through the ages, from Basques to Romans to Goths to Instagram influencers. I fended off a wave of wobbliness and steadied myself against the embedded bronze plaque. Perhaps the Amsterdam-Cuba connection was too winning.

"This is our one and only chance, isn't it? We gotta go, go far, go wide. When it's over, it's over." I nodded in full agreement with myself, thinking perhaps I'd missed my calling as a barroom philosopher. Hemingway's expression remained unchanged, a monument to composure, but I got the feeling he'd have agreed if he could.

"Right. Well, you were a legend. You did something right. What do I know? I'm just a guy standing here, by myself, talking to a statue."

Zaragoza

The timetables showed a daily regional train to Zaragoza, hidden between the high-speed lines, covering two-and-a-half hours and making 15 calls over old Iberian gauge. It didn't require reservations despite what the station attendant in Irun had insisted. Perhaps the blunt-nosed and boxy old electric slow trains were Aragón's little secret.

While louder and decidedly clunkier than their high-speed cousins, cube-shaped slow trains had grown on me. Riding them felt nostalgic, a throwback to a time, well, I never really knew, being a child of high-speed Europe. It comforted me knowing these rapidly declining nods to the Old World still exist. Plus, riding the slow train had exposed me to so much more local flavor. Slow trains stopped frequently, inevitably turning over more passengers, the vast majority of whom were locals. And now, over two weeks into my journey, I hardly noticed the fitful stops and starts, slow turns and graceless track changes.

After leaving the Pamplona plains, the train dropped into a parched and lunar depression. The only green emanated from the River Ebro's narrow banks. As I grappled with the arid transition, I staggered at the site of the ultra-modern Zaragoza-Delicias train station.

Designed by Carlos Ferrater and José María Valero, the station was fascinatingly repulsive. Instead of a unified facade, five white blocks with prison windows were stepped back from one another so they met at their corners. Something resembling the St. Louis Arch spanned the combined roof lines. As we approached, I couldn't fathom how this design won approval. After alighting, however, I found the interior positively delightful. Warm. Welcoming. Yet sleek. A massive glass atrium ceiling flooded the platform with sunlight. The slate flooring contrasted beautifully with the aluminum railings, round retro Roman numeral clocks and birch plywood paneling.

A 45-minute walk from old town, the gleaming metal-and-stone Delicias station's fringe location offered one benefit: the chance to stop at Moorish Aljafería Palace. The palace represents one of three fundamental forces influencing Zaragoza's culture, history and architecture: Roman establishment, Islamic rule and Catholic reconquest.

The massive Aljafería occupied at least 10 city blocks, yet I was shut out. No ticket! And they'd sold the day's allotment. So, I strolled the perimeter, contenting myself with the outside view. The rectangular Troubadour Tower crowned a geometric amalgamation of cylindrical towers interspersed with ogee-arch gateways. Modern block apartment buildings with window air conditioners and sunshade-covered balconies loomed a few blocks away.

The Aljafería, the Mosque-Cathedral of Córdoba and Granada's Alhambra form the triumvirate of Hispano-Muslim architecture. Like the Alhambra, Moors built the Aljafería in Iberian Islam's waning days. The fortress-palace fell to Catholic forces less than 50 years after its completion. In 1118, Alfonso I of Aragón expelled the Berber Almoravids, ending 400 years of Islamic rule in Zaragoza.

Twenty minutes later, I stood in Plaza del Pilar, an alfresco nave that stretched for 1,200 feet over immaculate tiles and flagstones. Walking from the serene Fuente de la Hispanidad monument to several charming Goya statues decorating the other end, I'm awed. Flanked by two massive cathedrals, La Seo and Basílica del Pilar, and lined with six-story buildings with ground-floor restaurants and shops, the plaza appeared endless, arresting and like an outdoor church. Unable to confess my sins, instead, I ducked into the glass-cubed TI.

"So...I should ride the bus to get to the train station." I switched to English, which the TI clerk readily spoke, to ensure I understood her perplexing advice to ride the bus, not the train, to Canfranc train station tomorrow.

"To reach Canfranc for the 10 a.m. tour, I should ride the bus?" I asked,

"Sì, for the tour, yes. Then, take the afternoon train back to Zaragoza," she reassured me with an unrelenting grin.

"So, to make the train station tour, I must ride the bus. The tour doesn't sync with the train timetable, correct?" I pressed.

Canfranc, once derided as the "Titanic of the Mountains" (props for honoring the analogy, I suppose), now sees but two round-trip trains a day to Zaragoza, a far cry from its forecasted heyday that never materialized. This meager 13-stop slow train makes the call at Canfranc just to keep the lights on. That's it. No international journeys. No pleasure trips into the Pyrenees. Just an obligatory four-hour milk run from Zaragoza to nowhere, population 454. It was as if authorities didn't want people knowing what they'd left rotting in the Pyrenees foothills.

"Yes, this is correct. The tour starts at 10, but the morning train arrives at 10:30. We recommend you take the 8:45 bus and return on the 15:40 train back to Zaragoza from Canfranc." She blinked her big, round, brown eyes, her smile never flinching.

"Vale. That's my plan. A little surprising, but, no worries." I scooped up the tourist brochures. Silly me for thinking a train ride would be the logical way to reach a train station. "Gracias por su ayuda. Hasta luego."

* * *

After 200 years of warfare at the conclusion of the Cantabrian Wars, the Romans finally conquered all Iberia (minus that Basque bit we previously scoured) and settled their battle-hardened legions atop a former Celtic village on the Ebro River sometime around 20 BCE. They named the city Caesaraugusta for their triumphant leader, Caesar Augustus. Then, in a centuries-long game of telephone, Arabic-speaking Muslims twisted the name into Saraqusṭa, which morphed into Çaragoça after the Catholic Reconquista and settled into the modern-day Zaragoza. Say Caesaraugusta ten times fast, and it'll turn into Zaragoza.

I pondered Zaragoza's over 2,000 years of history, while nibbling a jamón bocadillo and sipping an ice-cold Cerveza Zaragozana, at a café terrace overlooking what remains of the Roman theater, Teatro de Caesaraugusta. Unearthed by archaeologists in 1973, the ruins sat preserved in an atrium museum. Pre-bocadillo, I studied the aisles and ran my hands over the pockmarked arena seats, appreciating indestructible Roman construction. I imagined 6,000 rowdy spectators, a third of Caesaraugusta's total population, cheering gladiatorial combats, watching historic plays and celebrating pagan holidays.

I reflected on this engrossing city as I sauntered through the old town toward my Airbnb. Zaragoza exuded an Islamic feel rare among Spanish cities north of Cordoba. Yet, as its three massive cathedrals attested, it's also among its staunchest Catholic capitals. Plus, Roman ruins—theater, forum, walls, baths and port—remained in striking condition. Despite Iberia's penchant for ransacking their cities every couple hundred years, Zaragoza's history has seen shockingly peaceful power transitions. It's kind of their thing. (Stout Roman walls certainly helped.)

The Visigoths chased off the Romans, taking Zaragoza peacefully in

472 CE. Two hundred years later, after destroying the Visigoth army in pitched battles, the North African Umayyads entered a vanquished Zaragoza without a fight. When Alfonso I came a-reconquering with bands of Christian knights in 1118, the Moors, however, wouldn't vamoose. Understandably so. The Muslim *taifa* ruler was enjoying life in Aljafería Palace. (No ticket necessary.) A six-month siege followed, and two more horrific sieges ensued upon Napoleon's doomed Peninsular War with Spain. But that's about it, only three notable sieges over 2,000 years. Even during the Spanish Civil War, Francoist forces wrested control from Republicans one day after the 1936 coup d'état.

A grandmother-grandson duo Airbnb-ed the spare bedroom in their first-floor apartment in old town's southern labyrinth a couple blocks from the Rio Huerva. Twenty-year-old Alvaro managed the Airbnb side, while Carmen enjoyed meeting new people after her husband passed away two years ago. We spoke in her white-plaster dining room over a spotless red tablecloth clamped tight to the round table. Jesus Christ watched from paintings, statuettes and a disconcertingly detailed crucifix.

Alvaro brought his grandmother the blue leather-bound scrapbook. I'd told them how excited I was to see Canfranc tomorrow when Carmen, born and raised in this very apartment, revealed she'd ridden from Canfranc to Pau, France, as a teenager in the 1960s, and her parents attended the station's grand opening in 1928.

She paused after each page flip to recount memories to Alvaro, which he summarized to me in simpler, deliberate Spanish. Faded black-and-white Kodachromes, their corners upturned and edges fraying, showed Carmen as a young mother, holding Alvaro's mother and uncles, at the beach, in Barcelona, and at various weddings and celebrations.

"Ah, here we are," she said, about one-third the way through the photo book. "Yes, Canfranc." She laid the book open on the table.

"This is me with my sisters, and that's my mother and father. They're all gone now. Just me." She ran her fingers over the photos.

"The station was beautiful and luxurious. My parents said it was the most beautiful building they'd ever seen...that wasn't a church!" She smiled. "They were 18 and just married. They saw the king and many famous Spaniards at the ribbon cutting. My parents had so much hope and optimism for Canfranc.

"I remember my father saying that after the war, Canfranc would see renewal. Canfranc would be a way for us to heal, for France and Spain to grow closer. But my father was wrong." She flipped the page. "I remember Canfranc felt so empty in 1963. My memories were not glamorous like my parents'. It felt old and dirty, like they couldn't keep up with cleaning and maintenance.

"By then, only two or three daily departures to Pau. That station was supposed to handle dozens of trains every day. One café sat empty, and the only passengers enjoying the departure lobby were the ones who embarked with me. I rode the railway from Canfranc to Pau with my older sister in 1963, and I've never returned. Please take a picture for me; I'd like to see what's left of the station."

* * *

As the name implied, El Tubo, Zaragoza's bustling tapas district, was a perplexing warren of narrow streets and dark alleys. Looming five-story buildings created an urban tunnel from which I could barely discern the sky. On the ground, deep inside The Tube, it was party time as usual among the tapas bars at El Tubo's nexus of voraciousness, Calle Cuatro de Agosto, Calle Libertad and Calle Estébanes. Bricks, tiles and cut granite blocks paved the streets. Half-collapsed pale brick walls revealed garden bars covered in creeping vines and overgrown plants. Graffiti smothered every bare wall or metal security door, some of it good, most of it not. The district bristled with tapas bars, their imbibers spilled into the streets. I navigated through pinched choke points every few feet.

Revelers had darker skin and inkier hair than their Basque neighbors. I overheard the Spanish dialect, Castellano Septentrional. Pronouns and indirect objects were shuffled, diphthongs appeared, "R"s disappeared and elongated final vowels were almost their own words. The electronic music pulsating through El Tubo didn't help my fledgling attempts at deciphering the northern Spanish, which became flat-out incomprehensible when I lost count of my cañas.

After devouring paper plates of jamón, prawns, mushrooms and goat cheese, I escaped El Tubo to the seven-arched, 15th-century Puente de Piedra bridge, Zaragoza's Instagram icon. Darkness enveloped the city as I crossed the bridge. Modern aluminum pedestrian lights ran along the bridge's sidewalk, bathing the overpass in white light against the ebony night sky and yellow-floodlit cathedrals.

On the east bank, I plodded through the Balcón de San Lázaro viewing area, where couples kissed and teenagers smoked hash, to a triangular strip of gravel jutting into the Ebro. All alone, I captured the unobstructed nighttime view I'd sought: The Puente de Piedra under a starry sky with the floodlit Baroque domes and towers of Basílica de Nuestra Señora del Pilar in the background. The night sky turned the Ebro's languid waters dark blue as they flowed through the bridge's arches that hopscotched across the Ebro. It was breathtaking, the rare viewpoint that exceeds those lofty Instagram expectations. And, standing alone on the sandbar, I had it all to myself, not a selfie stick in sight.

While dark, it wasn't late, so I returned to El Tubo. Zaragoza wears its nighttime lights like fine jewelry, a celebrity ready for their red-carpet closeup with every sunset. A day trip to Zaragoza would be a waste, for it's at night when the city becomes most beautiful, a rival to any of Spain's fairy-tale metropolises. The streets are clean and welcoming.

White granite, ivory tuft, polished cobblestones and bleached limestone bounced the jaundiced glow of street lights in all directions. Every turn of the corner revealed glowing medieval stone ramparts, bronze statues or vibrant Mudéjar tiles. It was a treasure hunt with no map.

From Calle Don Jaime I, I turned right on Estébanes then left on Cinegio and reached El Tubo when my peripheral vision got blurry. Swirly and seething, the ancient city spun into an abyss. I could see through a pinhole in front of me, but the buildings of El Tubo and the street revelers eddied around me. El Tubo had morphed into a vacuum tube, churning frothy colors. I followed a pinhole of lucid light, leading me forward through El Tubo's claustrophobic reverie. I stopped where Cinegio became Cuatro de Agosto and stood still, but the swirling continued. Wait, was I standing pat or was I still walking and everyone else was standing in place? It was impossible to discern. I took shallow breaths as my heart rate increased and El Tubo's hazy periphery closed in. What was once a 10-foot-wide street became five feet wide, then two. I pushed through the collapsing El Tubo, but no one else noticed the implosion. They ate and drank, oblivious to the gyrating carnage all around us.

Maybe I'd stood downwind of the riverside hash smokers too long. I don't know what caused El Tubo to morph into a psychedelic wonderland, but I fled as El Tubo spun off into another universe and the seething district spit me out on Calle del Coso. A sign advertising all-night Taco Bell brought me back to reality as the pinhole of clarity expanded and my peripheral vision returned. I didn't wait around for another bout, though, and beat a hasty retreat toward my Airbnb where the *abuela's* preponderance of Catholic art, innumerable crosses, pink upholstery and white doilies would surely safeguard me.

* * *

Our two-and-a-half hour bus ride, not train, departed and arrived on schedule, dropping me and one other passenger at the bridge spanning the Aragón River, opposite Canfranc International Railway Station. The tour group assembled, a five-person group spoke Spanish while two fair-skinned young men stood to the side.

The village purpose built to service Canfranc station clung to the N330A motorway that climbed the 5,354-foot Somport Pass into France. In the distance, the Aragón River's headwaters cascaded from an escarpment. The rounded Pyrenean summits, bedecked in silvery granite cliffs and verdant scrub-oak slopes, perched a few vertical miles away. The white stucco and gray stone building closest to Canfranc station displayed "Se Vende" (for sale) signs. A group of cyclists, clad in rainbow Lycra, pedaled past, oblivious to the decaying depot's existence. Poor Canfranc, a beached battleship, cannons raised toward an imagined enemy.

Tall pine trees had blocked a full view of Canfranc, but as we crossed the entrance bridge with our guide, the decay was unmistakable. Everything needed fresh paint. Debris and trash blew across the front entrance. Dirt and acid-rain-etched, white-stone window sills begged for power-washing. Temporary security fencing and polycarbonate panels covered unused entrances, gates and doorways. Mold grew on corner pilasters while weeds stretched to the sun through every nook and crack. Canfranc wasn't collapsing, had all windows intact and a flawless roof, but the minimal maintenance being done couldn't hide the once-mighty hub's sad deterioration.

Still, Canfranc was arrestingly winsome, Wes Anderson's lost movie set, maybe the most beautiful train station I'd ever seen. Mold, fading paint, weeds and general neglect couldn't hide its ravishing curves, smashing proportions and elegant symmetry. Forget train stations. I was thinking Canfranc was as perfect a building as I'd ever seen, especially given its natural setting.

Somehow the bonny decorative elements blended with the natural terrain, the silvers and greens pouring from the Pyrenees Mountains into Canfranc's backyard complemented the earthy slate roof, beige stucco and curly wrought iron. I'd never witnessed such an exuberant, patterned facade blend with such a dramatic natural setting. A virgin valley before the railway, the gargantuan station coalesced with the green mountains, streaked by long, steep springtime drainages.

"It's 4,000 feet long, has 356 windows and 156 doors, which I think is an underestimate. They did not build it large just to be large, vale? It has twice the facilities of a typical border crossing because it's a combination French-Spanish one, okay? France controlled the north end and Spain operated the south end," said Sophia, our tour guide.

"Okay, each crossing had border control, train maintenance, gauge switching, everything needed to run as a standalone international station. So, it's twice the size by necessity. And it was more than a station, okay? It was a partnership between France and Spain."

As we approached the front, I noticed Sophia wasn't wearing her tour-issued hair net under her tour-issued white hard hat. I lagged the group, taking photographs and studying the elegant green doors. The young man from this morning's bus, a Canadian judging by the maple leaf patch sewn to his Wolfskin backpack, approached me.

"Do you speak English?" he whispered.

I snorted, "Gee, how could you tell?"

"Do you understand her," he pointed to Sophia.

"Yes, mostly," I said.

"So you speak Spanish," he asked.

The poor, lost Canadian soul who shadowed me from that point on was tall and thin, appeared college-aged and wore khaki shorts rolled once and a blue pinstriped, short sleeve collared shirt. He rubbed his chin as his backpack hung from his right shoulder.

"A little," I replied. "Do you?"

"None," he said, smiling. He held his face aloft. "But I had to see this place!" He raised his arms.

"I know, right?" I agreed, also in awe. "It's wonderful."

"Will you translate a little for me? Help me with the gist. After she's done speaking, of course," he asked.

"Yeah, no worries. Rory," I extended my right hand. "Nice to meet you."

"Ah, thank you. Jacob," he said. "Likewise."

We entered the building through the main green doors with two-by-six glass panes, identical to the several dozen other green doors, except it had an arched transom window with a sunburst design. The others had rectangular transoms matching the panes. The smell of dust prevailed as we gathered in the lobby.

Sophia tucked black hair strands behind her ear and under her white construction helmet. I resisted advising her that a lovely hair net would do that for her.

"Welcome to the lobby," Sophia said, once again tucking hair strands under her hard hat. Sans hair net, I had genuine concerns about how her thick, unkempt hair might accelerate Canfranc's demise. A millennium from now, would archaeologists excavating Canfranc stumble across her errant hairs and surmise a lackadaisical hair-net policy ruined this once magnificent edifice? "This was the central passenger hub with cafés and shops."

Photographs and dioramas made the station feel like a museum to itself. The grandeur of the past was evident with fine plaster moldings, hardwood wainscoting and vintage ticket booths. Gargantuan glass windows and skylights, brushed cement, classicist pillars and déco woodwork and ironwork marked the interior's inspired design.

"The idea for an alternative rail route through the Pyrenees had been discussed since the 1850s. Two companies—Midi Francés and Norte de España—jointly developed the proposal. From there, the idea for

Canfranc was born."

Sophia lectured for another few minutes about the private-public endeavor and how World War I slowed construction before the eventual 1928 ribbon cutting. Three years later, it caught fire. That's when folks introduced the derisive moniker "Titanic of the Mountains," and Canfranc has spiraled downward ever since.

"Okay, we can't go beyond the lobby, unfortunately. There are construction projects ongoing," she said.

Construction? I stifled a laugh. I saw no construction workers, no construction materials, no scaffolding, no engineers, no flags, no chalk lines, indeed, no evidence of construction, ongoing or not. "Construction projects," I could only assume, was code for "the roof may fall down on you."

Jacob nodded at my translation, then looked around for corroboration of ongoing construction.

"What construction," he wondered.

"Indeterminate," I replied, opening my eyes wide.

French influences abounded, from the mansard roof to the interior fleur-de-lis ironwork, the abundance of natural light and seamless woodwork. Lead architect Ramírez de Dampierre studied in Paris, which could explain why the style and the structure of the station resembled the Musée d'Orsay. The interior was designed with all the recognizable elements of classical Romanesque, though it screamed French. I couldn't shake the feeling Canfranc belonged in Paris, not the Pyrenees.

As Parisian as it felt, the overarching impression remained one of neglect. The lobby was taking an unearned retirement, a public employee who skipped 50 years of work but still received a golden watch. In my head, I christened the style "exuberant desolation."

"Are you traveling alone?" I asked Jacob as we trailed the group through semicircular arches toward the rail yard.

"No, I'm with two friends from university. They missed the bus, sleeping off hangovers...El Tubo last night."

"Yup, tell me about it. I tumbled into an intergalactic time warp in El Tubo last night," I commiserated.

"A what?"

Sophia straightened her hard hat, cramming more wild hairs behind her ear.

"During World War II, okay, Canfranc was an important smuggling route for French Jews and others persecuted by Nazi Germany. Max Ernst and Marc Chagall were spirited from France through Canfranc.

"Spain was neutral, but used Canfranc to play both sides, okay? The Nazis traded French wheat for Spanish iron ore. Hitler also sold German gold bars for Spanish foreign currency the government received from selling tungsten to the Allies. As a key crossing point and center for spies and espionage, okay, Canfranc earned a new nickname: Casablanca in the Pyrenees.

"And, yes, before you ask, because I said Nazis and gold in the same sentence, of course, Canfranc has a Nazi gold conspiracy. Happy hunting. Okay." Sophia and the group laughed.

"Huh?" murmured Jacob.

"She said there's Nazi gold buried here, so watch your step," I winked.

Two rusted rail cars sat abandoned on the second track. Graffiti covered the machine shop/workshop walls, and the equipment shed roofs had partially collapsed. Though another security fence prevented further inspection, I imagined they'd make superb candidates for those promised construction projects. Ruptures, weeds and missing brick trim signaled the decline of Canfranc's massive 650-foot-long platforms awaiting passenger throngs that will never return.

"This was the scene of utter chaos," Sophia said.

Sophia told an animated tale, punctuated with many a "vale," of late trains, misplaced luggage and interminable border waits. Instead of easing transfers, Canfranc became a bottleneck. Then the post-WWII animosity between de Gaulle's democratic France and Franco's Spanish dictatorship spurred a quarter century of border militarization, marked by myriad bunkers and trench lines dotting the landscape around Canfranc. Investment declined and the line became disused.

I tilted my head toward Jacob's ear and whispered, "The rail yard was a cluster, an abject failure. Plus, after World War II, the two countries hated each other."

Sophia brought it all home. "A derailment on the French side in March 1970 destroyed a critical bridge and the French shut the unpopular, money-losing line. The French absconded and this is what we have today: A nearly abandoned Canfranc, Spain's most beautiful mistake."

Only 45 minutes after it started, hardly enough time to appreciate anyone's most beautiful mistake let alone Spain's, the tour concluded. Sophia ushered us from the station grounds, shepherding the group over the Aragón River. Lingering alone in Canfranc is forbidden. Because of all the ongoing construction, I'm sure.

But I wasn't done with it.

"Hey, are you taking the train to Zaragoza?" I asked Jacob. He nodded.

"Vale," I said, mimicking Sophia's verbal crutch. "I'm going for a hike up there," I pointed to a stone pile on the mountainside behind Canfranc, a pile my phone's GPS app told me was a *refugio*, or hiker's hut. "Would you like to come?"

"Up there, eh? Think we can make it?" Jacob asked.

I laughed, "Doubtful, but let's try."

"Looks pretty steep," he said. Using GPS, the route to the 7,000-foot mountain refuge gained 4,000 feet over five miles, with more switchbacks than I cared to count.

"Um, it's not so bad," I lied.

Just a few minutes from the trailhead, we came across bunkers, as Sophia had promised. Franco's soldiers built the concrete fortifications into the hillside, camouflaged with trees and mossy stones. The embrasures pointed at Canfranc station with reinforced cement trenches running parallel to the train tracks. Pines, oaks and beech trees filled the forest canopy. A couple miles in, the trail switchbacked up a dry ravine to a leafy ridgeline, and the hut came into sight. The 8,439-foot La Moleta Mountain monitored our ascent.

Jacob sweated and gasped for breath. I extended my hand and pulled him over a rocky outcrop blocking the trail.

"Thanks Rory. I'm in terrible shape. Not used to this heat," he said, gulping air.

We reached the mountain hut about an hour later, collapsing against an outside stone wall and guzzling our water bottles as sweat permeated our t-shirts. The afternoon sunshine blistered through a cloudless sky. The three-week heat wave had abated elsewhere, but with temperatures in Canfranc pushing 90 degrees, Spain's stubborn summer refused to relent.

The ramshackle stone hut could've been a storm refuge for shepherds in centuries past. Whether it had, the hut was now a hiker's paradise. The mortar between the irregular, uncut stones had been recently repointed and a green metal roof kept the rain out. A knotty pine door and matching window shutters sealed out the wind, offering the exhausted hiker an overnight respite, complete with unparalleled views of mountains and one spectacular, forgotten train station.

The perspective was incredible. Across the valley, waterfalls fed tributaries of the Aragón, while ski lifts dangled from cables up the valley near 5,354-foot Somport Pass, a full thousand feet lower than where we now stood. The Pyrenees were captivating, but I had climbed till my feet burned not for mountain views, but for a bird's-eye perspective of Canfranc. Only from above could I truly grasp its scale.

"That's the hardest hike I've ever done," Jacob said, still catching his breath.

"Yup, it was a beast. Where are you from? Toronto?" I asked.

"A town not far from Toronto. How'd you know?" he replied, pouring his water bottle over his head.

I chuckled. "Lucky guess. But you did great, man. A little hotter, more mountainous than Ontario. Do much hiking in Canada?" I asked, grinning.

"No, never. I'm a, I'm not much of an outdoors person. But this," he said, nodding in agreement with himself and expanding his arms wide. "This is amazing. I can't believe we made it up here."

"Yeah, it's pretty great. And, hey, now's your chance to become a hiker," I said.

Earlier, between wheezing and wiping sweat from our faces, he'd divulged details about his yearlong, round-the-world adventure. Joined by his two best friends, they had started two weeks ago in Great Britain. After Spain, they would cross the Straits of Gibraltar to Africa then to India and Asia.

"You're traveling, mate. You can be whatever you want. This trip is your chance. Maybe you're a hiker now," I encouraged, and he shrugged.

"You never know. Your trip is just beginning. Mine's ending, but I could continue traveling forever. Oh, lucky you, to be 23 and traveling the world. I swear if I close my eyes," I closed my eyes. "I'm 23 again. I'm stepping on the tarmac in Langkawi, Malaysia. Oppressive heat and humidity hits me like a gut punch. All around the airport, green, tree-covered limestone crags on one side, the turquoise waters of the Andaman Sea on the other. Nothing but adventure ahead, a trip with no return date."

Jacob nursed multiple heel blisters as we waited outside Canfranc for our departure train. I made one last set of notes, observing the elegant intersection of the mansard roof and central pendant's curved slate roof, sloping inward, with four pinnacles arrayed on the flanks. The third-floor gabled dormer windows with eclectic Beaux-Arts style trim work could've been stripped from a French palace or Paris' 7th arrondissement. Out front, a lonely Renfe sign was tacked over the outer gated entrance, as if reminding people that, yep, it was still a railway station.

The diminutive train pulled into the platform, releasing three passengers before Jacob and I hopped on the lone passenger carriage. The red-and-white rectangular box lurched forward, and soon Canfranc was out of view, the mountaintops growing smaller in the distance.

I leaned against the window glass and pondered Canfranc's lessons. An overzealous Spain overbuilt an overzealous train station that was already obsolete when it opened. Is that it? What else could I learn from this handsome debacle?

Is the lesson purely ideological? Expecting a democracy (France) that was invaded and occupied by a Fascist neighbor (Germany) to fix a bridge with their other Fascist neighbor (Spain) comes across as a wee bit optimistic.

For all its symbolism, Canfranc failed for practical reasons, namely its impracticality at solving a complex border crossing. Canfranc isn't a failure in international relations or cross-border European cooperation. It was just a bad idea, executed with stunning brilliance. Canfranc is the Belgium of European railway infrastructure, the Continent's most successful failed station.

Renewing the international line would be a welcome sign (as would letting modern computers take a crack at that whole border-crossing logistics problem). And a revival sure seems possible if not inevitable. In 2014, France and Spain agreed to refurbish the line, paving the way for international service. EU funds arrived in 2019 and officials want the rail line operational by 2026. Of the myriad projects restarting the line requires, including revamping old bridges, earthworks and viaducts, both countries quickly agreed to fund a critical piece of new infrastructure: A modern, smaller train station to replace Canfranc.

Barcelona

Other than a few nighttime revelers keeping the party alive, Zaragoza slumbered at 6 a.m. as I trekked through old town toward Zaragoza-Goya train station. My beard itched, reminding me I hadn't shaved all trip. Outside old town, Zaragoza's boulevards grew broad, leafy and as straight as their Roman predecessors'. I walked the empty tram tracks that sliced through the median. Ten-story buildings with ground floor shops lined either side of Gran Via, but nothing was open. That's okay, I told myself. The station, like all European train stations, would have an open café serving espresso and pastries.

Opened in 2012, subterranean Zaragoza-Goya station was a steel-and-glass portal sitting beneath a wavy green roof. This miniature station offered a gorgeous example of blending contemporary, organic, formless design with the squares and rectangles of central Zaragoza. Yet few tourists will ever see Goya since it serves regional trains, not the high-speed lines leading to Madrid and Barcelona.

As I descended the escalator, I wondered if anyone—tourists or locals—ever see this station. It was ghostly quiet. Not a soul around. Most distressingly, not a café or coffee counter in the whole place. I hunted everywhere with the few minutes remaining before the train arrived, but Goya station shattered Europe's universal truth, which now required an asterisk: You can always find a decent pastry and espresso drink in European train stations, except Zaragoza-Goya.

I had stocked up on train-picnic supplies last night. In my backpack, I had lunch, snacks, wine and sparkling water, but neither coffee nor breakfast. Somehow, I'd survive the five-hour slow train. The high-speed AVE trains demolish this leg in less than two hours, but the slow trains ply the old Iberian gauge, first laid in 1861, making two dozen stops over five hours. It would mark the longest single leg of my trip.

Despite their clunky cars and inefficient routes, dawdling slow trains offered a slice of local life not found on the tourist- and business-heavy high speed routes. I enjoyed watching families and commuters board, noting how they dressed, acted and what languages and dialects they spoke. By forgoing reservations, the slow trains also encouraged spontaneity, without which I may not have ventured into Brittany and Basque Country. Plus, well, I was coming around to the journey-is-the-destination way of thinking. Why not pack a picnic and milk every rail jaunt for as long as possible? European train rides feature fabled rural views of farms, mountains, stone villages, so why would I deprive myself of that on a high-speed train? Slowness, I'd realized, is a privilege, and speed for speed's sake is a distraction.

Sleeker and more aerodynamic than the commuter train serving Canfranc, the diesel-powered articulated Renfe train pulled into Goya. The cars featured interiors straight from the 1980s with the 2x2 seating plans smothered in aquamarine. Upholstery, window curtains, arm rests, carpeting, everything aquamarine.

I passed rows of unoccupied seats until I found the café car and ordered a coffee from the half-asleep bartender. The indifferent barista jerked and cranked a drinkable espresso, which I brought two cars forward. Soon, my laptop and notebook received the caffeine's business end when an email arrived from my Airbnb host in Barcelona:

Hi Rory,

Im doing the camino of Santiago but i hurt my foot and will be back in bcn tonight. Would you share the apartment and book a single room? The only thing now i have to try to change price if is ok with you. It would be 40 eu per Day. It will be only me in the apartment. hope its no problem. :-)

...

Hola Francesca,

No worries. 40 euros is good. Excited to meet you!

Cheers

It wasn't a question; she was informing me the two-bedroom I booked for myself was now a private room in a shared apartment. Such is Airbnb life. Forty euros a night, though, roommate or not, was a killer deal in Barcelona's uber-hip El Born neighborhood. While Francesca was apologetic, sort of, about crashing my stay, I genuinely looked forward to meeting the Gothic Quarter's rare local. At the very least, I expected solid restaurant recommendations.

I just hoped Francesca wasn't crazy.

The train paralleled the Ebro, meandering only slightly less than the serpentine river, into Catalonia before breaking east at Mora La Nueva. From here, the Ebro flows south into the Mediterranean Sea while the train chugs northeast to the coast at Tarragona before pulling into Barcelona-Sants station.

At every stop, the car gained and lost passengers, maintaining near-peak capacity the whole route, though no one had sat next to me when we jerked into Samper. Two older Moroccan men, with sun-worn skin like leather work boots and wearing embroidered white *djellabas*, slid into the row one ahead and over from me. They exchanged thoughts in soft-spoken Arabic. A pair of middle-aged, smartly dressed couples with roller bags boarded in Caspe, sitting behind me. Two young men wearing green mechanic jumpsuits departed the seats across the aisle after riding half-awake for two stops. Then at Flix, a fair-skinned mother, wearing a blue knee-length skirt, carrying a toddler on her right hip and corralling a six-year-old boy in front of her, took their place.

The six-year-old held a soccer ball and eyed me, unable to resist my red hair's magnetic draw, while his mother slipped into the window seat, cooing the toddler. The woman's white, short-sleeve blouse revealed thin, defined arms. She asked her son to sit down, which he ignored, continuing to peer at me and juggling the ball back and forth in his hands. He wore a minion's t-shirt, jeans and retro-Adidas kicks.

As the train staggered from the station, then found its iron footing, the brown-haired boy could no longer wait. He dropped the black-and-green soccer ball, let it bounce once, then blasted it straight through the empty aisle seat's foot well into my calf.

"Goooooooooaaaaaal" I said, dribbling the ball before it ran into the aisle.

He fell into his seat head-first, roaring with laughter. His mother looked up and smiled, then continued cooing the toddler lounging in her lap. The six-year-old regained his composure as I tilted my head and looked at the soccer ball. His eyes followed mine to his prized possession, now pinned under my left foot.

"Cuántos años tienes?" I asked him, as he debated his next move.

"Seis," he replied, holding up five fingers with his right hand before quickly adding his left pointer.

"Ah, seis. Eres muy viejo, no?"

He closed his eyes, nodded and said, "Sí," with great conviction.

He bent his knees and guarded his foot well like a goalie. I pointed to the luggage rack above his seat and said, "Qué es eso?" Then I flipped the ball into the air with my left big toe.

However, unlike the very accomplished six-year-old athlete, my return volley flew astray, caromed off the overhead luggage bin, and knocked the fez hat off the Moroccan man sitting in the aisle seat before settling on his lap. He flinched and shouted, "Akk!," then looked at me while searching the aisle for his hat. I waved my hand, taking credit for the errant lob, then covered my face with both hands as the boy fell backward laughing, nearly taking his toddler sister with him.

The silvered Moroccan man laughed and smiled, reapplied his hat and bounced the ball, not to me, but behind him to the six-year-old, who blasted it at me once again. This time, however, I used my hands and bounce-passed the soccer ball back to him. This continued until they departed at beachfront Vilaseca. I waved adiós as a wave of nerves washed over me. My skin tingled, thinking about kicking a soccer ball with my son and hugging my wife in a few days.

In short order, however, my taste buds tingled, thanks to a succulent picnic spread. I uncorked a red Somontano wine from Pirineos Winery, the Ebro River valley's northernmost vineyard. I poured the tempranillo-moristel-parraleta-cabernet blend into a disposable plastic cup I'd requisitioned from my Airbnb. The ruby red Somontano tasted like char-roasted jam as I unwrapped the cheese, sausage and bread, a crusty round farmhouse demi-loaf that I'd sealed tight in its brown paper bag.

I sliced through the white Penicillium candidum mold that gives the Benasque cheese its chalky rind. The artisan cheese promised it was "*moldeado a mano,*" molded by hand. The hard, unpasteurized cow's milk had a buttery texture and a tangy, salty flavor. Its earthy aroma filled the carriage. I swished the slice down with a sip of Somontano and removed the casing from the wild boar ("*jabali*") sausage. The 330-gram link opened with little effort after pulling the blue-yellow starter string. The informative sausage wrapper showed precisely how the sausage gets made, depicting a hunting dog assaulting an irate wild boar. The chorizo-style link tasted robust and nutty with a hint of paprika. I sliced the sausage and cheese and placed them on bread chunks, chasing each wedge with a gulp of wine. For dessert, I bit into a *melocotón de calanda,* Aragón's famous peach variety. It exploded in my mouth, sending juices down my chin. Oh, so this is what a peach should taste like, I thought.

As I refilled my plastic cup, an elderly man embarked at Tarragona, and I had my first seat mate of the entire journey. He slid a well-used cerulean-blue suitcase into the overhead storage.

"Want some?" I asked, pointing to the Somontano. It was several minutes after 11 a.m. and the morning wine had awakened my Spanish.

"Yes, thank you, but only a little," he replied, pinching his forefinger and thumb together.

I withdrew the other clear plastic cup I'd re-appropriated and filled it an inch high with the currant-colored tipple. Víctor savored the Somontano, remarking, "Bien, bien," after each sip.

"I'm visiting my son in Barcelona," he said. "And you?"

"Visiting Barcelona for a couple days, then flying home to the States."

"Ah, yes, okay. That explains your American Spanish. At first, I thought you were English," he smiled and sipped his wine.

We chatted about our families, my colonial Spanish colliding with his Castilian, and showed each other photos, which I did on my phone while he pulled out prints from his wallet. He had two sons and a daughter. One son and the daughter lived in Germany. The conversation moved to Spain's economy ("*patético*"), politics (he voted for Podemos) and history, a topic for which he displayed particular enthusiasm. We discussed Canfranc, Basques, Catalans and, of course, the Franco dictatorship, a cloud which seems to hover over all Spanish history discussions.

"Spain is a country," he said, finishing his wine refill and dabbing his lips with a cocktail napkin, "where the past is always present."

* * *

From Barcelona Sants station, notable only for its forgettable office-building appearance and vast connections elsewhere in Spain and throughout Europe, I emerged from the Jaume I Metro station into what I can only describe as a rolling bachelor party. Barcelona's Gothic Quarter was packed with travelers, young and old, cruise-ship tourists, European, American and Asian, and every European Millennial not living in Berlin. This was Amsterdam levels of tourist merrymaking. Dodging vast groups and intoxicated revelers, I patrolled the Gothic Quarter, looping around the Barcelona Cathedral to the grungy-brick Basílica de Santa Maria del Pi en route to Las Ramblas and my favorite spot in all Barcelona, the Boqueria Market.

Ramblas, however, streamed with people. It was like crossing a raging river, a torrent of sunburned cruise-ship tourists, African immigrants selling plastic souvenirs, swerving pedicabs and Instagrammers framing the perfect photo. I almost bailed then and there, but the Boqueria was only a block up and so I persevered, wading through the morass until I stood under the open-air market's heavenly metal roof.

The market, unofficially opened in the 13th century, gained government recognition in 1853. Added in 1914, Catalan Modernist Antoni de Falguera designed the trademark iron arches and metal roof, dotted with colored glass. Falguera isn't as well-known as his contemporary Antoni Gaudí, but his work along with that of his mentor, Josep Puig i Cadafalch, is just as significant in Catalan Modernist architecture. Of the many city buildings and townhouses the two designed, the Boqueria roof is their crowning achievement.

But that's as close as I got. Tourists streamed out from under the roof drinking smoothies and beers in plastic cups as additional travelers plowed into the overcrowded market. There was pushing and shoving. Market sellers looked stressed and tired. I heard English more than Spanish. The bars were bustling. Cocktails, tapas and smoothies sat in piles on counters. Somewhere in there, from past trips, I recalled fishmongers, green grocers, cheese sellers and other ingredient-based stalls, but today it looked like one rollicking bar with tourists toting takeaway chorizo-on-sticks.

I backtracked, avoiding the Boqueria Disneyland, and crossed back over Ramblas and gathered myself after stumbling across Sant Felip Neri Square. A bronze plaque explained why this rustic square goes unnoticed by tourists. But I needed to catch my breath after reeling through the Ramblas. I sat on the Romanesque fountain's white-granite capstone. This idyllic square revealed its ghosts, as I scanned the pockmarks on Church of Saint Philip Neri and a bronze remembrance plaque. On January 30, 1938, during the Spanish Civil War's Siege of Barcelona, Franco's Fascist friends, Nazi Germany and Mussolini's Italy, joined forces to carpet bomb the city. Two bombs fell on this square, killing 42 people, most of whom were children holed up inside the church's makeshift orphanage.

I felt their presence in that wounded square. They huddled in despair, the first humans to experience war's new toy: carpet bombing. I heard their cries, saw the blood pooling on the cobblestones. I saw the pain and terror in their souls as they wailed, cries interrupted by concussive explosions and the sound of metal shrapnel ricocheting off stone and eviscerating flesh.

The past...ever present in Spain.

* * *

After dark, I searched for tapas. Or were they pintxos? Pintxos are a Basque creation, but Barcelona isn't Basque. It's Catalan. In fact, it's the capital of Catalonia. While Catalonia's Roman ancestry gives it an identity, greater Aragon, however, was an expressly French creation with no real ethnography. To check Islamic incursions, the Franks set up militarized rump states south of the Pyrenees, one being the County of Barcelona which would merge with the Kingdom of Aragon.

However, while Catalans have their own culture and Romance

language, Barcelona has always been a Mediterranean melting pot. So, travelers will find tapas being served next door to authentic pintxos down the street from pasta joints, sushi bars, taco restaurants, vegetarian North African stands and, of course, ubiquitous burger restaurants. In boozy, bacchanalian Barcelona, few seem to understand, notice or care about the tapas-pintxos distinction. Jamón is jamón, after all.

Barcelona's Gothic Quarter was partying at 9 p.m., but the streets were markedly less crowded after sundown as revelers migrated inside packed bars. The sunburned set, presumably, had returned to cruise ship buffets, where they were certainly not respecting the dissimilitude between tapas and pintxos.

I sated my appetite and thirst at several stops along Carrer de la Boqueria and made for El Born and my Airbnb, somewhere north of Mercat de Santa Caterina. This area is a neighborhood called La Ribera, whereas El Born is closer to the coast. Both are subsets of the Sant Pere district. Although, nowadays, even locals refer to the entire neighborhood as El Born.

Along the way, on a dark, cobblestone alley, I smelled weed smoke wafting down the street. I paused and realized that a Barcelona cannabis club, private bars where it's legal to buy and smoke marijuana, held court on the other side of the bronze-handled door. After a mere nanosecond, a tall, thin man in his 20s made eye contact with me.

"Do you want a card? I live here. I can take you inside," he said in perfect English. Barcelona's cannabis clubs are limited to residents and their friends. Anyone with a membership can sponsor their "friends" with a day pass. Ten euros buys a friendship.

"Ahhh," I was curious what was happening behind that door, but I could imagine it—overpriced weed, green clouds, googly-eyed tourists. "Gracias, mate. I'm tired."

He smiled and passed me a business card, introducing himself as a "fixer," with his WhatsApp on it. "If you change your mind," he said.

I trudged to the fifth floor and tiptoed into the dark, silent Airbnb around midnight, following Francesca's WhatsApp directions to my bedroom just past the kitchen. I pulled open the room's double doors and flopped into bed, careful not to awaken her, whoever she might be.

* * *

Lucid morning sunshine illuminated the room, rousing me from slumber as I squinted at my phone. It said 7:03 a.m. I sat up and examined the room. The white walls and white sheets were the only things not splashed in color. The comforter was a checkerboard of blue, green and orange. A lime green beanbag chair sat in the corner. Above me, Buddhist prayer flags and exuberant red, orange and yellow tapestries embellished the walls and ceiling. It was as if the entire Holi Festival, India's pigment party, had gotten derailed in Mumbai and exploded here.

The room was scorching already, a puddle of sweat soaked the sheets. I pulled on a t-shirt and shorts and stepped into the short hallway outside my bedroom, rubbing my eyes as I stumbled toward the living room. My eyesight focused, and I realized I wasn't alone. I stopped a half-step short of striding into my host, who was bent over backward in an arch projecting her pelvis upward. She was barefoot, had long, curly black hair and wore lilac yoga pants with a white sports bra over her svelte body, looking rather spry for someone with an injured foot.

"Oh, gosh, I'm sorry. Didn't see ya there." I spun around and retreated to the kitchen as she laughed and followed. Six glass bulk food bins containing grains and nuts sat on the kitchen counter. She skipped into the kitchen. It seemed her injured foot had miraculously recovered.

"Francesca," I shook her right hand. "Mucho gusto."

"Yes, welcome," she said in a deep voice with accented English, her

"Y"s containing a hint of "J."

We faced each other at the rectangular, pressed-wood IKEA table. She had a faded blue tattoo on her left index finger and round brown eyes with spindly eyelashes.

"So, how was the Camino? Are you sad about leaving early?" I asked as she pulled her right knee to her chest.

"Yes, it was wonderful. I walked for six days." Her big brown eyes circled the room. "And I'm okay leaving early. You know, I had the most amazing experience," she said and paused.

"Two days ago, I was walking, and I came upon a cow standing by a fence, looking at me. And I looked him straight in the eyes," she continued, pointing to her eyes and mine, assuming I was the cow in this scenario. "We had a moment, through our eyes, an understanding. I found a truth in his eyes. It was magic!"

"A cow?" I scratched my head. "What did it say?" I smirked.

"He's a cow. Cows don't talk," she replied matter-of-fact.

"Oh."

"What did you do yesterday?" she asked.

"Last night I walked around a bit, tapas and beers. It's been years since I've been to Barcelona and I couldn't believe how busy it is. So many tourists. Wow." She rolled her eyes and nodded. "Oh, I went to the Boqueria. It was so crowded I didn't even go in."

She looked at her watch. "Yes, now is the time for la Boqueria. Come!"

I rose from the table and she was already pulling on a tank top and holding her purse.

* * *

Today's 8 a.m. Boqueria was a much different market than yesterday afternoon's Boqueria. Vendors tidied their displays, and butchers sharpened knives on long steel rods as delivery men and the market's first shoppers streamed through the fragrant and frantic maze. The wet concrete floor was divided by a central oval surrounded by 11x11 rows of stands of various shapes and sizes fitted together like Tetris pieces. Other than dedicating the central oval to seafood, the layout followed little rhyme or reason. "Photos No!" signs adorned some counters. We nipped lattes at Quiosc Modern, a standalone bar-café near the seafood oval, letting the market and ourselves awaken before strolling the aisles.

"Maybe the milk came from your Camino cow!" I grinned, pointing at my latte. She rolled her eyes.

Fishmongers set their shiny catches upon beds of crunchy pellet ice while charcuterie shops racked jamón legs. Inquisitive abuelas toted two-wheeled metal shopping carts behind them, carefully examining meat, seafood and produce. The world of food springing up around us was mesmerizing as more and more stands filled their coffers: poultry, dried and candied fruit, ham hocks, olives, seafood, fresh fruit, vegetables, offal, bread. Over 250 vendors slung local and foreign fare with a seemingly equal mix offering prepared hot foods, takeaway and groceries.

At a bar on the opposite side of the oval, I gobbled a small plate of eggs, caramelized foie gras and wild mushrooms dusted with fresh herbs while Francesca filled her canvas shoulder bag with onions, leeks and peas from farmer's stands.

"Rory, oranges from Valencia," she ushered me toward a three-foot-tall, sloping battlement of citrus. "Do you want one?"

"I don't know, citrus gets sticky," I replied, still savoring the lingering forest-mushroom piquancy.

"Pfft. Smell one. We can't worry about stickiness when something smells," she inhaled, "and tastes this incredible."

The aproned fruit seller stood by, smiling. Francesca lifted the orange to my nose. The aroma hit me from inches away, like pungent nose poetry. It smelled like a Mediterranean sunrise over a whitewashed *costa* village.

"Okay, you're right. I must have one. Maybe just to smell it," I said, caressing the marigold orb.

"Señor, una naranja por favor," she said, in wildly sexy Spanish.

"Hey, I can handle that." I said and turned to the fruit vendor. "Ah, una naranja por favor," I said in wildly pedestrian Spanish. I faced Francesca. "Oh, you do it better."

She scoffed, tossed back her thick raven hair and continued hunting fresh fruit and veggies at another farmer's stand, while I sniffed my new orange. Francesca sorted through piles of vegetables, scooping up organic purple garlic, rainbow-colored chilis from North Africa and pitted-brown mushrooms freshly harvested from Catalan forests.

I stalked picnic supplies. A husband-wife charcuterie team sliced my 100 grams of *jamón iberico* into delicate shavings while I watched, then thoughtfully wrapped it in waxed-brown butcher paper. I gathered roasted *largueta* almonds, grown in western Catalonia, a wedge of earthy caved-aged Garrotxa goat cheese, one seed-covered demi-baguette, dried strawberries from Andalusia and a chocolate-caramel bar.

We sipped Cava and reviewed our morning haul at a bar near the Rambla entrance. The cresting morning sun brought the day's first tourists, gripping smoothies and smartphones.

"Man, Francesca, the hordes of people pouring into this market yesterday were insane. People bumping into each other and huge groups standing in the aisles. Yeesh," I said, recounting yesterday's horrors.

"I know. This is why I come early, always before nine and gone by 10," she sipped her golden bubbly. "Last year, the city passed a rule banning tour groups in Boqueria. But, look," she waved her left hand at the open-air market that lacked doors, walls or really any enclosure other than Falguera's glorious roof. "How can you stop them?"

We chatted about our families and backgrounds. She was astounded to hear I had a nine-year-old son at home.

"We are the same age, but you have a nine-year-old. Ay yai yai," she said, eyes wide.

"And how about you? Do you have siblings? And your name, Francesca, sounds Italian, right?" I asked.

"Yes, it's Italian," she replied.

"Oh, is your mother or father Italian?"

"Yes, my mother and my father are Italian. So are my two brothers. So am I." She grinned.

"Oh, okay, wow, you speak perfect Spanish. I didn't know. Where in Italy are you from?" I asked.

"Perugia," she answered.

"And is that where your family is? Your parents still live there?" I asked.

"Yes, my father and brothers live there. One of my brothers," she sighed, "he still lives at the house of my father. But my mother is in heaven."

"Ah, I'm really sorry. Losing a family member is so hard. I know how you feel. I lost a brother many years ago."

"Oh, Rory, I'm also sorry. Yes, my mother passed many years ago, too."

"Cheers to those who can't be with us." We clinked Cava glasses in silence.

"Do you believe you'll see your brother again?" she asked.

"No," I said, shaking my hand and gazing through the market. "Will you see your mother again?"

"Yes, of course, in heaven," she replied, twisting a curl that had fallen between her eyes. We sipped in silence and appreciated the now-bustling Ramblas.

"Rory, I'm sorry I showed up like this. Thank you for being cool about it. I really wasn't expecting to leave the Camino." She rolled her eyes and exhaled. "Well, before the Camino, I had an argument with my boyfriend because he is moving back to Italy. I regretted it and left the Camino early to make up and say goodbye. He leaves in a couple days. But after I asked you, I was like, oh no, what if he's crazy?"

"Haha, no worries. But, yeah, I thought the same thing—hope she's not crazy." I swirled the Cava remnants in my glass.

"Well, I'm not crazy," she said, tilting her head and staring at me.

"Not yet," I corrected her while raising my eyebrows.

As the Cava ran dry, I noticed fast-food stands, timing their opening with the tourist arrival, setting up deep-fried takeaway. They opened cardboard boxes and Tupperwares of chicken nuggets, calzones, ribs, falafel, crepes, jamón in cups, chorizo on sticks, round personal pizzas, hot dogs, French fries, fruit cups and smoothies, all of it but the smoothies arrived packaged and precooked from somewhere off-site. I contemplated how long El Mercat de San Josep de La Boqueria, as it's properly known, can balance this split personality—local grocery market in the morning and throbbing technicolor tourist daydream in the afternoon.

I checked my watch. Parc Güell opened in 30 minutes, so we split with a hearty "ciao," Francesca to stash her farm bounty and save her relationship and me to wander Antoni Gaudí's perplexing masterpiece.

* * *

Parc Güell opened in 1914, just in time for its architect Antoni Gaudí to turn his full attention to his magnum opus, the still-under-construction Sagrada Família church. Parc Güell is perhaps the best completed vision of Gaudí's genius that's open to the public. The park comprises two areas: the free forest zone and the pay-to-play monument zone. Two sandcastle towers flank the main entrance on Carrer d'Olot, both with vaporous lollipop crowns, guiding visitors up the swooshing Dragon Stairway to the famed terrace and Gaudí's Greek theater.

Catalan Modernism's most famous practitioner, Gaudí pushed the style to its breaking point, fusing his love for Gothic with his obsession for perverting ruled geometric surfaces. To grasp Gaudí's genius requires understanding this obsession with twisting and warping ruled facets, surfaces through which straight lines connect from edge to edge. Ruled surfaces are obvious in squares and rectangles, where every surface is a flat plane, but can be impossible to detect in wavy works like Gaudí's.

Gaudí's free-flowing, curvy organic shapes, dripping in ornamental style, look irrational, playful and as impromptu as the Mediterranean's surface currents when they're the opposite. Every undulating surface in Parc Güell is planned with mathematical precision, every kinked plane remains geometrically ruled and scrupulously measured, maintaining proportional symmetry and alignment. Add in Gaudí's ebullient tile and glass ornamentation, inspired by North Africa's dye markets, Moorish Mudéjar art and Catalonia's coastal-mountain geography, and Parc Güell is an outdoor space unlike anywhere else in the world.

Plus, it offers breathtaking views. Meandering to the park's summit, the Turó de les Tres Creus observation point rewarded me with a Barcelona that unfolded from my toes to the Mediterranean Sea. The city's tight 18th- and 19th-century urban grids crashed into the Gothic Quarter's tangled warren while the 583-foot Montjuïc, dangling a cable car, overlooked the urban sprawl, as if daring the city to scale its forested slopes. I ate my picnic, the silky jamón one dainty shaving at a time, in the northern forest zone.

Returning to El Born, I bought my wife a shirt and skirt from Biaitee

Master Blaster, one of El Born's many boutiques. I could tell from the window display that I couldn't go wrong shopping for my hippie-chic wife here. Master Blaster's owner, Beate, besides being a fan of *Mad Max Thunderdome* (I assumed), was stitching away at her sewing machine in a cramped loft above the retail floor.

"Yes, everything is handmade here. I source many second and leftover fabrics from larger makers. So, describe your wife, her size." She said before sorting through racks of lightweight Bohemian textiles with earthy colors. Luckily, my wife looked a lot like the lean, strong and about-my-height Beate.

I also couldn't go wrong buying my son a Barcelona Football Club jersey, which I did at a gaudy souvenir shop on Avenue de Francesc Cambó en route to the Airbnb.

The brutal afternoon heat demanded I grab my bathing suit (not the vending-machine Speedo) and make tracks for the *playa*. Barcelona's beaches, south of the Olympic Port in the old fishing village of Barceloneta, were almost as crowded as the Gothic Quarter. Dark-skinned immigrants hocked hash, baubles and beach accoutrement. One lanky fella sold sugar-covered donuts, a dozen of which sat balancing on his head. I hid my apartment key in my t-shirt and dove head first through the surf zone. The cool Med hit the spot, and I floated around, careful not to swallow water.

The temperature finally dropped with the sun, and I walked home through Parc de la Ciutadella. I paused at the Baroque Cascada del Parc de la Ciutadella, a triple-level waterfall fountain covered in sandstone statues of mythical creatures, like Venus in a clamshell and griffins that spat water from their mouths.

"Rory?" I heard Francesca's voice behind me.

"Hey, Francesca! What are the odds?" I remarked, turning around.

"Hello! Rory, this is Marco, my friend. He's also Italian you should know."

"I hope that's okay," he added.

Marco and I exchanged greetings and handshakes. We chatted for a minute beside the fountain. Their reconciliation was successful.

"Oh, wow, you went swimming...in the sea." Francesca seemed worried. Marco listened and nodded disapprovingly.

"Well, uh, yes, I did. Probably not the cleanest, huh?"

"I don't know. I don't swim here," she said, looking anxiously at the sea.

Marco interjected, "I swim here. Sometimes. It's fine, Rory."

"Don't worry, I'm going to the apartment for a shower." I stepped back from them and they laughed. Marco wrapped his arm around Francesca's neck and muttered something in Italian that sounded familiar to which Francesca replied, "Sí."

"Rory, Marco moves from Barcelona in two days. Back to Italy. Rome. We are having a beach party tonight, and he asks if you'd like to join us. I know it's your last night, and it's been a long trip, so it's okay to say no. You want to party-party in the Gothic Quarter, right?" She smirked and swung her hips into Marco, grabbing his bicep.

My tongue nearly twisted itself into a pretzel accepting the offer.

"Yes, yes, I'd love to. Thank you so much! What can I bring?" Marco smiled and gave Francesca a see-I-told-you-so look.

I couldn't have dreamt of a better way to spend my last night in Europe.

"Just yourself. And some beer," said Marco, laughing. "Not too much."

"I can do that. Thank you, thank you," I gushed.

"Meet us here," she looked at the fountain, "about 20," Francesca said.

* * *

I clutched two plastic grocery bags bulging with beer cans in each hand as I was introduced to Francesca's and Marco's friends. We'd assembled on Platja del Somorrostro between the Olympic Port and Barceloneta, near to where I swam earlier.

"I swear I'm not an alcoholic. These," I lifted the plastic bags, "are for everyone."

Except everyone ignored me at first. I was not the curiosity I'd assumed or hoped I was. Instead, they lamented Marco's impending departure, then calmly integrated me into proceedings, introducing themselves and their friends and partners. We formed a figure-eight in the sand, opening food containers, passing around paper plates and plastic forks (Francesca cursed the waste) and sweaty beers. I helped Francesca dish out the goods as two Spaniards sitting beside us opened bottles of wine. Someone played pop music on a portable speaker.

I asked Francesca to describe the food as we served it. The first box contained a charcuterie platter of pre-sliced sausages and jamón.

"Oh, not that one yet," she said, popping the lids. "Here, this one first; they go together. This is pà amb tomàquet, like Catalan bruschetta. Hmm, my favorite." She handed me two boxes of Barcelona bruschetta. I slid several pieces on my plate and passed them around. She then shared the charcuterie platter before popping open another container, this one lined in aluminum foil.

"Ha, amazing. Rory, these are calçots, very special onions from Catalonia, roasted in the fire. Very flavorful. See how big they are!" She held up a charred green onion about an inch thick with an eight-inch edible bulbous bottom. "Peel off the burnt layer and enjoy." I took one—its fire-roasted smell was luxurious—and sent the platter forward.

"Oh, the sauce! Drizzle this on the onion," Francesca said. I did as instructed and handed the cup of tomato *romesco* sauce, made with pepper, garlic, almonds and olive oil, to my neighbor.

"Rory, are you ready for this one? Prawns in saffron stew." Francesca's eyes grew wide and she licked her lower lip. The smoky saffron filled the air as soon as she opened the lid. I slid two fist-sized prawns onto my plate.

Francesca opened the next Tupperware and howled, inhaling deeply as she presented the stew.

"Samfaina, Rory. Gorgeous."

"Ah, my favorite," said Marta, a Spanish woman who leaned over Francesca's shoulder. Blonde-streaked brown curly hair fell over her round, wireframe glasses. "This is very popular in Valencia, where I come from. When I smell it, I can remember my mother making it."

"Smells wonderful. What is it?" I asked her.

"Heaven," Marta laughed. "Typically, eggplant and zucchini, cut in very small cubes, added to a sofrito. It's like ratatouille."

"Sofrito...what's that?" I asked.

Marta thought for a moment, her eyes scanned Barcelona's skyline. Lights flipped on in the mid-rises.

"Sofrito is a vegetable base of, typically, garlic, onion, peppers, tomatoes sauteed in olive oil. Cook it on low heat."

"I will also put bay leaves and leeks in my sofrito," added Marta's friend, Julia, as she uncorked a rioja blend.

Steam and earthy aromas rose from the harlequin fare as my paper plate strained under the weight of prawns, veggie stew, an onion as thick as a bicycle handlebar, tomato bread and charcuterie. Soon, I juggled a paper cup of red wine and an opened yellow can of Moritz beer. I rotated between the two drinks, biting into the juicy onion that revealed a mineral-rich flavor. The prawns were fleshy and spicy, a perfect complement to the salty charcuterie.

Through satisfied bites and cherished moans, conversation spun from the delicious food to matters at hand.

"Marco," asked Max, an overdressed 20-something from Essen in

Germany's populous Rhineland. "Why are you leaving us? And why are you leaving so quietly? I just found out from Francesca yesterday. And, wow, the prawns are amazing."

Marco smiled and snapped into a *calçot*, releasing flecks of ash into the air.

"Well, it's a bit last minute. The person renting my apartment in Rome is leaving, and I have to leave my apartment here. They are raising rent. I love living here, but Barcelona has become too expensive. I can work anywhere with my job, as you know." Marco was an IT trainer who worked for corporations all over the world. "And my mother is not doing well. I should be close to her. But, mostly because Barcelona is just too expensive. I can always move back...if you miss me." Marco's permanent grin showed signs of collapsing as he thanked his friends for coming to the party.

The group formed a nearly perfect casserole of Western Europeans: three Spaniards, two Germans, two Italians, one French-Algerian, one Dane, one Belgian and a Brit. And I was the American ginger saffron sprinkled on top. Everyone nodded and agreed about Barcelona's rising cost of living. Several worked for companies that transferred them to Barcelona, a couple bankers and corporate marketers for which the living costs weren't a factor. But the rest chose Barcelona for its lifestyle, including a yoga instructor, language teacher and two salespeople, and they were feeling the pinch. They could live anywhere in the EU, and they'd chosen Barcelona.

"Why Barcelona," I asked. "Why are you all here? I've been through all your countries on my trip. Well, except the UK, but that doesn't count, right?" I turned to Francesca. She smiled and nodded. Everyone agreed: The UK didn't count.

"But why Barcelona?" I pressed.

"Because everyone wants to be in Barcelona," Anders, the Dane, eagerly offered. He turned to one of his local comrades. "Right, Marta?"

Marta nodded in agreement and added, "Por supuesto," before he continued, "Here we have it all: sun, weather, beach, mountains, beautiful people, the best food in Europe." The Italians raised their eyebrows upon hearing this declaration. "And..." He considered Barcelona's last ingredient, something he struggled to put into words, at least English words.

"Una...buena onda?" I suggested.

The Spaniards and Italians nodded in agreement, while the Anglos scratched their chins and considered the proposition.

"What about all the tourists?" I asked.

Eyes rolled, people fell backward into the sand, guffaws thundered like autumnal storms pouring in from the Med.

"Yes, the tourism is crazy," said Marco, "but Barcelona still has, yes, a special onda. Here, they are a little French, a little Spanish, a little Italian and a lot Catalan. Barcelona has a lifestyle unlike anywhere else in Europe."

"Yeah, and jobs," said Marta, her blue shirt sleeves rolled once above the bicep.

Everyone laughed and nodded. Jobs, food, weather. Why not Barcelona?

"And creativity!" said Francesca, chuffed at being the first to say it. "Barcelona's artists are the most creative in the world."

This launched a conversation into Barcelona's gallery artists, street artists, architects, clothiers, chefs. Everyone named recent art exhibitions and films they'd attended or would attend soon, agreeing that Barcelona was Europe's creative volcano.

"Rory, why are you here?" Anders asked. "And where have you been on your journey?"

"I'm just passing through, mate, leaving tomorrow, even before poor Marco here." I rubbed Marco's right shoulder, and we laughed. The pressure fled from Marco's shoulders. He looked at the sky, and

Francesca leaned into his chest. I gave them the 60-second spiel, starting in Copenhagen (Anders' Danish ears perked up), about riding slow trains through France to northern Spain.

"I bought a Eurail Pass, like Interrail, you know, for the first time in 15 years and decided to go, I suppose, with the flow, and not plan much. I went places less popular with Americans and did less-popular things in popular places, like Paris and here.

"And I'm a writer, so I hoped to meet people and have experiences worth writing about. I, ah, I want to tell fun stories from Europe, Europe in 2016." I trailed off, hoping that was sufficient.

"And what did you find? Did you find something to write about, Rory?" Anders said. Christ almighty, his English was better than mine.

I stared at the stars. "Yeah, I'm not so sure. I mean, other than this thing with cats in Amsterdam."

"Cats?"

I chuckled. "Let this be your warning: Beware of cats in Amsterdam." Everyone chuckled and turned to me. "Yeah, a buncha cats got into my Airbnb..." But I'd already lost the crowd.

I shook my head and my grin settled. "But, yes, yes, I think I have a few decent stories. I've met lovely people, like you all. I've learned so, so much, mate. And I, yeah, I found a Europe I thought still existed. Beyond the selfie sticks and tour groups, Europe's the most amazing, interesting continent on Earth because of its people. Because of you." I refrained from launching into a lecture on those mysterious Basques.

"What is your favorite part, Rory?" Anders asked.

The unavoidable question—favorite, best, most memorable, greatest, Instagram-worthy. I knew it was coming.

"Definitely not the cats..." I muttered and opened my eyes wide. "It's right here, right now." I pointed to the sand and smiled. "It's silly, yeah. But over the last few weeks, every day is always the best day. It doesn't really matter where I am or what I'm doing, exactly. The best part is always the here and now, good or bad." I frowned and shook my head. Everyone silently nodded.

"Like today. Today was a perfect day." I looked up. "And after three weeks, this is the perfect ending. Thank you for asking. Thank you for inviting me, Marco."

I raised my beer can. "Salud and ànims!" I had googled how to say cheers in Catalan back at the apartment, thinking it might come in handy.

The party erupted in cheers-ing, using languages near and far.

"Prost!"

"Saluti!"

"Skol!"

"Cheers!"

"Santé!"

"Tchin-tchin!"

After a couple hours, we'd lost a few fellow revelers and had reached the end of the wine and the bottom of the Tupperwares. The beach sat below street level fronting a two-story concrete building with patio restaurants on top and nightclubs on the beach. Francesca corralled us toward the pounding nightclubs.

"We will dance!" she promised. Or threatened, depending on your perspective.

We high-stepped through the beach sand and into a row of dark, cheesy, horrid little dance clubs spilling onto Platja del Somorrostro. Several people remonstrated when faced with Francesca's intended destination, a couple of whom departed. Our remaining revelers had to be cajoled inside with only minor mockery and peer pressure. But we made it inside and danced. Francesca and Marco fit together like two puzzle pieces. Much to my surprise, both my feet actually coordinated their progress across the parquet floor, sand, salt and spit flying in my harmonious wake.

Two bass-heavy electronica songs and one appallingly overpriced draft beer later, I decided against repeating the Reeperbahn performance. This being my last night and all, I preferred to remember it. Good and lubricated, I bid an Irish goodbye to the crew, Francesca and Marco were locked in rhythm and I'd lost track of everyone else, except Anders, who towered over everyone on the dance floor. I smiled and saluted him. He lifted his beer toward me, and then I shuffled out the front door.

I ambled Barceloneta's beachfront and sat on the concrete foundation of L'Estel Ferit (The Wounded Star) statue, four stacked steel-and-glass cubes that leaned over like a doomed Jenga tower, feigning disrepair as if they could crash down at any moment. The statue commemorates fisherman's shacks that once lined the beachfront serving fresh seafood and drinks. The *xiringuitos* were torn down during Barcelona's gentrification program preparing for the 1992 Olympics.

Barcelona's crescent-shaped skyline was alive from the forested heights of Montjuïc to the inland apartment buildings overlooked by the Torre Agbar skyscraper, a doppelganger of London's Gherkin. Before I turned into Barceloneta's latticework of alleyways and slender mid-rises, I kicked a pile of sand under the star-soaked sky and scrutinized the Mediterranean's reflection of Barcelona's skyline. My eyes filled with salty tears as I whispered, "I love this life so much. I hope I never forget it."

* * *

The rising morning heat and unobstructed sunlight in the many-hued bedroom once again rendered sleep impossible. I checked the time, intending to wring one last experience with my few remaining hours on the Continent. A few blocks away, the local market, Santa Caterina, was opening for business in about 30 minutes.

A beautifully remodeled market building, El Born's Santa Caterina Market is among the grandest modern renovations in Western Europe. Santa Caterina has operated here since 1848, receiving its stunning face-lift in 2005. The original structure needed but a light touch. Workers whitewashed the 24-arch portico and reimagined the interior layout. The real magic happened not so much in the building but above it.

Architects Enric Miralles, Barcelona's native son, and his Italian partner-wife Benedetta Tagliabue, designed an undulating steel super-structure that appeared like frozen ocean swell. But instead of painting the canopy a pretty color or two, Tagliabue and Miralles decorated it with a mosaic comprising 325,000 multicolored, ceramic hexagonal tiles that mimic the colorful fruit, vegetables and other edibles found inside. The effect was mesmerizing to behold. I walked under and looked up, cozy wood panels were nailed to the underside.

A Dominican monastery, the Convent of Santa Caterina, was built here during the Middle Ages, but succumbed to neglect (and Catalan resistance fighters) in 1835. But during the 2005 renovation, workers stumbled on something much older while setting the footings for that handsome new roof: a ruined Roman necropolis. The Christian convent, it was discovered, had rested upon pagan Roman foundations, a house of God erected over a city of the dead.

On a bench at the ruins' viewing area, I ate my final breakfast in Europe: gossamer shavings of jamón ibérico laid upon juicy Lleida pear slices and a double espresso chased with two *xuixos*, deep-fried, custard-filled pastries similar to a cannoli. While the market buzzed with locals piling produce, meats, bread and seafood into metal baskets and canvas shoulder bags, I ate my Catalan breakfast and drank Ethiopian coffee alone by the quiet Roman ruins.

A leisurely, roundabout circuit led me through El Born's tangled streets, alleyways and leafy plazas. At a corner bodega, I bought a razor and shaving cream and mixed-fruit juice before reluctantly climbing the Airbnb's stairs and beginning the de-traveling process of packing and showering. I slathered the prickly 21-day beard in white foam and stared into the mirror, hesitating, when my phone buzzed. It was a WhatsApp message from Francesca:

Heyy, we missed goodbyes last night. leaving soon?

...

Yup, packing now. Catch the Metro in 20 mins.

...

I'm with Marco. join us for lunch and a movie?

...

Ha, well, yes, but I'd miss my flight!

...

I know.

...

Impossible.

...

Yes. ;>) At Carrer de Blai if you change mind.

Was it impossible? Fifteen years ago, I would've accepted their offer and canceled my flight, consequences be damned. However, that was a different life.

I stood at the mirror, holding the razor a few inches from my face. I had enough time for a quick shave and shower before catching the Metro to the airport. My eyes darted from the razor to my phone sitting beside the sink. I dropped the razor, picked up my phone and Google Mapped their location. Carrer de Blai sits at the base of Montjuïc on Barcelona's west side en route, coincidentally, to the airport.

The bathroom smelled of mildew and the shower curtain swung halfway open, revealing a tiny square window that looked into the neighbor's kitchen. I again lifted the razor to my face, pressing into the shaving foam, then pulled back and rested the razor back on the sink counter.

Maybe I could live with a beard. Maybe a beard was just the beginning. Maybe I had changed and there was no returning now that I had cracked the code, Europe at ground level. This milk run could be just the beginning. Perhaps Francesca's invitation was the fateful opening I needed to start a new life. I could fly my family to Spain and apply for a visa. We could live an uncompromising life of adventure from Europe to Africa to Asia, a hashtagging lost generation, with kiddo in-tow. Maybe someday I too would end up with a granite bust beside a Spanish bullring. I wiped the foam from my beard and dropped the razor in the trash can.

Or perhaps it was time to go home.

The humid September air formed sweat beads on my brow the second I hit the sidewalk, shouldering the jungle-green backpack while walking to the Jaume I Metro station on Plaça de l'Àngel. A smooth chrome railing mounted to a brushed cement knee wall led to the subterranean station. I gripped the aluminum, hesitating. From Jaume, I could still go either way: the airport or Carrer de Blai. While pulling my wallet from the daypack, my hand grazed something in the interior pocket. It was the red lighter with three yellow dots I'd bought in Christiania, Copenhagen. A green garbage bin sat a few steps away, and I almost dropped the lighter inside it, but instead placed it atop the can's curved cover. The three-dot lighter stood upright, awaiting its next owner. I descended the steps just as my Metro arrived.

Epilogue

The WhatsApp messages had collected, unnoticed, unread for months after I returned to the States because I don't use WhatsApp at home. While taxiing at Denver International Airport, I turned off notifications and moved the app into a forlorn folder called "Misc" where I put unused applications out to pasture. On a whim one snowy December day, months after returning home and feeling nostalgic for the solo road, I tapped open WhatsApp, and the messages flooded in:

Hans from Hamburg:

Hey Rory! Just wanted to say hi. How was the rest of your trip? Are you home now? Do you know any good photo editors? Ya'll!!!

Farid from Amsterdam:

Hello friend. Do you know these bikes, Ibis?

Madeleine from Paris:

Hey Rory. Again, great meeting in person. Finally! I launched my tour website, please look. And I'm working on a new article...coming to your inbox soon!

Christine from Bayeux:

Hello Rory. Jean and Marie come for dinner last night. They say again they enjoy meeting you. We meet again!

Jacob from Canfranc:

Hey bud! Hope you're well. Good news: I'm a hiker now! I did a trek in Nepal. It took seven days! It was so hard and wonderful. I'll look you up next time I'm "down south."

Francesca from Barcelona:

marco and i say HELLO! we meet in sardinia for the month. it is halfway!
;) ru home? do u miss bcn? we think costa rica trip in spring. is that close to
colorado? haha ;) maybe you and your wife can join us. we let you know.
besos.

Flushed with memories and effusive apologies for my months-long tardiness, I replied. I couldn't stop there, flipping open my laptop and scrolling my Airbnb history, reminiscing about the perfect balcony on Estafeta in Pamplona, the prostitutes on the other side of the wall in Paris, the roof-cat invasion of my Amsterdam writer's nest and the serene courtyard dinner in Bayeux. Oh, that heavenly boeuf en croûte! I opened Christine's Airbnb listing in Bayeux, clicked through the photos—the courtyard, my room, her hardworking kitchen, before exclaiming, "What the hell? Let's see what's available this spring!" But when I punched in the dates, a message in stark red font read: "Property turned off."

The room, however, wasn't what I missed. It was Christine's open heart. It was Pascal's reluctant kindness. It was Francesca inviting me to a beach party even though she'd known me less than 12 hours. It was Madeleine, divulging her immigrant experience. It wasn't the storybook rooms or even the unforgettable meals (although the food finished a close second). It wasn't the museums, churches or history tours. No, it was none of those things I'd typically structure an itinerary around. In reflection, my mind raced to the smiles, jokes, stories, conversations, and limitless generosity. (Okay, and the food!)

My ground-level approach to traveling Europe had revealed the Continent's greatest treasure: its people.

Some say European travel has become too cookie-cutter, like my dinner host at this book's outset. Between the preponderance of tour groups and Instagram-driven bucket list-chasers, I admit, they have a point. But scratching the tourist veneer requires little effort and reveals a friendlier, more rewarding Europe. A very real one. Slow trains and family-run restaurants and lodging put you in front of real locals. Even in big cities, off-beat neighborhoods show enduring reality. And for a countryside hop, where great food, welcoming hosts and idyllic hiking among scattered ruins awaits, a train ticket remains all that's required. Ground-level travel in Europe is, in every sense of the phrase, "real travel."

I dropped my phone and dug out my original "milk run" manifesto, scribbled in my frayed notebook late at night almost a year ago. I reread it:

- Go solo.
- Ride slow trains. Or walk.
- Eat at markets, small cafés.
- Find Airbnbs and guesthouses owned by locals.
- Be spontaneous.
- Take setbacks in stride.

Had I done it? Had I obeyed my declarations? Mostly, yes. (Especially that last one.)

So, now, a confession: My manifesto is wholly unoriginal. The ideas are rooted in slow travel philosophy, an over 30-year-old outgrowth of the slow-food movement. Yes, I riffed the plan one night while tossing and turning in bed, but I didn't invent the concept of slow, ground-level tourism. Slow travel advocates traveling by environmentally friendly means and exploring local history, cuisine and culture. It's a conscious alternative to mass tourism.

I held a romanticized notion that slow travel required studying some obscure lost dialect in a remote Swiss valley, learning how to train truffle dogs in Istria or volunteering at a derelict cherry farm in central Portugal. Boy, was I wrong. The time frame doesn't matter. What matters is having patience and curiosity—learning why the wine or fish tastes that way, why the old houses look the same or what caused a place to be abandoned.

This realization lit an ember that soon became an obsession. I read everything I could find about slow travel—articles translated by Carlo Petrini, father of the slow-food movement, Bradt Guides and myriad books, blog posts and magazines. All the articles and books formed a general ethos, but I sought a fully conceived and relatable list of European slow-travel tenets. Eventually, I found it.

A couple of weeks after I sent my apologetic, inexcusably tardy WhatsApp replies, on December 25, I received the one and only gift on my Christmas list, a subscription to *Hidden Europe* magazine, the slow-travel connoisseur's guide to Europe. My subscription came with three back issues of my choosing. That night, after setting up my online account, I scrolled through the *Hidden Europe* archive until a headline from issue #25, March-April 2009, caught my eye: "A slow travel manifesto." I couldn't add it to my order fast enough.

Three weeks later, I tore open a flat-rate media envelope from Berlin containing my *Hidden Europe* back issues. Issue #25's cover featured an ordinary, gray apartment building in Oostende, Belgium. Not a great start, I thought. However, I thumbed to page 10 and devoured the slow-travel manifesto, penned by *Hidden Europe* publishers, Nicky Gardner and Susanne Kries. My heart connected with every word, every sentiment, as if they'd written it just for me. A rosy-background sidebar listed Europe's slow-travel guiding principles:

"The key to slow travel is a state of mind...Avoid planes, and instead enjoy ferries, local buses and slow trains...Don't let the anticipation of arrival eclipse the pleasure of the journey...Check out local markets and shops...Savour café culture...Do what the locals do, not only what the guidebooks say...Savour the unexpected. Delayed trains and missed bus connections create new opportunities."

I latched onto the five-page manifesto, carefully cutting out and pinning the sidebar to the bulletin board over my desk. Now, every time I dream about a trip, I review it.

* * *

The deeper I studied slow travel, the more I learned about the social and environmental consequences of modern tourism. It left me grappling with the fundamental idea of travel, movement for pleasure's sake. I felt something larger happening, an understanding that how I traveled and how I interacted mattered far more than where I went. In *Europe by Milk Run*, I proved Europe still constituted "real" travel. But in the months since returning home, I'd spent my time waging an existential battle over what kind of traveler I wanted to be.

During these internal debates, my thoughts about *Europe by Milk Run* returned to people, food and transportation. It boils down to those three things. Slow trains and walks peppered my thoughts. I reminisced about the hikes in Normandy, Pamplona, Dinan and Canfranc. What if I combined slow trains and foot travel? What if I hiked to villages and slept and ate in family-run hotels and restaurants?

Late one night, as winter turned to spring in my small mountain town, I spread maps and old books across my oak coffee table. I set my sights on France, its many villages connected by the extensive footpath system I had sampled in Bayeux and Dinan. I sought a route or even a fragment of an unknown hiking route I could turn into something special. Surely, there was an overlooked trail I could dredge up, polish and call my own.

But of the country's over 100,000 miles of marked and maintained trails, my research suggested most hikers stuck to a handful of pre-defined routes found in marketing brochures and hiking guides: The Robert Louis Stevenson Trail, the Brittany and Normandy coastlines, the Loire and Dordogne valleys, Camino de Santiago and, of course, the high-elevation Mont Blanc routes.

I scanned the maps and thumbed through the guidebooks. Some books were 40 years old. A village hike not yet detailed in any modern guides or tourism pamphlets was out there somewhere. I just had to find it. Or invent it. What was I seeking? A once-popular now overlooked route, or a newly established one or two nearby trails I could connect by road. I needed to find something different.

In a 20-year-old, large-format paperback, I stumbled across it, that something different, a path through Provence that hadn't yet been commodified. Thinking there couldn't possibly be anywhere left exploring in tourist-saturated Provence, I almost skipped right past the page. Instead, I gave it a shot. The author, a Franco-American, described several trails in Provence, but one gripped my imagination: "The walk on the GR 6 through the Luberon is one of the great French walks...takes the visitor into the heart of a Provence that is far from glitzy, into a land of quiet narrow streets, hill towns, *petanque* and friendly, independent people."

Three months later, I shouldered my backpack in Place Genty Pantaly, Gordes, and embarked on a 12-day trek, sleeping in medieval "perched" villages and eating at farm-fresh, family-run restaurants. Reveling in an invisible Provence, I scoured the Luberon from forested mountains and mossy stone bridges to valley-floor lavender fields overlooked by hillside vineyards. I forged a modern route along ancient paths.

* * *

A *Walk in Provence*—coming spring 2023.

Subscribe for updates from the author: rorymoulton.com/subscribe

* * *

Enjoyed this book? Please leave a review. It really helps indie authors like me. Plus, leaving a book review a day keeps Amsterdam's roof-cats away!

—*Rory*

Bits & Bobs

Get Two Free Paris Books

Smarter European travel starts now!

Download two free Paris books—*10 Perfect Days in Paris* and *Paris for €10*—and receive the author's free newsletter. In it, he reveals European travel tips and news, book updates and his myriad personal shortcomings. He'll probably send it every couple weeks, usually on Thursdays, but would prefer you don't hold him to a set schedule.

Subscribe: rorymoulton.com/subscribe.

The Milk Run Map

Follow the milk run route

From Copenhagen to Barcelona, this digital map lists every restaurant, destination, attraction, diversion, ruin, park, etc. mentioned in *Europe by Milk Run*. That quaint, unnamed Parisian restaurant? The ruined church in Normandy and fortress-prison in Pamplona that aren't "very closed?" Yeah, they're in here. (Don't tell your mom.)

Start milkin': rorymoulton.com/milk-map

Travel Consultations

Get help planning your own milk run with author Rory Moulton

If the complexities of rail passes, itinerary building, French etiquette, lodging options or even packing are stressing you out, I can help. If you have lots of questions and/or a complex trip to plan, or if you're a first-time traveler and are not sure even where to begin, consider a personalized, in-depth trip consultation. I'll answer all your travel questions (possibly by Googling them), help you construct an itinerary (that may or may not make your head spin) and deconstruct the mysteries of public transportation. I specialize in Western Europe, but can offer help from Lisbon to Istanbul. Except Liechtenstein.

Book a consultation appointment: rorymoulton.com/consultation.

About the Author

I'm a travel writer and editor living in the Colorado Rockies with my wife and son. When away from my desk, I'm passionate about travel, food and the great outdoors. I travel independently on a ground-level budget to Europe and South America. Send me an email at rory@rorymoulton.com. I'd love to hear about your travels.

You can connect with me on:
- 🌐 https://rorymoulton.com
- 🐦 https://twitter.com/roryam
- 📘 https://www.facebook.com/EuroExperto
- 📷 https://www.instagram.com/rorymoulton

Subscribe to my newsletter:
- ✉ https://rorymoulton.com/subscribe

Also by Rory Moulton

Rory Moulton writes memoirs and guidebooks about European travel.

Essential Paris Travel Tips

"Author presents idea after idea and ways to save anyone time and money... Worth every penny for this easy to use guide." (Available from your favorite bookseller.) 4.4/5 stars, Amazon Best Seller

Buy Now: books2read.com/essentialparis

Essential Amsterdam Travel Tips

"Highly recommended with plenty of useful information. Well worth the price." (Available from your favorite bookseller.) 4.5/5 Stars, Amazon Best Seller

Buy Now: books2read.com/essentialamsterdam

Essential Rome Travel Tips

"I have been to Rome several times but still learned about places...a very enjoyable, informative book with splashes of humor that made me smile." (Available from your favorite bookseller.) 4.3/5 stars, Amazon Best Seller

Buy Now: books2read.com/essentialrome

Hiking France

"The best book for helping to organize a French hiking trip. Contains many interesting in-France travel tips which will be helpful to anyone... " (Available from your favorite bookseller.)

Buy Now: books2read.com/hikingfrance

Across Europe with Satanella

Lost for almost 100 years, Rory Moulton found, edited and annotated this classic Motorcycle trip From England to Russia in 1924. (Available only on Amazon.)

Buy Now: amzn.to/3sUGKaG

Manufactured by Amazon.ca
Bolton, ON